International Trade
and Economic Growth

HARRY G. JOHNSON

Professor of Economic Theory
University of Manchester

International Trade
and
Economic Growth

STUDIES IN PURE THEORY

HARVARD UNIVERSITY PRESS
CAMBRIDGE, MASSACHUSETTS
1961

PRINTED IN GREAT BRITAIN

To My Mother

PREFACE

THE studies collected in this volume embody the results of research conducted during the past four years into various theoretical problems in international economics. They fall naturally into three groups—comparative cost theory, trade and growth, and balance of payments theory—although these groups are not mutually exclusive, the first and third interacting and extending in the second. In addition, they are linked by a common purpose—the consolidation of the work of previous theorists and its extension to new problems—and by a common method—the application of mathematically-based logical analysis to theoretical problems thrown up by discussion of current topics among economists, generally those relating to economic policy. The motivation, explicit and implicit, has usually been to see what could be made of the tools available, in analysing the problem that suggested itself as an interesting one.

Theoretical analysis of the type pursued here has two major functions, both of which are comprised in the scientific objective of simplicity of generalization. The first is to push the application of known and tested techniques into new areas, thus extending the range of the analytical apparatus built up by the labours of successive economic theorists. The second is to review the existing literature with the double object of verifying the accuracy of accepted conclusions and synthesizing the methods and results of previous writers into a simpler, more readily usable analysis. Both types of endeavour are represented in this volume.

The analysis of the relation between factor endowments, direction of trade, and the effect of trade on factor prices which begins the volume belongs to the second group. My interest in this topic originated in a vague feeling of dissatisfaction with Samuelson's 1948 article on factor price equalization; this was resolved by Pearce's article on the same subject, in the editing of which I had a share in 1951, and a number of other writers have since made the correct analysis available in a number of journals. But the puzzlement which greeted Harrod's attempt to explain to the Association of University Teachers of Economics why incomplete specialization does not necessarily imply factor price equalization convinced me that some useful work remained to be done in the way of simplification and tidying-up of loose ends, while Harrod himself provided one of the instruments required for the purpose. The argument of Chapter I is the result. It is intended as a systematization of one branch of the

B

theory of comparative costs, and should be regarded as no more than that, since not only is a large part of international trade accounted for by differences in factor quality, differences in technology, and economies of scale, from which the argument abstracts, but factor endowment is itself a variable, influenced by investment in equipment and human skill and by international factor movements.

The analysis of optimum tariff retaliation which completes Part I started as a study of the first type, but grew into one of the second. The problem left unsettled by other writers was the conditions under which an optimum tariff would pay, even if the other country retaliated; the analytical difficulty was that the imposition of tariffs shifts the offer curves, altering the optimum tariffs, while the gains or losses depend on the utility functions underlying the offer curves. It occurred to me that these difficulties would be overcome in the case of a utility function generating a constant-elasticity offer curve; this proved to be so. Publication of the results required a re-statement of the theory of optimum tariffs, in the course of which I was led to the conclusion that many of the propositions in Scitovszky's classic article on the subject were unfounded. Since then, Gorman has shown that my original assumption that a utility function could be uniquely identified with an offer curve was erroneous—the direction of shift with income changes having to be specified as well. The argument has accordingly been revised to include the richer and more interesting results which follow from the correct analysis of the problem.

The studies which make up Part II are all of the first type, and appear in the reverse order in which they were written. My interest in the theoretical aspects of growth in an international economy began with curiosity as to how the Machlup-Metzler foreign trade multiplier analysis might be applied to the Harrod-Domar problem of equilibrium growth at full employment. While Keynesian analytical methods suggested international investment as the mechanism for equilibrating the balance of payments, it was logically necessary to consider the alternative mechanism of exchange-rate or price-level adjustment. The crux of the Harrod-Domar analysis, the knife-edge requirements of self-justifying growth, has, however, ceased to interest economic theorists, in consequence of the recognition that the savings ratio and the capital-output ratio are not parameters but variables amenable to economic policy or subject to equilibrating forces; correspondingly, the international aspects of the original problem have become less worth pursuing. The analysis of them is nevertheless included here, partly because some of the details of Part I are still interesting, and partly because Part II contains my first attempt at bringing together the income and price effects of economic growth.

The apparatus developed for the analysis of the relative price movement required to preserve equilibrium between growing economies suggested itself as a ready-made tool for analysing another problem, that of the effects of increasing productivity on the balance of payments, which at the time (1953-4) was the key element in a popular explanation of the dollar problem among economic theorists. This was an entirely monetary analysis, which took the fact of growth as a datum. The next step was to follow the path laid down in Hicks' *Inaugural Lecture* into a full-scale analysis of the real effects of various causes of economic growth on the economic relations between growing economies, an endeavour for which the stimulus and opportunity were provided by an invitation to deliver a series of three lectures at the University of Manchester. A highly condensed and rather difficult version of these lectures was published in *The Manchester School*; the opportunity has been taken here to revise some of the concepts, make explicit the mathematical argument underlying part of the reasoning, and include a treatment of international transmissions of productive power which was only briefly sketched in the published version.

Part III is composed of essays devoted to the second purpose, consolidation and simplification of existing analysis. All three grew out of a course of lectures on International Monetary Economics first delivered at the London School of Economics in the session 1954-5. Chapter VI outlines a general framework for the analysis of balance-of-payments problems, which integrates the 'elasticity' and 'absorption' approaches and includes the use of controls on trade, and into which both more advanced theoretical analysis and specific practical problems can be readily fitted. Chapter VII began with the discovery that the transfer problem and the exchange stability problem are formally one and the same problem; since this discovery was published, I have verified a suspicion that trade controls could be treated by exactly the same method as exchange rate changes—insertion into the transfer formulae of the effects on demands of the policy change—so that the argument now demonstrates that all the possible methods of correcting a balance-of-payments disequilibrium are special cases of the transfer problem, and that the one technical apparatus will handle the analytical side of all the policy methods discussed in general terms in Chapter VI. Chapter VIII reduces the formal corpus of foreign trade multiplier theory to its barest essentials.

The essence of the theoretical method exemplified in this volume is the utilization of the work of previous theorists as a foundation for new construction; continuity and multiplicity of effort are the rule in this as in other academic disciplines. I should like to express grateful acknowledgment not only to those writers whose contributions of leading ideas are recognized in the footnotes and the texts of the studies which follow, but also to the wider body of scholars who create a climate of opinion and thought from which one often plucks ideas without realizing it, to the graduate students from many universities and countries whose enthusiasm and high standards have been a constant stimulus, and not least to the editors of journals, whose many helpful suggestions and whose kindness in permitting me to reprint articles from their pages are poorly rewarded by the laconic footnotes to chapter titles. I should also like to record my debt to my teachers at Toronto, Cambridge, and Harvard, who first aroused my interest in the field of international trade; and to James Duesenberry, Paul Samuelson, and Franco Modigliani, who favoured me with a very helpful discussion of the contents of this volume.

In conclusion, I should like to thank Miss Margaret Hitchen for performing the labour of typing and preparing the manuscript, and my wife for checking and proof-reading it.

HARRY G. JOHNSON

University of Manchester
October 1957

CONTENTS

PART ONE

COMPARATIVE COST THEORY

CHAPTER I

Factor Endowments, International Trade and Factor Prices[*]

IN the past few years, there has been a revival of interest in the Heckscher-Ohlin model of international trade, and a closer scrutiny of two propositions associated with its analysis of the principle of comparative costs.[1] The first is that the cause of international trade is to be found largely in differences between the factor-endowments of different countries; the second that the effect of international trade is to tend to equalize factor prices as between countries, thus serving to some extent as a substitute for mobility of factors. The result, very briefly, has been to show that neither proposition is generally true, the validity of both depending on certain factual assumptions about either the nature of technology or the range of variation of factor endowments which are additional to, and much more restrictive than, the assumptions of the Heckscher-Ohlin model itself.

My purpose here is to survey the related problems of the relation between factor-endowment and international trade and the effect of trade on relative factor prices, with the aim of clarifying the nature and simplifying the explanation of some of the results of recent theoretical research. The main instrument employed to this end is

[*] *The Manchester School of Economic and Social Studies*, XXV, no. 3, September, 1957, 270–83.

[1] See in particular: Abba P. Lerner, 'Factor Prices and International Trade', *Economica*, N.S., XIX, no. 1, February 1952, 1–15; I. F. Pearce, 'A Note on Mr Lerner's Paper', loc. cit., 16–18; S. F. James and I. F. Pearce, 'The Factor Price Equalisation Myth', *Review of Economic Studies*, XIX(2), no. 49, 1951–2, 111–20; Romney Robinson, 'Factor Proportions and Comparative Advantage: Part I', *Quarterly Journal of Economics*, LXX, no. 2, May 1956, 169–92; R. W. Jones, 'Factor Proportions and the Heckscher-Ohlin Theorem', *Review of Economic Studies*, XXIV (1), no. 63, 1956–7, 1–10; also Lionel McKenzie, 'Equality of Factor Prices in World Trade', *Econometrica*, 23, no. 3, July 1955, 239–57, which handles the same problems by linear programming methods.

a diagrammatic representation of the technological side of the economy, developed from one originated by Mr R. F. Harrod.[2]

In common with other models of international trade, it is assumed, on the consumption side, that tastes and the distribution of the means of satisfying wants (property ownership, or claims on the social dividend) are given; and that, on the production side, technology and the supply of factors of production in each country are given (the latter implying that factors are immobile between countries). Production functions and factors are assumed to be identical in all countries; the outputs of goods are assumed to depend only on inputs of factors into the production processes for those goods, and factors are assumed to be indifferent between uses. Further, production is assumed to be subject to constant returns to scale, so that the marginal productivities of factors depend only on the ratios in which they are used. Finally, perfect competition and the absence of trade barriers (tariffs and transport costs) are assumed. The argument is simplified still further by assuming, initially, the existence of only two countries, I and II, two goods, X and Y, and two factors of production, labour and capital,[3] the available quantities of the factors being given independently of their prices.

The given technical possibilities of production, summarized in the production functions, imply a definite relationship between the optimum capital : labour ratios in the two industries, relative factor prices, and relative costs of production of commodities. This relationship is represented in Fig. 1. For any given relative price of labour in terms of capital (such as w_I) there will be an optimum ratio of capital to labour in the production of each good ($r_{x.e}$ in X and $r_{y.e}$ in Y) which equates marginal productivities to factor prices, and a relative cost of X in terms of Y (c_I) which embodies the ratio of their costs of production at the given factor prices with the associated capital : labour ratios.

An increase in the relative price of labour above the given level will make it profitable to substitute capital for labour in both industries, thus raising the optimum capital : labour ratio in both;[4]

---

[2] Presented at the conference of the Association of University Teachers of Economics, January 1957. Mr Harrod's diagram was a rudimentary version of the top half of the diagram used here.

[3] The simplicity of these assumptions is a virtue rather than a defect, in an argument whose purpose is to show how little can be said.

[4] The shapes of the curves relating optimal capital : labour ratios to the relative price of labour assume increasing difficulty in substituting capital for labour as the capital-output ratio rises, and continuous substitutability of labour for capital in response to changing relative factor prices. On linear programming

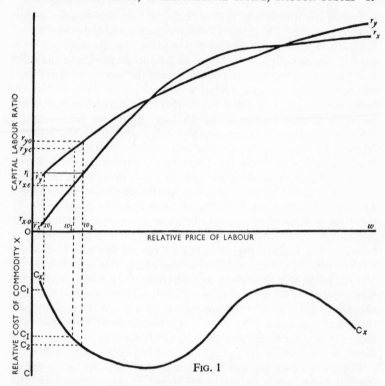

FIG. 1

it will also increase the relative cost of the labour-intensive good (X in the neighbourhood of w_1), since its costs will be raised more than those of the capital-intensive good by the increase in the relative price of labour.[5] Further increases in the relative price of labour will continue to raise the optimum capital: labour ratio in both industries; but either one of two possibilities may be the effect on the relative cost ratio, depending on the relative ease of substituting capital for

assumptions the curves would be step functions, the steps representing discontinuous changes in capital intensity. At their left extremities, the curves will cut the Ow axis if labour can entirely replace capital in production, and the Or axis if it cannot.

[5] If the capital: labour ratios in the two industries remained constant as the relative price of labour was increased, the relative cost of the labour-intensive good would obviously increase; and the effect on relative costs of the substitution of capital for labour in both industries induced by the increase in the relative price of labour can be neglected, since in the neighbourhood of the minimum cost point substitution of one factor for the other does not alter cost.

labour in the two lines of production. The first, and simpler, occurs when one commodity remains labour-intensive and the other capital-intensive, whatever the relative factor price. In this case, one commodity can be definitely identified as labour-intensive and the other as capital-intensive; and the relative cost of the labour-intensive good will continue to rise as the relative price of labour rises, so that the latter can be deduced from the former. The second occurs when, owing to greater facility in substituting capital for labour in the initially labour-intensive good, the difference in capital-intensity between the two goods narrows and eventually reverses itself, so that the labour-intensive good becomes capital-intensive and *vice versa;* such a reversal of factor-intensities may occur more than once (as illustrated in Fig. 1), as variation in relative factor prices induces variation in the capital-intensity of production of both goods. In this case, a commodity can only be identified as labour-intensive or capital-intensive with reference to a range of relative factor-prices or (what is the same thing) a range of capital-intensities; and the relative cost of a commodity will alternately rise and fall as the relative price of labour rises, as that commodity varies from being labour-intensive to being capital-intensive. Consequently more than one factor price ratio may correspond to a given commodity cost ratio, and the factor price ratio cannot be deduced from the commodity cost ratio alone. The distinction between the two cases, which turns on the facts of technology, is fundamental to what follows.

The analysis so far has been concerned with the relationships implicit in the given technological possibilities of production. But only a limited range of the techniques available can actually be used efficiently by a particular economy with a given factor endowment; and the possible range of relative factor prices and relative commodity costs is correspondingly limited. The factor endowment of the economy sets an overall capital : labour ratio, to which the capital : labour ratios in the two industries, weighted by the proportions of the total labour force employed, must average out. At the extremes, the economy's resources may be used entirely in the capital-intensive industry or entirely in the labour-intensive industry; and the relative prices of factors, and the relative costs of commodities, must lie within the limits set by these two extremes.[6]

---

[6] At the extremes, the country is completely specialized on one or other commodity; in a closed economy, there would therefore be no exchange ratio between commodities, though the non-produced one might have a 'virtual' price (equal to or less than its cost of production); in an open economy, the price of the non-produced good would be an international one (equal to or less than the domestic cost of production).

The restrictions imposed by the factor endowment on the techniques the economy can employ and on the possible variation of factor prices and relative costs of production are illustrated in Fig. 1, where r_I represents the economy's overall capital:labour ratio. If all resources are used in the production of Y, the relative price of labour will be w_1, if all are used in the production of X the relative labour price will be w_2; the corresponding relative costs of commodity X are c_1 and c_2. As w rises from w_1 to w_2, the capital : labour ratio in Y rises from r_I to $r_{y.o}$ and the ratio in X from $r_{x.o}$ to r_I; the increases in these ratios are reconciled with the constancy of the overall capital : labour ratio by a shifting of resources from production of Y to production of X, which frees the capital required for the increases in the ratios. It can easily be shown that, for any relative factor price, the proportions of the total labour supply employed in one of the industries is equal to the ratio of the difference between the other industry's capital : labour ratio and the overall ratio, to the difference between the capital : labour ratios in the two industries; thus, for example, the proportion of the labour force employed in producing X at the relative labour price w_I is $(r_{y.e}-r_I)/(r_{y.e}-r_{x.e})$.

As can readily be seen from the diagram, the range of variation of relative factor prices and commodity costs possible in the economy depends broadly on two technological factors: the spread between the optimum capital:labour ratios in the two industries (reflected in the vertical distance between the r_y and r_x curves), and the difficulty of substituting capital for labour (reflected in the gentleness of the slopes of the two curves). The greater the difference between optimum factor-intensities and the greater the difficulty of substituting capital for labour, the greater the range of variation of factor prices and commodity costs possible between the extremes of specialization on one or other product. If, on the other hand, capital : labour ratios were the same in the two industries or factors were perfect substitutes, there would be no possibility of variation of relative factor prices and commodity costs.

Before proceeding, it may be as well to notice that the assumption that the quantities of factors available are fixed, can be relaxed without trouble. Dependence of factor supplies on their relative prices can be readily introduced by making the overall capital : labour ratio depend on the relative price of labour; in the normal case the curve representing the relationship will be downward-sloping, reflecting the reduction in the supply of capital and increase in the supply of labour as the price of the former falls relatively to the latter. The effect (in the normal case) would be to restrict the range of possible variation more than would otherwise be the case; in the extreme case of perfect elasticity of factor supply, only one relative factor price ratio and commodity cost ratio would be possible.

Within the range of variation permitted by technology and factor endowment, the factor price and commodity cost ratios will be determined by the forces of demand. For a closed economy, this determination is most readily conceived as follows: to any given relative price of labour will correspond a certain pattern of production, a certain distribution of income, and a certain price ratio between the commodities at which the recipients of the income will be just willing to consume the quantities of both goods produced at the given price of labour. As the relative price of labour rises and resources are shifted out of producing the capital-intensive commodity into producing the labour-intensive commodity, the equilibrium demand price of the latter is very likely to fall,[7] while its relative cost is rising. The equilibrium levels of commodity prices (costs) and factor prices will be determined by the condition that the relative costs of production should be just equal to the relative prices at which the outputs of the two commodities will be absorbed.[8]

The next stage of the argument is to introduce the possibility of international trade and examine its effects. This is done in Fig. 2, which reproduces Fig. 1 with the deletion of certain parts of it no longer necessary to the argument. In the diagram, the country previously analysed ('country I') is represented by its factor endowment ratio r_I, and its closed-economy equilibrium factor price and comparative cost ratios w_I and c_I. The possibility of trade is introduced *via* another country ('country II') similarly represented on the diagram by its factor price and cost ratios w_{II} and c_{II}, with a different closed-economy equilibrium comparative cost ratio. It is assumed in all cases that country II is endowed with a higher ratio of capital to labour than country I.

[7] The exceptional case is that in which the reduction in the supply of the capital-intensive good is offset by a reduction in demand because the owners of labour have a stronger preference for the labour-intensive good than the owners of capital. It makes no fundamental difference to the analysis unless the effect is so strong that the equilibrium demand price of the labour-intensive good rises more rapidly than its cost of production, a possibility of instability which will be ignored here.

[8] The determination of full general equilibrium could be represented by drawing in the bottom half of Fig. 1 a curve expressing the equilibrium price of X as a function of the relative price of labour (and, implicitly, of the factor endowment), whose intersection with the relative cost curve would determine the equilibrium of the system.

So long as the closed-economy equilibrium comparative cost ratios of the two countries are different, international trade will be profitable, and each country will export the good in which it has a comparative cost advantage (as measured by equilibrium commodity price ratios in the absence of trade). In the assumed absence of trade barriers, the effect of trade will be to equate the price ratios in the two economies at a level (c_e in the diagram) somewhere between the two closed-economy comparative cost ratios, this level being determined by the demand and supply conditions in the two countries taken together.

At the new international price ratio, both countries may continue to produce both commodities, or one may specialize completely in the production of the commodity in which it has the comparative advantage, or both may specialize. Which will be the case is governed by two principles—that the new price ratio will lie between the two closed-economy price ratios, and that a country will not specialize at a price ratio between the extremes of its comparative cost range—and is determined by the relations between four cost ratios—the maximum cost ratio in the country with the lower maximum, the minimum cost ratio in the country with the higher minimum, and the two closed-economy equilibrium price ratios. The following four propositions can be deduced from the two principles stated above; for diagrammatic simplicity, they are illustrated only for cases in which the two countries' capital : output ratios lie in the same range, so that there is a one-to-one relation between cost ratios and factor price ratios.

(i) If the minimum cost ratio in the country with the higher minimum exceeds the maximum cost ratio in the other country, so that the comparative cost ranges of the two countries do not overlap, one country at least must specialize completely. This would be the case if country II's endowment ratio coincided with r_a in Fig. 2.

(ii) If the cost ratio ranges of the two countries overlap, at least one of the countries will not specialize. This would be the case if country II's endowment ratio were either r_b or r_{II} in Fig. 2.

(iii) If one country's cost ratio range includes the other's closed-economy equilibrium price ratio, the former country will not specialize. For example, if country II's endowment ratio were r_b and its closed-economy equilibrium labour price w_b, the labour price ratio corresponding to the new price must fall

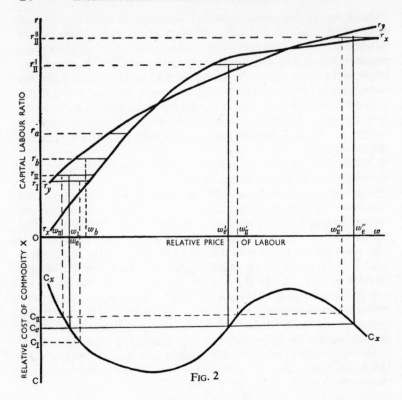

FIG. 2

between w_b and w_I, so that country I would produce both goods.

(iv) If each country's closed-economy equilibrium price ratio falls within the other's cost ratio range, neither will specialize completely. For example, with country II's endowment ratio r_{II} and closed-economy equilibrium labour price w_{II}, the labour price ratio corresponding to the new equilibrium price must fall between w_I and w_{II}, in which range both countries would produce both goods.

In the explanation of the causes of international trade presented above, comparative advantage was measured by equilibrium prices in the absence of trade. Such an explanation, amounting to the statement that those goods are traded which it is profitable to trade, is little more than a tautology. The next problem requiring analysis, and the one which the apparatus built up earlier in this chapter is designed to elucidate, is the relation between comparative advantage so defined and differences in factor supplies. Closely related to this problem is the problem of the effect of international trade on the prices of factors, which can be dealt with by modifications of the same argument.

To begin with, it is necessary to notice a difficulty: relative scarcity or abundance of a factor may be defined in either of two ways—relative cheapness, a matter of price, and relatively high endowment ratio, a matter of physical quantity. These two definitions may not be synonymous, and it is necessary to investigate the relationship of differences in factor supplies on both definitions to differences in comparative advantage.

The investigation is most conveniently divided into two parts, corresponding to the two cases distinguished in the discussion of the technological data above.

The first case is that in which there is no reversal of the factor-intensities of commodities in the range of capital : labour ratios between the endowment ratios of the two countries. This situation (exemplified by the combination of r_I with $r_a, r_b,$ or r_{II} in Fig. 2) may be the consequence either of technological conditions which exclude the possibility of such a reversal, or (as in the diagram) of sufficiently similar endowment ratios in the two countries. In this case, owing to the one-to-one relation between comparative cost and factor price ratios, a relatively lower commodity price in one country necessarily implies a relatively lower price there of the factor used relatively intensively in the production of that commodity. Hence comparative advantage is necessarily associated with factor abundance, and disadvantage with factor scarcity, when abundance and scarcity are defined in terms of cheapness or dearness of the factor concerned in one country as compared with the other.

But scarcity and abundance in this sense are not necessarily the same as scarcity and abundance as measured by factor endowment ratios, since factor prices depend on demand as well as on supply, and the influence of demand may outweigh the influence of supply.

Thus a country with relatively abundant labour, judged by its endowment ratio, may be a country with a relatively high price of labour, and hence export the capital-intensive commodity. This possibility is illustrated in Fig. 2 by the combination of $r_I\, c_I$ with $r_{II}\, c_{II}$: country I is at a comparative disadvantage in the production of X, the labour-intensive commodity ($c_I > c_{II}$), labour being more expensive there than in country II ($w_I > w_{II}$); but this is quite

c

consistent with country I having a relatively more abundant endowment of labour, and less abundant endowment of capital, than country II $(r_{II} > r_I)$.

For this possibility to occur, two conditions must be fulfilled. The first is that each country's comparative cost range must overlap the other's closed-economy equilibrium price ratio, which entails (proposition (iv) above) that international trade will lead neither country to specialize completely. The second, and more important, is that each country must have a strong preference for the good which uses intensively the factor with which the country is relatively abundantly endowed.[9]

The effect of trade on relative factor prices in this case is a comparatively simple matter: owing to the one-to-one relationship between commodity cost ratios and relative labour prices, the equalization of commodity prices through trade will tend to equalize relative factor prices.[10] If both countries continue to produce both goods under international trade, equalization will necessarily be complete. (In the case shown in Fig. 2, the relative price of labour in both countries will be w_e, the price corresponding to the common commodity price ratio c_e).[11]

The second case is that in which the endowment ratios of the two countries are separated by one or more reversals of factor-intensities in the production of the goods. In this case, there is no possibility of the country with the higher capital : labour endowment ratio having a lower relative price of labour, since by assumption the ranges of relative factor prices possible in the two countries do not overlap: factor scarcity and abundance can therefore be measured indifferently by endowment ratios or relative factor prices. But because of the intervening factor-intensity reversal(s) and the associated reversal(s) of direction of the effect of a relative factor price change on the commodity cost ratio, it is not possible to relate

[9] Using the ratio measure of the proportions of labour employed in the two industries referred to above, it can easily be shown that at the pre-trade country I price of labour country II would have a smaller proportion of its labour force engaged in the production of the labour-intensive good than country I; at the lower pre-trade country II price of labour, the proportion must be still smaller. At the common price-ratio established by trade, country II must devote a larger proportion of its resources to the capital-intensive industry than will country I.

[10] Since production functions are identical in the two countries, equalization of relative factor prices also means equalization of absolute factor prices (marginal productivities).

[11] If the equilibrium price ratio lies outside a country's range of commodity cost ratios, its relative factor price will be that corresponding to the cost ratio in the range nearest to the equilibrium price ratio.

comparative cost advantage in the production of a particular good to relative abundance (in either sense) of the factor utilized relatively intensively in producing that good—or even, in some cases, to identify goods as relatively labour- or capital-intensive in the world as a whole. The commodity in which the labour-abundant country has a comparative advantage may be either labour-intensive or capital-intensive in that country, and either capital-intensive or labour-intensive in the capital-abundant country. And since the effect of trade is to raise the relative price of the commodity in which the country has a comparative advantage, and therefore the relative price of the factor used relatively more in the production of that commodity, its effect on relative factor prices may be to move them in the same direction in the two countries, towards each other, or away from each other. Moreover, in equilibrium both countries may continue to produce both goods, even though factor prices are different in the two countries.

Two sub-cases may be distinguished for analysis of the effect of trade on factor prices, according to whether the factor-endowment ratios of the two countries are separated by an odd or an even number of reversals of factor-intensities.

If the number of reversals is odd, a commodity which is labour-intensive in one country will be capital-intensive in the other, so that the export commodities of the two countries must have the same relative factor-intensity in the country of origin, being either both capital-intensive or both labour-intensive. The effect of trade will be to move factor prices in the same direction in both countries, and the difference between them may either narrow or widen according to circumstances. If the relatively labour-abundant country has a comparative advantage in its labour-intensive commodity, trade will raise the price of labour in both countries; conversely, if its comparative advantage lies in its capital-intensive commodity, trade will lower the price of labour in both countries. The latter case is illustrated by the combination $r_I\ c_I$, $r'_{II}\ c_{II}$ in Fig. 2, where country I, the relatively labour-abundant country, has a comparative advantage in its capital-intensive commodity Y: the effect of trade is to lower the relative price of labour in both countries, from w_I to w_e in country I and from w_{II} to w'_e in country II. In the particular case shown, both countries continue to produce both commodities, though their relative factor prices are different.

If the number of intervening reversals of factor-intensities is even, a commodity is either labour-intensive or capital-intensive in both countries. The effect of trade is therefore to move factor prices in the two countries in opposite directions; but the movement may be convergent or divergent. If the labour-abundant country has a comparative advantage in the production of the labour-intensive commodity, factor prices in the two countries will move towards each other; if it has a comparative advantage in the production of its capital-intensive commodity, factor prices will move away from each other. This latter case is illustrated by the combination r_I c_I, r_{II}'' c_{II} in Fig. 2, where country I has a comparative advantage in its capital-intensive commodity Y and the effect of the equalization of commodity prices through trade is to lower the relative price of labour in country I from w_I to w_e and raise it in country II from w_{II}'' to w_e''. In the case shown, both countries continue to produce both goods though with different relative factor prices.

The conclusions to be drawn from the foregoing analysis with respect to the influence of differences in factor supplies on the pattern of international trade, and of trade on relative factor prices, may now be summarized and illustrated by reference to the three cases shown in Fig. 2. First, it is not necessarily true that a country will export the commodity which uses relatively intensively the factor with which the country is relatively heavily endowed; in all three cases shown, the country endowed with the lower[12] ratio of capital to labour exports the capital-intensive good. Second, it is not necessarily true that a country will export the commodity which uses relatively more of the factor which would be relatively cheaper in the absence of trade. This proposition will be valid only if, as a consequence either of the nature of the available technology or of the endowment of countries with factors in not too dissimilar proportions, the relative factor-intensities of goods do not reverse themselves as the capital : labour ratio varies between the endowment

[12] A corollary of this result is that the so-called 'Leontief scarce-factor paradox' —that the U.S.A. is a labour-abundant, capital-scarce country, deduced from the statistical finding that U.S. exports are more labour-intensive and less capital-intensive than U.S. import-competing products—rests on a theoretically invalid assumption since the nature of a country's factor endowment, relative to that of the rest of the world, cannot be inferred from the relative factor-intensities of exports and import substitutes in its domestic production. See W. Leontief, 'Domestic Production and Foreign Trade; The American Capital Position Re-Examined', *Proceedings* of the American Philosophical Society, 97 (September 1953), reprinted in *Economia Internazionale*, VII (1954); ibid., 'Factor Proportions and the Structure of American Trade: Further Theoretical and Empirical Analysis', *Review of Economics and Statistics*, XXXVIII, no. 4, November 1956, 386–407. To the list of critics in Footnote 2 of the latter should be added Jones, loc. cit. The theoretical analysis is not, of course, the only questionable feature of Leontief's argument.

ratios of the two countries—the condition required to exclude the possibility of cases like r_I, r_{II}' and r_I, r_{II}'' in Fig. 2. Thirdly, the proposition that trade will tend to equalize relative factor prices, and will in fact do so if both countries continue to produce both goods, is valid only on the same condition; otherwise, trade may have any effect on factor prices, and production of both goods in both countries is consistent with widely different factor prices.[13] Consequently, it is only on the assumption that this condition is fulfilled that it can be maintained that trade is a partial or complete substitute for factor mobility, and free trade a substitute for removal of restrictions on factor movements. Thus the conclusions of the Heckscher-Ohlin model depend not only on the assumption of competition, absence of trade barriers, constant returns to scale, and so forth, but also on an empirical assumption about the nature of technology or the degree of variation in the factor endowments of countries.

In conclusion, something must be said about the extension of the technique of analysis beyond the simple two-country, two-commodity, two-factor case.

Analysis of cases involving more than two countries requires merely the representation of the additional countries by their endowment ratios and pre-trade comparative cost ratios. Similarly, additional goods can be represented by additional curves showing the relation between the optimal capital : labour ratios used in their production and the relative factor price. Little can be said about the effect of allowing for a number of countries, since this depends on the dispersion of their endowment ratios. The effect of allowing for a number of commodities, however, is to strengthen the proposition that a country will tend to export those goods which use relatively most of the factor which would be relatively cheaper in the absence of trade, and that trade will tend to equalize factor prices. The reason for this is that the more goods there are, the more likely it will be that two can be found whose relative factor intensities do not reverse at a capital : labour ratio between the endowment ratios of the two countries.

The relatively labour-intensive commodity of such a pair must be cheaper in the country with the relatively lower price of labour, and

[13] Compare P. A. Samuelson, 'International Trade and the Equalisation of Factor Prices', *Economic Journal*, LVIII, no. 230, June 1948, 163–84, and ibid., 'International Factor Price Equalisation Once Again', loc. cit., LIX, no. 234, June 1949, 181–97. The condition required for equalization, that factor-intensities do not reverse between the endowment ratios, is assumed implicitly in the first of these articles, and stated explicitly in the second. See James and Pearce, loc. cit.

conversely, in the pre-trade situation; and the effect of trade in establishing a common price-ratio between the pair must therefore be to raise the price of labour in the labour-abundant country and reduce it in the capital-abundant country. If both goods continue to be produced in both countries, factor prices must be equalized completely.

While the technique can be easily adapted to handle more countries and more commodities, it cannot easily be extended to allow for a larger number of factors of production, since each additional factor introduces an additional factor price and endowment ratio. Two points can, however, be made with respect to the conditions under which countries will necessarily export the commodities intensive in their relatively cheap factors, and trade will tend to equalize factor prices. The first is that, unless the number of goods is at least equal to the number of factors, no relationship between commodity prices and factor prices such as that assumed in Fig. 1 will exist, so that it will not be possible to establish conditions on which factor prices are in a one-to-one relationship with commodity prices. The second is that, once the number of factors (and goods) exceeds two, the conditions required for the one-to-one relationship to hold cannot be stated in any economically meaningful way, because the concept of 'factor-intensity' loses its simplicity.

CHAPTER II

Optimum Tariffs
and Retaliation*

DURING recent years the proposition first advanced by Mill and formalized by Bickerdike, that a country can improve its welfare as compared with the free trade position by imposing a tariff on imports, has achieved general recognition in the literature of international trade theory. There is still, however, some confusion over what happens if other countries retaliate by imposing tariffs in their turn. Although Kaldor,[1] in his classic revival of the proposition, referred explicitly to the possibility that a country might gain by imposing a tariff even if other countries retaliated—a possibility which is also indicated by considerations of general monopoly theory—the possibility is often overlooked: it being assumed, and argued against the 'optimum tariff' theorem, that once retaliation occurs all parties are bound to lose as compared with the free trade position. The *locus classicus* of this error (and some others) is probably Scitovszky's analysis of retaliation in his 'Reconsideration of the Theory of Tariffs'.[2]

My purpose in what follows is to reassert the proposition that a country *may* gain by imposing a tariff even if other countries retaliate; and to determine the conditions under which it *will* gain in a special group of cases. In the process, the theory of optimum tariff retaliation is restated. The argument is conducted throughout in terms of a two-country, two-commodity exchange model, in which country *I* exports commodity *Y* in exchange for imports of commodity *X* from country *II*. It is assumed—as is necessary for drawing any definite welfare conclusions from international trade theory—that each

* *The Review of Economic Studies*, XXI(2), no. 55, 1953–4, 142–53.

[1] N. Kaldor, 'A Note on Tariffs and the Terms of Trade', *Economica*, N.S., VII, no. 28, November 1940, 377–80.

[2] T. de Scitovszky, 'A Reconsideration of the Theory of Tariffs', *Review of Economic Studies*, IX, no. 2, Summer 1942, 89–110, reprinted in *Readings in the Theory of International Trade* (Philadelphia, 1949), chap. 16, 358–89; Part IV analyses retaliation.

country pursues a definite social welfare policy (maximizes a given social welfare function) so that its willingness to trade under various conditions can be summarized in a set of community indifference curves (community preference system); these curves are assumed to have the customary convexity and non-intersection properties.

In the analysis itself, it is assumed that 'retaliation' takes the form of the imposition of an optimum tariff, on the assumption that the other country's tariff will remain unchanged;[3] and attention is confined to cases in which each country's demand for imports as a function of its terms of trade is elastic, so that the imposition of a tariff by either country reduces the total volume of imports it receives.[4]

The optimum tariff theory may be briefly summarized by reference to Fig. 1. In the diagram, U^I and U^{II} are the preference systems of countries I and II, $O.I$ and $O.II$ their respective offer curves, and P the free trade equilibrium point. Unless country II's offer curve is a straight line, country I can gain by imposing a tariff which brings the trade equilibrium point anywhere within the range PQ on country II's offer curve, Q being the point on country II's offer curve which lies on the same country I indifference curve as P. Country I's optimum tariff is that which brings trade equilibrium at the point P' on the highest country I indifference curve touched by country II's offer curve. The rate of tariff which produces this result is $t_I = j - 1$, where j is the elasticity of country II's reciprocal demand curve $\left(\dfrac{EY}{EX}\right)$ at the point P' and is measured on the diagram by the ratio $\dfrac{OB}{AB}$.[5]

---

[3] This assumption obviously begs the question of rationality if the world is really assumed to consist of only two countries; following Scitovszky, the two-country analysis may be taken as representative of a monopolistically-competitive situation. The assumption that the interaction of trade policy proceeds by the successive imposition of optimum tariffs, rather than by slight changes in existing tariffs, is a simplification which would affect the result only if multiple trade-policy equilibria existed. Finally, while a country might 'retaliate' by imposing a tariff other than the optimum, either from 'good-neighbourliness' or from vindictiveness, such behaviour would imply that its welfare depended in part on the welfare (or illfare) of other nations as well as on its own consumption, and would therefore fall outside the strictly self-regarding assumptions of optimum tariff theory.

[4] This does not, however, restrict the validity of the conclusions to such cases.

[5] For the derivation of this and other formulae, see H. G. Johnson, 'Optimum Welfare and Maximum Revenue Tariffs', Review of Economic Studies, XIX(1), no. 48, 1950–1, 28–35 (Appendix to this chapter).

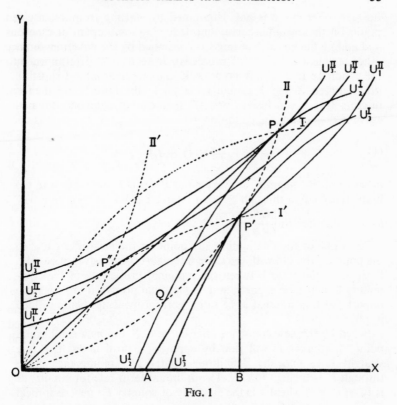

FIG. 1

The imposition of the tariff t_I alters country I's offer curve to $O.I'$, which intersects $O.II$ at P'. It is worth noting that, in contrast to the procedure employed in general tariff theory, $O.I'$ is not found by simply shifting $O.I$ to the south-east to an extent proportional to the tariff rate. This is because, in general tariff theory, the consumers are assumed to give up the tariff proceeds, which therefore do not affect their behaviour,[6] whereas in this case the tariff proceeds are assumed to be redistributed to the consumers (directly or indirectly) and so do influence their behaviour. Consequently, the location of

[6] L. A. Metzler, however ('Tariffs, the Terms of Trade, and the Distribution of the National Income', *Journal of Political Economy*, LVII, no. 1, February 1949, 1–29), assumes that the tariff proceeds are distributed to consumers and analyses the effects of the distribution on the location of the offer curve in terms of the marginal propensity to import; and J. E. Meade, in *A Geometry of International Trade* (London, 1952) employs the same construction as that used here.

the new offer curve is not determined by starting from successive points on the old offer curve, and deducting the amount of exports and adding the amount of imports consumed by the government (or other recipient of the tariff proceeds). Instead, it is determined by the condition that, at any point on it, the marginal rate of substitution between X and Y should be equal to the ratio between their internal (i.e. tax-inclusive) prices.[7] In terms of symbols, the new curve is defined by the condition

$$(1) \qquad \frac{dX}{dY} = -\frac{U_y^I}{U_x^I} = (1 + t_I)\frac{p_x}{p_y};$$

in terms of the diagram, at every point P' on $O.I'$ the tangent to the indifference curve through P' must intersect OX at A in such a way as to make the ratio $\dfrac{OB}{AB} = t_I + 1$.

The slope of the line joining any point on the new offer curve to the point on the old with the same internal (tax-inclusive) price ratio is equal to the ratio between the marginal propensity of the community to consume exports, and its marginal propensity to consume imports, at that internal price ratio, both propensities being defined in physical units.[8]

Faced by the new country I offer curve $O.I'$ and new equilibrium point P', country II will gain by imposing a tariff unless $O.I'$ is a straight line, since by definition country II's indifference curve through P' is tangent to OP'. The optimum tariff rate for country II is $t_{II} = k - 1$, where k is the elasticity of country I's new reciprocal demand curve $\left(\dfrac{EX}{EY}\right)$ at the point P''.

P'' may or may not be a position of final (commercial-policy) equilibrium, since the new country II offer curve through that point may or may not make it advantageous for country I to revise its tariff rate. To pursue the matter further, let us turn to Fig. 2, which concentrates on the situation at P''. In the diagram, AA' has been drawn tangent to the country I indifference curve through P'', and

---

[7] It follows from the assumed convexity of the community indifference curves that the reciprocal demand curve traced out by a higher tariff rate will always lie inside the curve traced out by a lower tariff rate, whether the latter is inelastic or not. Consequently, the imposition of a tariff cannot, on our assumptions, turn a country's terms of trade against it.

[8] On the assumption that tax proceeds are spent by the Government, the slope of this line is equal to the ratio of export to import quantities in the purchases of the Government out of tax proceeds.

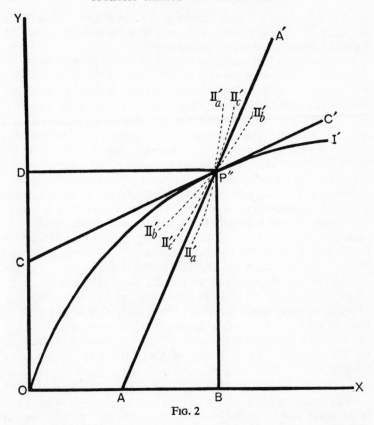

FIG. 2

II'_a, II'_b, and II'_c have been drawn to represent possible positions of $O.II'$.

From Fig. 2, it is obvious that if $O.II'$ intersects AA' from the north-west (II'_a) country I will gain by increasing its tariff rate; if it intersects AA' from the north-east (II'_b) country I will gain by lowering its tariff; if $O.II'$ is tangent to AA' (II'_c) country I cannot gain by changing its tariff. Since the slope of $O.II'$ at P'' is an indicator of the elasticity of country II's new (post-retaliation) reciprocal demand curve at that point, and the slope of AP'' reflects the elasticity of country II's original reciprocal demand curve at the point P', it follows that country I will raise its tariff if the elasticity of $O.II'$ at P'' is greater than the elasticity of $O.II$ at P'; lower its tariff if the elasticity of $O.II'$ at P'' is less than the elasticity of $O.II$ at P'; and leave it unchanged if the elasticities of $O.II'$ at P'' and $O.II$ at P' are the same. This conclusion, of course, may be arrived at directly from the formula for the optimum tariff.

The conclusion just stated contradicts that arrived at by Professor Scitovszky, who concludes that at P'' country I either cannot gain by altering its tariff, or finds it advantageous to raise its tariff still higher. His conclusion, which seems to derive from an uncritical extension of the argument for the situation at P' to that at P'', implicitly assumes that the elasticity of country II's tariff-ridden reciprocal demand curve at P'' is always higher than the elasticity of its free-trade reciprocal demand curve at P', an assumption for which there is no justification in the nature of the problem.[9]

This point is easily understood when translated into more general terms. The imposition of the original tariff gave country I the benefit of an improvement in its terms of trade, secured at the cost of some reduction in the volume of trade. The imposition of a retaliatory tariff by country II both worsens country I's terms of trade and further restricts the volume of international trade. In the new situation, three courses are open to country I: it can raise its tariff, improving its terms of trade at the expense of a further restriction of trade volume; it can lower its tariff, increasing the volume of trade at the cost of a further worsening of its terms of trade; or it can leave the tariff and the volume of trade unchanged. Depending on the circumstances, any one of the three may be the most advantageous.

If P'' is not a position of commercial policy equilibrium, further

[9] This assumption seems to be related to the argument developed by Scitovszky in connection with his welfare criterion, that as restriction increases trade is confined to goods for which the demand is less elastic (on the usual definition of elasticity), so that the possibility of exploiting the foreigner increases with restriction. However, both Scitovszky's analysis and ours assume that at some price-ratio country II would cease to gain from trade; and at this price-ratio the elasticity of its demand for country I's goods must be infinite (i.e. unity on the definition of elasticity employed here). Consequently, the elasticity of country II's demand for imports cannot be presumed always to decrease as trade is restricted, and the argument referred to would not be sufficient to establish the validity of the conclusion disputed in the text. This argument—that the more trade is restricted, the more inelastic the foreigner's demand becomes and the more he can be exploited—has been applied to the parallel case of import restriction by J. R. Hicks ('Free Trade and Modern Economics', a paper read to the Manchester Statistical Society on March 14, 1951), who deduces from it a successive tightening of import restrictions. His argument seems to overlook the consideration that by the same reasoning domestic demand for imports becomes less elastic as trade is restricted, so that the sacrifice of imports entailed in exploiting the foreigner further becomes more burdensome.

successive adjustments of the tariffs of the two countries will take place. Before the possible outcomes of the adjustment process are considered in detail, two general points about it may be noted. First, the outcome will be unique, in the sense that, given that country *I* has made the first move, each succeeding step in the adjustment process is uniquely determined.[10] Second, each of the trade equilibrium points reached in the adjustment process must involve a volume of trade which is positive but less[11] than the trade volume under free-trade conditions. That the adjustment process will never end in the elimination of trade is a logical consequence of the classical proposition that some trade is always better than no trade;[12] that the volume of trade will be less than it would be under free trade may be inferred from the argument presented above.

Both of these points are denied by Scitovszky, who asserts that the outcome is not necessarily unique, and that retaliation may end in the termination of trade. The former assertion is probably a verbal slip;[13] the latter seems to involve a confusion of optimum tariff theory with pessimum tariff history, and of trade in particular commodities with trade in general.

The process of adjustment may be studied in detail by means of a reaction-curve technique which is presented in Figs. 3(*a*) and (*b*).[14]

[10] Though the other country's reciprocal demand curve might be so shaped that it is touched more than once by the same indifference curve of the tariff-imposing country, it is reasonable to assume that one tangency point is consistently chosen in preference to the others. Problems of discontinuity of choice implied by this possibility are ignored in what follows.

[11] If the demand for imports as a function of the terms of trade were inelastic for one or both countries, trade in one commodity might be greater than under free trade.

[12] Except in a limiting case excluded by the definition of the present problem.

[13] It is difficult to be certain, since Professor Scitovszky does not define the term, though he uses it in the same context as the present writer. Also, while his diagrammatic treatment proceeds on the same assumption as that adopted here —that adjustment is effected by the imposition of optimum tariffs—his verbal argument allows the possibility that he is assuming adjustment by small tariff changes; this alternative assumption might allow a variety of paths to be followed from the same starting-point.

[14] Although the problem is formally one in bilateral monopoly, the technique of analysis employed below bears a strong family resemblance to the Cournot solution of the duopoly problem. Relaxation of the Scitovszky assumption that each country ignores the reactions of the other could lead to a Stackelberg type of analysis in terms of a policy-leader and a policy-follower. Thus, if country *I* proceeds on the assumption that country *II* will impose whatever tariff is optimum given the tariff imposed by country *I*, the tariffs imposed by the two countries will be determined by the tangency of a country *I* indifference curve with the country *II* welfare-reaction curve depicted in Fig. 3(a). Country *I* might in this

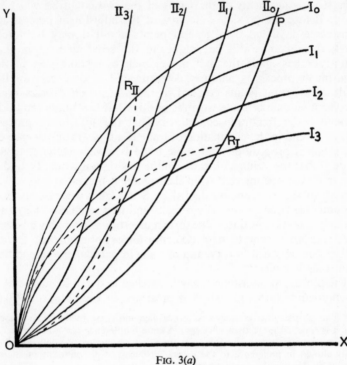

FIG. 3(a)

In Fig. 3(a) are plotted the offer curves of the two countries at various levels of tariffs, as determined by the procedure outlined earlier; $O.I_0$ and $O.II_0$ represent the offer curves under free trade (zero tariff) conditions. The tangency points of one country's in-difference curves with the other's offer curves trace out *loci* of optimum-tariff equilibrium points (welfare-reaction curves) for the respective countries. Thus OR_I shows the optimum point for country *I* for each tariff that might be imposed by country *II*, the tariff

case be worse off than it would be if it could use its leadership to maintain free trade; but, by reasoning analogous to that presented below, this result is by no means inevitable. A more interesting 'leadership' model might be constructed on the assumption that country *I*'s tariff-rate sets a maximum to the tariff-rate which country *II* can impose; this assumption would define a locus of potential trade-equilibrium points, of which country *I* would choose the one which maximized its welfare.

This footnote was suggested by comments from Solomon Adler and Robert Solow.

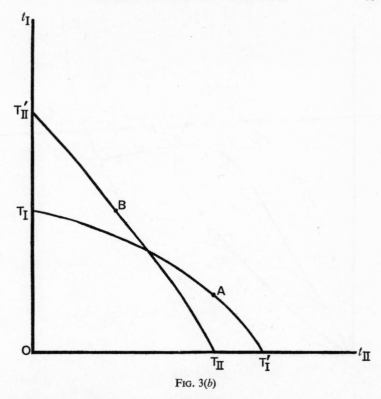

FIG. 3(b)

required to bring country I to that point being given by the index of the $O.I$ curve through that point. The curve OR_I must pass through the origin, lie inside $O.I_0$ (except in the neighbourhood of the origin, where it coincides with $O.I_0$), move steadily to the right (i.e. Y must be a single-valued function of X), and meet $O.II_0$ below P; otherwise it may take any shape. Similar conditions apply to OR_{II}. Each country is better off the farther along its welfare-reaction curve it is from the origin.

The welfare-reaction curves show the optimum trade-equilibrium points for each country, for all possible tariffs imposed by the other. A movement away from the origin on such a curve may imply either an increase or a decrease in the country's (optimum) tariff,[15] and it is convenient to supplement these curves with reaction curves

[15] As Fig. 3(a) is drawn, higher welfare for either country is associated with the imposition of a higher tariff.

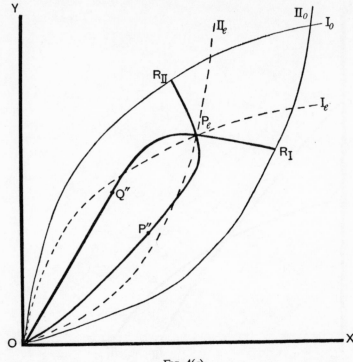

FIG. 4(a)

showing the tariff required to maximize a country's welfare, given the tariff imposed by the other. These are presented in Fig. 3(b). In the figure, $T_I.T_I'$ shows the optimum rate of tariff for country I for each actual tariff imposed by country II, and $T_{II}.T_{II}'$ gives the corresponding information for country II. T_I, the starting point of $T_I.T_I'$, must be positive; $T_I.T_I'$ must move continually to the right (i.e. t_I must be a single-valued function of t_{II}); it must pass through some point A vertically above T_{II}; it must meet the $O.t_{II}$ axis somewhere beyond T_{II}, at the point corresponding to the tariff-rate which would eliminate trade;[16] and T_I must always be less than the latter

[16] The tariff-rate which would eliminate trade is the same, whichever country imposes it, and is equal to one less than the ratio of the slope of the country I indifference curve through the origin to the slope of the country II indifference curve through the origin, both slopes being taken relative to the X-axis. More simply, it is the proportional excess of the price of X in country I over its price in country II, in the absence of trade. I am grateful to R. M. Goodwin for clarification of the restrictions on the shape of the tariff-reaction curve.

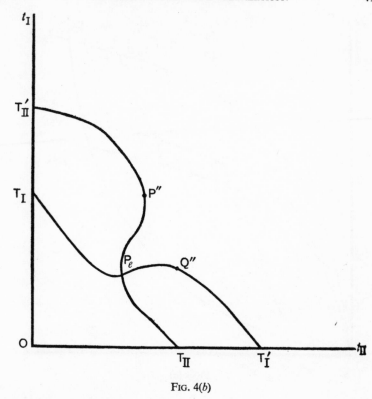

FIG. 4(b)

rate. But $T_I.T_I'$, and similarly $T_{II}.T_{II}'$, may take any shape which fulfils these conditions. Country I is worse off the farther along $T_I.T_I'$ it is from T_I, and country II is worse off the farther along $T_{II}.T_{II}'$ it is from T_{II}.

With the aid of this apparatus it can easily be seen that, starting from an interruption of free trade by the imposition of an optimum tariff by country I, the adjustment process may lead to either one of two possible outcomes. First, it may lead to a position of policy equilibrium, characterized by the tangency of one of each country's indifference curves with the other country's tariff-inclusive offer curve. Such a position would be represented by the intersection of the two countries' reaction curves [OR_I with $O.R_{II}$ in Fig. 3(a), $T_I.T_I'$ with $T_{II}.T_{II}'$ in Fig. 3(b)]. In equilibrium, the tariff of either country may be either higher or lower than it was at the first stage

D

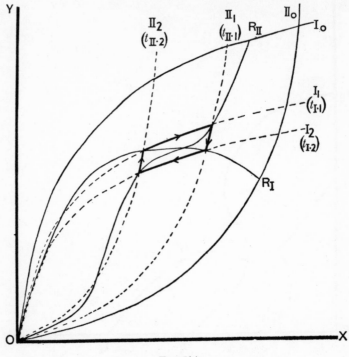

FIG. 5(a)

of retaliation (P'' in Figs. 1 and 2) when country I had imposed an optimum tariff and country II had retaliated. The possibility that the tariff rates finally arrived at may be lower for both countries is illustrated in Fig. 4.[17]

The second possible outcome of the adjustment process is that policy equilibrium will never be reached;[18] instead, the adjustment

[17] The figure is drawn so that the same result follows whether country I or country II makes the first break from free trade. P'' and Q'' represent the first stage of retaliation in the two cases; P_e, I_e and II_e the equilibrium point and equilibrium tariffs.

[18] I am indebted to a discussion with M. J. Farrell for elucidation of this possibility.

[19] Such a tariff cycle will ensue if the shapes of the tariff-reaction curves make it possible to draw about their intersection a rectangle with sides parallel to the axes and corners on the two reaction curves, such that:

   (a) the product of the slopes of the country I curve at the corners through which it passes is less than the product of the slopes of the country II

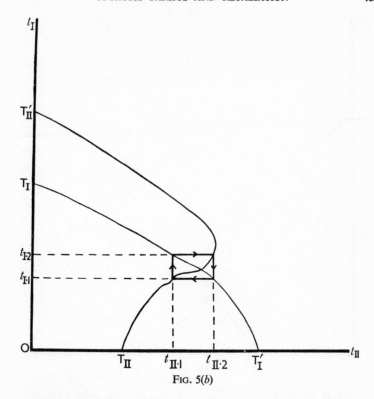

FIG. 5(b)

process may converge on a 'tariff cycle',[19] with (for example) an increase in country I's tariff leading to an increase in country II's tariff, which in turn provokes a decrease in country I's tariff which leads to a decrease in country II's tariff which leads country I to raise its tariff again. Such a 'tariff cycle' is illustrated in Fig. 5.[20] In the diagrams, an increase in country I's tariff from $t_{I,1}$ to $t_{I,2}$ leads

curve at the corners through which it passes, both slopes being taken relative to the t_I axis; and

(b) T_I does not lie within the segment of the t_I axis cut off by the projection of the sides of the rectangle.

In the limiting case the 'rectangle' may be the intersection point itself [as in Fig. 5(b)]; then condition (a) becomes the usual slope condition for an explosive cobweb cycle, and condition (b) excludes the possibility of unstable policy equilibrium.

[20] Since the cycle depends on an increase in one country's tariff making it advantageous for the other to lower its tariff, it could not arise if it were always

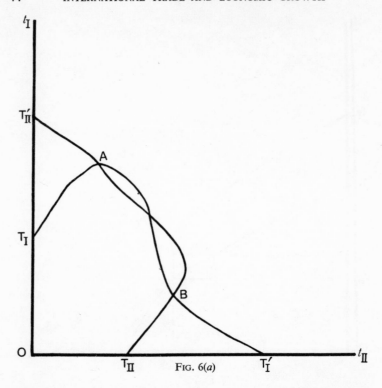

FIG. 6(a)

country II to raise its tariff from $t_{II.1}$ to $t_{II.2}$; country I retaliates by lowering its tariff to $t_{I.1}$; country II follows by lowering its tariff to $t_{II.1}$; country I raises its tariff again to $t_{I.2}$ and the cycle repeats itself.

To summarize, there are two possibilities; the adjustment process may converge on a policy equilibrium point, or it may converge on a tariff cycle. The analysis thus far has assumed that the adjustment process begins with the interruption of free trade by the imposition of an optimum tariff by country I. Free trade may equally well be interrupted by the imposition of a tariff by country II; and the outcome—whether a tariff cycle or policy equilibrium—may be different from the outcome when the process begins with a move by country

advantageous for one country to respond to an increase in the other's tariff by an increase in its own. Thus the Scitovszky assumption excludes the possibility of tariff cycles. It may be remarked that a continued tariff cycle would eventually demonstrate the irrationality of the model's assumptions.

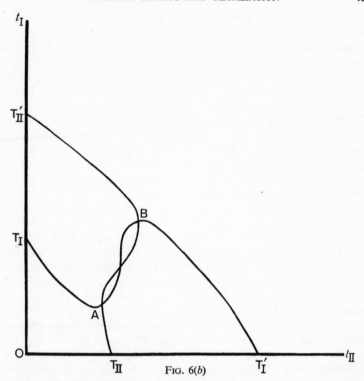

FIG. 6(b)

I.[21] In short, the outcome of tariff retaliation may depend on which country first imposes a tariff.

This does not, however, as assumed by Scitovszky and others, imply that a country necessarily winds up in a better position if it is the first to impose a tariff than if the other country begins the erection of tariff barriers. In those cases in which a position of policy equilibrium is reached,[22] it is also possible for a country to end up better off if the other country imposes the first tariff than if it makes the first move itself; or for *both* countries to be worse off if one of them starts the tariff-erection process than if the other does. The first of

[21] It may be remarked that in cases in which policy equilibrium is not achieved in the first two steps, and the Scitovszky assumption that adjustment *always* involves tariff increase or no change holds good, the same position will be reached whichever country imposes the first tariff.

[22] The argument can be extended, with appropriate modifications, to cases in which the outcome is a 'tariff cycle' rather than a policy equilibrium, by considering the least favourable position on the tariff cycle.

these possibilities is illustrated in Fig. 6(*a*), and the second in Fig. 6(*b*). In each diagram, policy equilibrium is reached at *A* if country *II* imposes the first tariff and at *B* if country *I* imposes the first tariff. In Fig. 6(*a*) each country ends up closer to the starting point of its reaction curve, and therefore better off, if the other country rather than itself imposes the first tariff. In Fig. 6(*b*), both countries end up better off if country *II* imposes the first tariff than if country *I* does. Both of these cases involve reaction curves with ranges in which an increase in one country's tariff makes an increase in the other country's tariff advantageous; if an increase in one country's tariff always prompted a decrease in the other's (the opposite of the Scitovszky assumption) a country would always be better off if it were the first to impose a tariff.

The foregoing argument has been devoted to a restatement of the theory of retaliation; our central concern, however, is with the question of whether, as Scitovszky and others assert, both countries are necessarily worse off when retaliation is allowed for than they would be under free trade. In considering this problem, we shall for simplicity confine the argument to cases in which a policy equilibrium is attained.[23] Let us assume that P'' in Figs. 1 and 2 represents such an equilibrium. Then from Fig. 1 it is apparent that country *I* would be better off after both countries have imposed (consistent) optimum tariffs if the indifference curve through P'' passed to the right of *P*, the free-trade equilibrium point; similarly country *II* would gain as compared with the free-trade situation if the country *II* indifference curve through P'' passed to the left of *P*. Whatever the final equilibrium point, one country *must* lose under tariffs as compared with free trade, since gain depends on obtaining an improvement in the terms of trade sufficient to outweigh the loss of trade volume, and this is impossible for both countries simultaneously; and both countries *may* lose, as is in fact the case in Fig. 1; but it is not necessarily true that both *will* lose.[24]

[23] See previous footnote.

[24] It is, however, true that both countries together will lose under tariffs as compared with free trade, in the compensation-principle sense that both could be made better off by a return to free trade, possibly coupled with an income transfer, since the trade equilibrium point with tariffs is off the contract curve. This may indeed be what Scitovszky had in mind, though his argument is certainly not explicit; if so, apologies are in order for misinterpretation. P. A. Samuelson has pointed out to the writer, in support of this interpretation of Scitovszky's argument, that the latter's remark that 'if foreigners produced perfect substitutes, their reciprocal demand would be perfectly elastic and the optimum tariff rate would be zero, and would remain zero even after other countries have imposed tariffs of their own' (*Readings*, 376) implicitly recognizes the possibility of a country gaining even with retaliation.

The same point emerges from Fig. 2, which represents the commercial-policy equilibrium point, but does not show the free-trade equilibrium point. All that is known about the latter is that it must lie to the north-east of P'': if it lies to the left of AA', country I must, by the usual index-number logic, be better off than it would be under free trade;[25] if it lies to the right of CC', country II must, by the same argument, be better off than it would be under free trade; if it lies between AA' and CC', either country may be better off or both may be worse off than under free trade, depending on the location of P and the shapes of the indifference curves through P''.[26]

Unfortunately, while it is easy to demonstrate the possibility of one country being better off under (optimum) tariffs than under free trade, the conditions under which it will be so involve the relationship between the preference systems of the two countries,[27] and are too complex to express in terms of simple and objectively assessable concepts. Kaldor's statement,[28] for example, that:

> 'if the elasticity of the country's own demand for foreign products is markedly higher than the elasticity of foreign demand for its own products—an unusual case—this policy may be advantageous even if the "optimum degree of retaliation" of foreign countries is allowed for'

is imprecise and almost meaningless, since, as has been seen above, the elasticities involved in the analysis lie on different and not closely related curves—of which they may not be parameters—and in any

[25] By a simple geometrical argument it can be shown that a country's welfare is necessarily improved if the total proceeds of the tariff exceed the difference between the values of the free-trade quantity of imports at the new and the free-trade internal prices. Specifically, country I must be better off with tariffs if

$$\frac{t_I}{t_I + 1} \; \pi_x \, . \, X_1 > (\pi_x - p_x) \, . \, X_0$$

where X_o and X_1 are the quantities imported under free trade and in tariff equilibrium, p_x and π_x are the internal price of X in terms of Y before and after the tariff, and t_I is the tariff rate.

[26] Alternatively, the conclusion could be established by finding the rate of tariff for the other country which would leave the country in question exactly as well off, after it had retaliated, as it would be if both countries practised free trade, and marking the corresponding point on its welfare-reaction curve [Fig. 3(a)] or tariff-reaction curve [Fig. 3(b)]. The country's welfare would be greater under tariffs than under free trade if the policy equilibrium point lay farther from the origin than that point on the former curve, or closer to the origin than that point on the latter curve.

[27] There are also the difficulties discussed above that the outcome may be a tariff cycle instead of a policy equilibrium point and that the answer may depend on which country first imposes a tariff. [28] Loc. cit., p. 380.

case the answer depends on the preference systems lying behind the curves.

Parenthetically, this is a general problem in the application of the optimum tariff theory, since the elasticities incorporated in the various optimum tariff formulae (besides being 'total' and not 'partial' concepts) are likely to vary along the reciprocal demand curve, so that empirical observations on these elasticities may yield no useful guide to policy conclusions, except perhaps as to the desirable direction of change.[29]

There is, however, one group of cases in which the required conditions could be fairly readily established.[30] If in each country the community preference system were such as to generate an offer curve of the same, constant, elasticity, whatever the tariff the country imposed on its imports, each country's optimum tariff would be independent of the other's; and the same commercial policy equilibrium point would be reached, in only two steps from the free-trade position, whatever country first erected a tariff.[31] The free-trade and optimum-tariff equilibrium points could therefore easily be determined, and the utility levels enjoyed in the two cases by the two countries assessed from the community preference systems; and the condition for a country to be better off under optimum tariffs could be stated in terms of the relations between four parameters, two for each country—the (constant) elasticity of reciprocal demand, and the direction of shift of the offer curve with the imposition of the tariff.

A group of cases answering this description, which can be handled without great difficulty, is that in which the utility functions are of the form

(2a) $$U^I = f^I (k X^{\frac{a}{k}} - A^{\frac{a}{k}} Y^a) \quad (1 \leq a \leq k)$$

(2b) $$U^{II} = f^{II} (j Y^{\frac{b}{j}} - B^{\frac{b}{j}} X^b) \quad (1 \leq b \leq j)$$

[29] Cf. Graaff's strictures on R. F. Kahn's attempt to prove that the optimum tariff is likely to be high (J. de V. Graaff, 'On Optimum Tariff Structures', *The Review of Economic Studies*, XVII(1), no. 42, 1949–50, 47–59, especially 56).

[30] The argument of this and the following paragraphs has been drastically revised as a result of criticisms raised by W. M. Gorman ('Tariffs, Retaliation, and the Elasticity of Demand for Imports', *Review of Economic Studies*, XXV(3), no. 68, June 1958). The original version assumed, wrongly, that the utility function could be derived from the offer curve, and hence dealt with one of the particular cases of the group discussed below as if it were the only one consistent with constant elasticity.

[31] If one country only has a utility function of this special type, the equilibrium point would still be the same, whichever country started tariff-erection, and would be reached in either two or three steps, depending on whether the other or that country imposed the first tariff.

where the f's are any monotonically-increasing functions of the expressions in brackets, and for simplicity are henceforth omitted. Taking country I for purposes of illustration, the offer curve corresponding to any tariff t_I ($t_I = 0$ under free trade) is defined by the condition

$$(3) \qquad -\frac{U_x}{U_y} = \frac{X^{\frac{a}{k}-1}}{A^{\frac{a}{k}} Y^{a-1}} = \frac{dY}{dX} = (1 + t_I) \frac{Y}{X}$$

[equality of the marginal rate of substitution with the internal (tariff-inclusive) price ratio]; and its equation is

$$(4) \qquad X = A (1 + t_I)^{\frac{k}{a}} Y^k.$$

Hence the elasticity of the offer curve is a constant ($= k$) whatever the tariff rate.

The direction of displacement of the offer curve by the tariff is determined by the exponent $\frac{k}{a}$. Differentiation of (3), keeping the right-hand side constant, yields the result

$$(5) \qquad -\frac{\dfrac{dY}{Y}}{\dfrac{dX}{X}} = \frac{\left(1 - \dfrac{a}{k}\right)}{(a - 1)}.$$

This gives the ratio of the proportional reduction in the quantity of exports offered to the proportional increase in imports demanded at any given internal price ratio as the tariff is increased. Two extreme cases are of interest:[32] if $a = k$, the quantity of exports offered is independent of the tariff, which shifts the offer curve entirely in the import direction (east for country I in Fig. 1); if $a = 1$, the quantity of imports demanded is independent of the tariff, which shifts the offer-curve entirely in the export direction (south, for country I in Fig. 1). From the fact that the direction of shift reflects the relative magnitudes of the community's marginal propensities to consume the two goods, it can be inferred that in the former case exports are a pure necessity (zero marginal propensity to consume) and imports a pure luxury, whereas in the latter case imports are a pure necessity and exports a pure luxury.

[32] Cases of 'inferiority' of a commodity in a country's consumption are ignored in what follows.

Solution of equation (4) and the corresponding equation for country *II* yields the equilibrium quantities of goods traded,

(6a)
$$X = A^{\frac{1}{1-jk}} B^{\frac{k}{1-jk}} (1 + t_I)^{\frac{k/a}{1-jk}} (1 + t_{II})^{\frac{kj/b}{1-jk}}$$

(6b)
$$Y = A^{\frac{j}{1-jk}} B^{\frac{1}{1-jk}} (1 + t_I)^{\frac{jk/a}{1-jk}} (1 + t_{II})^{\frac{j/b}{1-jk}}.$$

From these are determined the utility levels enjoyed in the two countries,

(7a)
$$U^I = \left(k - \frac{1}{1 + t_I}\right) X^{\frac{a}{k}}$$

(7b)
$$U^{II} = \left(j - \frac{1}{1 + t_{II}}\right) Y^{\frac{b}{j}}.$$

The ratios of the utility levels enjoyed under optimum tariffs $(t_I = j - 1, t_{II} = k - 1)$ to those enjoyed under free trade $(t_I = t_{II} = 0)$ are

(8a)
$$\frac{U_t^I}{U_0^I} = \frac{k - \frac{1}{j}}{k - 1} j^{\frac{1}{1-jk}} k^{\frac{j\,a/b}{1-jk}}$$

(8b)
$$\frac{U_t^{II}}{U_0^{II}} = \frac{j - \frac{1}{k}}{j - 1} j^{\frac{k\,b/a}{1-jk}} k^{\frac{1}{1-jk}}.$$

In terms of the more usual conception of elasticities of international demand $\Big($elasticities of quantity demanded with respect to relative price, determined by the relations $\eta_I = \frac{k}{k-1}, \eta_{II} = \frac{j}{j-1}\Big)$ these equations for the ratios of the utility levels are

(9a)
$$\frac{U_t^I}{U_0^I} = \frac{\eta_1 + \eta_2 - 1}{\eta_2} \left(\frac{\eta_1 - 1}{\eta_1}\right)^{\frac{(\eta_1-1)\,\eta_2\,a/b}{\eta_1+\eta_2-1}} \left(\frac{\eta_2 - 1}{\eta_2}\right)^{\frac{(\eta_1-1)(\eta_2-1)}{\eta_1+\eta_2-1}}$$

(9b)
$$\frac{U_t^{II}}{U_0^{II}} = \frac{\eta_1 + \eta_2 - 1}{\eta_1} \left(\frac{\eta_1 - 1}{\eta_1}\right)^{\frac{(\eta_1-1)(\eta_2-1)}{\eta_1+\eta_2-1}} \left(\frac{\eta_2 - 1}{\eta_2}\right)^{\frac{(\eta_2-1)\,\eta_1\,b/a}{\eta_1+\eta_2-1}}.$$

Country *I* will be better or worse off under optimum tariffs than under free trade according as the right-hand side of (8a) [or (9a)] is greater or less than unity; and similarly for country *II*. These conditions unfortunately cannot be reduced to the form of more simple relations between the three variables—the two reciprocal demand elasticities *j* and *k* (or η_I and η_{II}) and the ratio of the shift parameters $\dfrac{a}{b}$ —on which they depend. Some idea of the border-line between cases of gain and of loss under optimum tariff retaliation as compared with free trade can, however, be obtained by calculation of numerical examples. This has been done for the following four special values of the ratio of shift parameters:

Case I: $\dfrac{a}{b} = \dfrac{1}{j}$. In this case, imports are a pure necessity and exports a pure luxury in country *I*, whereas imports are a pure luxury and exports a pure necessity in country *II*.

Case II: $\dfrac{a}{b} = \dfrac{k}{j}$. This case includes a range of combinations of magnitudes of the shift parameters for the individual countries; at one extreme is the case in which imports are a pure luxury and exports a pure necessity in both countries.

Case III: $\dfrac{a}{b} = 1$. This case also includes a range of combinations of shift parameters, one extreme being that in which imports are a pure necessity and exports a pure luxury in both countries.

Case IV: $\dfrac{a}{b} = k$. In this case, imports are a pure luxury and exports a pure necessity in country *I*, whereas imports are a pure necessity and exports a pure luxury in country *II*.

In each case, the border-line between cases of gain and of loss for country *I* was found by a trial-and-error process of computing the logarithm of the right-hand side of equation (9a), starting with $\eta_I = \eta_{II} = 1 \cdot 1$, raising the value of one elasticity by one-tenth intervals until the logarithm changed sign, increasing the value of the other by one-tenth, and repeating the calculation until one elasticity reached the value 5·0. The results (which also provide border-lines for country *II*) are presented in Fig. 7, which maps the

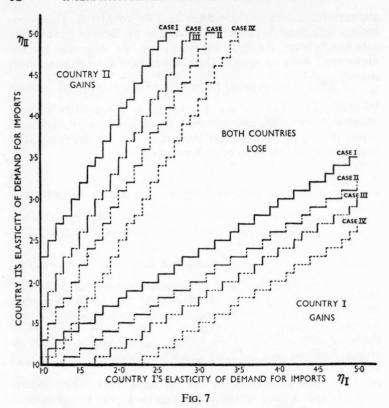

FIG. 7

combinations of elasticities which yield a gain for one country or the other or a loss for both, for the four cases.[33] Comparison of the results for the different cases suggests some interesting conclusions

[33] The method of computation yields two border-lines, that corresponding to definite gains from tariffs with retaliation and that corresponding to definite losses, with a range of indeterminacy between them corresponding to untested values of the elasticities. The border-lines in Fig. 7 link elasticity values showing a definite gain from retaliation. Despite the complexity of the right-hand sides of equations (9a) and (9b), the computed border-lines are very close to linear. In fact, the linear regressions of η_I on η_{II} for the mid-points between the two border-lines in the four cases are as follows, the correlation co-efficient in all four being in excess of 0.999:

$$\text{Case I:} \quad \eta_I = -1.1193 + 1.7035\,\eta_{II}$$
$$\text{Case II:} \quad \eta_I = -0.6530 + 1.7445\,\eta_{II}$$
$$\text{Case III:} \quad \eta_I = -0.2204 + 1.7366\,\eta_{II}$$
$$\text{Case IV:} \quad \eta_I = 0.3429 + 1.7471\,\eta_{II}$$

about the conditions under which a country is likely to gain from optimum tariffs as compared with free trade.

In Cases II and III, the economic character of the exports (and imports) of both countries is the same, which implies (since one country's import good is the other's export good) that tastes in the two countries differ and each commodity plays contrasting roles in the consumption of the two countries. In the extreme of Case II, a commodity is a pure necessity in the country of origin and a pure luxury in the country of destination, and vice versa in the extreme of Case III. Comparison of the two border-lines indicates that the scope for one or other country to gain from optimum tariff retaliation is greater, the more closely imports approximate to pure luxuries and exports to pure necessities. It also follows that, where tastes differ in the fashion described, a country cannot gain from optimum tariff retaliation unless its elasticity of demand for imports is substantially higher than that of the other country.

In Cases I and IV, the economic character of the exports (and imports) of the two countries is contrasting, implying that tastes are similar and each commodity plays the same role in the consumption of the two countries. In Case I, country I's export good is a pure luxury and its import good a pure necessity in both countries, and conversely in Case IV. Comparison of the border-lines indicates that the scope for a country to gain from optimum tariff retaliation is greater the closer its export good approximates to a pure luxury in world consumption, and conversely. This is a rather surprising result, since it might be expected that the country producing the more necessary good would have more power to exploit the foreigner; the clue to the explanation is probably to be found in the fact that the more necessary is a country's export good, the more will any gains from exploiting the foreigner be directed towards increased expenditure on imports.

Another conclusion that follows from Case I is that, contrary to the proposition of Kaldor's quoted above, it is not a necessary condition for a country to gain from optimum tariff retaliation that its elasticity of demand for imports should exceed the import demand elasticity of the other country. It can gain even if its elasticity of import demand is lower than that of the other country, provided both elasticities are low and the country's exports are of a sufficiently strong luxury character in world consumption. This is illustrated in

Fig. 8, which shows the maximum values of the ratio $\frac{a}{b}$ which will allow country I to gain from optimum tariff retaliation and the

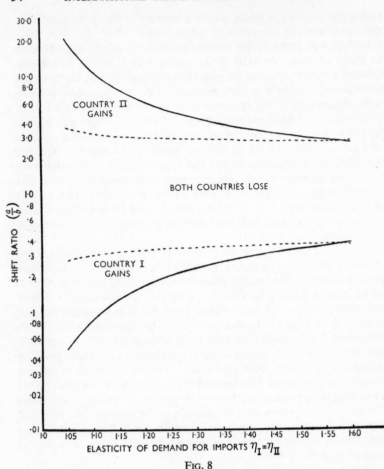

FIG. 8

minimum values which will allow country *II* to gain, when elasticities of import demand are the same in both countries.[34]

Taken as a group, the special cases just examined suggest that the scope for one country to benefit from optimum tariff retaliation is greater the more internationally traded goods are luxuries in the

[34] In the diagram, the solid lines represent the range of variation within which the ratio $\frac{a}{b}$ is confined by the condition that neither good is inferior in consumption; the dotted lines were obtained by setting the right-hand sides of equations (9) equal to unity and computing $\frac{a}{b}$ for $\eta_I = \eta_{II} = 1.05$, 1.1, etc.

country of destination, and that the likelihood of a country actually gaining is greater the more its exports are a luxury in world consumption and the higher is its elasticity of import demand relative to the foreign elasticity; but if both elasticities are low, the country may gain even though its demand for imports is less elastic than the other country's.

To summarize, it has been shown in this chapter that, contrary to a widely held opinion,[35] a country *may* gain by imposing an optimum tariff even if other countries retaliate by following the same policy; and the conditions under which it *will* gain have been investigated for a group of special cases. The implication,[36] as in many other problems in the theory of international economic policy, is that the answer depends on the circumstances of the particular case; and that anyone who asserts that one conclusion is universally valid is making an implicit assumption about the facts which ought to be explicitly defended—if it can be.

The possibility that a country may gain under tariff retaliation has an important bearing on the question of the international policy arrangements required to promote world welfare, which should be mentioned in conclusion. As Scitovszky points out, the fact that a country benefits from imposing a tariff, as against practising free trade, if other countries' trading policies are independent of its own, means that universal free trade would not be maintained automatically by self-interest, but would have to be enforced by international agreement. If it were true that each individual country lost under tariff retaliation, a return to free trade by itself would suffice to make each country better off, and all would have an incentive to come to an agreement to enforce it. But if, as the foregoing analysis shows is possible, not all countries lost under tariff retaliation, a return to free trade by itself would not suffice to make each country better off, and an agreement to restore and maintain free trade would have to provide incentives to participate, in the form of income-transfers from the others, to the countries which gained under tariff retaliation.

[35] See, e.g., S. Enke and V. Salera, *International Economics*, second edition (New York, 1951), 272–3, and C. P. Kindleberger, *International Economics* (Homewood, 1953), 195. D. B. Marsh, in *World Trade and Investment* (New York, 1951), 320 and 322, states the main point correctly, but his exposition is defective in other respects.

[36] A further implication of the general theory of optimum tariff retaliation presented here, and one which is too obvious to deserve elaboration, is that the optimum tariff theory is not a very useful approach to the explanation of tariff history. Contrast Scitovszky, loc. cit.

Appendix to Chapter II:

Alternative Optimum Tariff Formulae[*]

THE formula for the optimum welfare tariff is most readily derived as follows. Assuming one export good X and one import good Y,[1] the possibility of international trade gives rise to a foreign transformation curve ('reciprocal demand' or 'offer' curve) which represents the quantities of imports which can be obtained in international exchange for varying quantities of exports. The shape of this curve will depend on foreign tastes and technology, and the supplies and ownership of factors of production; or, in brief, on foreign demand and supply conditions.

Such a foreign transformation curve is represented by OF in Fig. 1. Any point on it, such as P, shows the quantity of imports OQ that the outside world will supply, and the quantity of exports PQ that it will demand in exchange, at the exchange ratio given by the slope of the vector OP.

The purpose of imposing the 'optimum' welfare tariff is to bring the community's foreign trade to that point on the foreign transformation curve at which its welfare is maximized. Suppose that P is that point.[2] Then, at P, the marginal rate of substitution between X and Y in domestic consumption will be equal to the marginal rate of transformation of X into Y through foreign trade, and both will be equal to the slope of the tangent PR to the transformation curve at P.

The domestic exchange ratio between the goods must also be equal to the marginal rate of substitution between them, and therefore

---

[*] Section I of 'Optimum Welfare and Maximum Revenue Tariffs', *Review of Economic Studies*, XIX(1), no. 48, 1950–1, 28–35.

[1] X and Y may be interpreted as composite bundles or 'bales' of goods, if the reader is prepared to ignore the index-number problems created by this procedure.

[2] For expositional purposes, the point P may be determined by the tangency of a community indifference curve with the foreign transformation curve. Since community indifference curves cannot in general be drawn independently of the position on the transformation curve, the argument of the text is presented without reference to them.

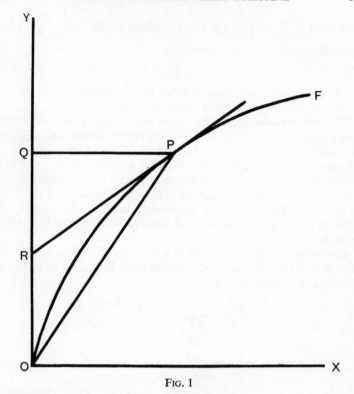

FIG. 1

to the slope of the tangent to the transformation curve. In terms of the diagram, the domestic price of Y in terms of X is PQ/QR; let p represent this price. The foreign price of Y in terms of X, however, is PQ/OQ; let this price be represented by π.

The optimum rate of duty t on the foreign price of Y is given by the equation $p = (1 + t)\pi$, whence

(1)
$$t = p/\pi - 1$$
$$= PQ/QR \cdot OQ/PQ - 1$$
$$= OQ/QR - 1.^{3}$$

The fraction OQ/QR is the elasticity of the foreign reciprocal

[3] This simple proof was furnished by J. de V. Graaff, in amendment of a more cumbersome and restricted proof by the writer which was derived from Edgeworth.

E

demand for X in exchange for Y, defined as $E_{frd} = \dfrac{Y}{X} \cdot \dfrac{dX}{dY}$. Hence the optimum tariff formula becomes

$$(2) \qquad\qquad t = E_{frd} - 1.^{4}$$

The optimum welfare tariff is equal to the elasticity of the foreign reciprocal demand for exports, reduced by unity.

This is a basic formula, from which others can be deduced. In the first place, from the reciprocal demand curve can be derived either an ordinary demand curve expressing the demand for exports as a function of the exchange ratio between exports and imports (the 'barter terms of trade') or an ordinary supply curve expressing the supply of imports as a function of that exchange ratio. The elasticity of reciprocal demand can be expressed in terms of the elasticity of either of these curves, and the result substituted in the optimum tariff formula.

The reciprocal demand curve is a functional relationship of the form $Y = F(X)$. The demand curve derived from it is of the form $X = f(X/Y)$ and its elasticity

$$(3) \qquad e_{fd} = -\frac{Y/X}{X} \cdot \frac{dX}{d\left(\dfrac{Y}{X}\right)} = -\frac{Y}{X^2} \Bigg/ \frac{d\,(Y/X)}{dX}$$

$$= -\frac{Y}{X^2} \Bigg/ \frac{X\dfrac{dY}{dX} - Y}{X^2}$$

$$= -\frac{1}{\dfrac{X}{Y}\dfrac{dY}{dX} - 1}$$

$$= \frac{E_{frd}}{E_{frd} - 1},$$

whence

$$(4) \qquad\qquad E_{frd} = \frac{e_{fd}}{e_{fd} - 1}$$

and

$$(5) \qquad\qquad t = \frac{1}{e_{fd} - 1}.$$

[4] The proof of this is obvious, since $\dfrac{Y}{X} \cdot \dfrac{dX}{dY} = \dfrac{OQ}{PQ} \cdot \dfrac{PQ}{QR}$, which appears in the second line of the derivation of t above.

That is, the optimum welfare tariff rate is equal to the reciprocal of one less than the foreign elasticity of demand for exports as a function of the barter terms of trade.

Similarly, the supply curve derived from the reciprocal demand curve is of the form $Y = g(X/Y)$ and its elasticity:

$$(6) \qquad e_{fs} = \frac{X/Y}{Y} \cdot \frac{dY}{d\left(\frac{X}{Y}\right)} = \frac{X}{Y^2} \bigg/ \frac{d\left(\frac{X}{Y}\right)}{dY}$$

$$= \frac{X}{Y^2} \bigg/ \frac{Y\left(\frac{dX}{dY}\right) - X}{Y^2}$$

$$= \frac{1}{\dfrac{Y}{X}\dfrac{dX}{dY} - 1} = \frac{1}{E_{frd} - 1},$$

whence

$$(7) \qquad E_{frd} = \frac{e_{fs} + 1}{e_{fs}}$$

and

$$(8) \qquad t = \frac{1}{e_{fs}}.[5]$$

That is, the optimum welfare tariff rate is equal to the reciprocal of the foreign elasticity of supply of imports as a function of the barter terms of trade.

It is more usual, however, to express the formula for the optimum welfare tariff in terms of elasticities of demand for exports and supply of imports conceived of as functions of money prices, rather than as functions of the barter terms of trade. To do this, it is necessary to assume the presence of a third good, which can be used as a *numéraire* in which to express the prices of exports and imports: with only two goods, there can be only one price, and the elasticities of demand for exports and supply of imports are necessarily related by the property of Footnote 5.

Assuming the presence of such a *numéraire*, the elasticity of reciprocal demand can be expressed in terms of price elasticities of demand and supply by making use of the fact that, at every point

---

[5] This result can also be derived from the familiar relationship between the elasticity of a demand curve and the elasticity of the supply curve into which it can be converted, i.e. $e_d - e_s = 1$.

on the reciprocal demand curve, the value of exports must be equal
to the value of imports. Denoting the price of exports by p_x, and
the price of imports by p_y, at every point on the reciprocal demand
curve

(9) $$X p_x = Y p_y.$$

Differentiating,

$$X \, dp_x + p_x \, dX = Y \, dp_y + p_y \, dY \quad \text{or:}$$

(10) $$p_x \, dX \left(1 + \frac{X dp_x}{p_x dX} \right) = p_y \, dY \left(1 + \frac{Y \, dp_y}{p_y \, dY} \right).$$

Denoting the foreign elasticity of demand for exports by

$$\eta_x = - \frac{p_x}{X} \frac{dX}{dp_x}$$

and the foreign elasticity of supply of imports by

$$\epsilon_y = \frac{p_y}{Y} \frac{dY}{dp_y},$$

this becomes

(11) $$\frac{p_x \, dX}{p_y \, dY} = \frac{1 + \dfrac{1}{\epsilon_y}}{1 - \dfrac{1}{\eta_x}}.$$

Substituting for p_x/p_y,

(12) $$\frac{Y}{X} \frac{dX}{dY} = \frac{1 + \dfrac{1}{\epsilon_y}}{1 - \dfrac{1}{\eta_x}} = E_{frd}.$$

Finally, substitution of this result into the optimum tariff formula
yields the result

(13) $$t = \frac{\dfrac{1}{\epsilon_y} + \dfrac{1}{\eta_x}}{1 - \dfrac{1}{\eta_x}}$$

which is the Bickerdike-Edgeworth-Kahn-Little-Graaff result.[6]

---

[6] This formula must be interpreted with care, since the elasticities are defined
in terms of the partial differentials of quantities with respect to prices, not in
terms of partial derivatives as the conventional price elasticities are. The two
definitions of elasticity are only identical when the good is independent of

Account may also be taken of the likelihood that the outside world will produce some of the goods which it imports, and consume some of the goods which it exports, so that the elasticity of its demand for imports will depend on the elasticity of its home supply of as well as the elasticity of its total demand for imports, and the elasticity of its supply of exports will depend on the elasticity of its home demand for as well as the elasticity of its total supply of exports. It can easily be shown that, in the above formula,

$$(14) \qquad \eta_x = d_{fx}\, \eta_{fx} + s_{fx}\, \epsilon_{fx}$$

and

$$(15) \qquad \epsilon_y = d_{fy}\, \eta_{fy} + s_{fy}\, \epsilon_{fy},$$

where η_f and ϵ_f refer to the foreign elasticities of demand and supply respectively, d_f and s_f denote the ratios of the amounts consumed and produced abroad to the amount internationally traded, and subscripts x and y denote the commodity.[7] These values can be substituted into the optimum tariff formula to give the result:

$$(16) \qquad t = \frac{(d_{fx}\, \eta_{fx} + s_{fx}\, \epsilon_{fx}) + (d_{fy}\, \eta_{fy} + s_{fy}\, \epsilon_{fy})}{(d_{fy}\, \eta_{fy} + s_{fy}\, \epsilon_{fy})\,(d_{fx}\, \eta_{fx} + s_{fx}\, \epsilon_{fx} - 1)}.$$

This result, however, is formal and rather useless, since d_f and s_f will vary with price except in the special case referred to in Footnote 7.

other goods in both consumption and production; otherwise, the elasticities of the formula must be interpreted as measures of the response of quantities to prices when all the repercussions of general equilibrium adjustment have been worked out. For a full discussion of this point, see Graaff, loc. cit. Cf. also the remarks by Charles Kennedy ('Devaluation and the Terms of Trade', *Review of Economic Studies*, XVIII(1), no. 45, 1949–50, 28–41) on the meaning of international elasticities.

[7] These formulae underline the need for caution in assuming constant elasticities of international demand and supply, as is frequently done in the literature, since a constant international elasticity generally implies a special kind of variation in the domestic elasticities of demand and supply for the internationally traded good. Constant international elasticity is only consistent with constant domestic elasticities in the special case in which the domestic elasticities are equal and opposite in sign, which implies that one of them is perverse. If the domestic elasticities are constant, the international demand function is of the form:

$$X_d = A_x P_x^{-\eta_{fx}} - B_x P_x^{\,\epsilon_{fx}}$$

and the international supply function is of the form $Y_s = B_y P_y^{\,\epsilon_{fy}} - A_y P_y^{-\eta_{fy}}$ (A and B standing for constants). From consideration of these expressions it is obvious that the international elasticities will only be constants if $\epsilon_f = -\,\eta_f$; the same conditions give constancy of d_f and s_f. These considerations, however, do not apply to the assumption of constant arc-elasticities.

PART TWO

INTERNATIONAL TRADE AND
ECONOMIC GROWTH

CHAPTER III

Economic Expansion and International Trade*

THE problem of the effects of economic growth on international trade has excited increasing interest since the war, in connection with discussions of 'dollar shortage' and the development of 'under-developed countries', and more recently of Britain's long-run economic prospects. This chapter examines, as a background to such discussions, the theoretical effects of economic expansion on the volume and terms of trade between manufacturing and primary-producing countries. By 'economic expansion' is meant the growth of output, whether as a result of population growth, capital accumulation, or technical progress: it is assumed that these causes of expansion can in principle be isolated one from another, and that certain technical difficulties in defining them can be ignored. The analysis is concerned with the disturbances introduced by different types of expansion and the adjustments required to maintain international equilibrium, on the assumption that full employment is maintained and that competitive conditions rule in the markets for goods and factors of production. For simplicity, the argument is presented in terms of two countries, Mancunia and Agraria; Mancunia is assumed to export manufactured goods, and Agraria to export foodstuffs. It is further assumed that manufactures are a luxury good and foodstuffs a necessary good, in the technical sense that the income-elasticity of demand for manufactures is greater, and the income-elasticity of demand for foodstuffs less, than unity.[1]

In Part I it is assumed that each country is completely specialized on the production of the type of good it exports, and completely

* *The Manchester School of Economic and Social Studies*, XXIII, no. 2, May 1955, 95–112. The text has been revised and extended to include additional material contained in the three lectures on which the original article was based (which were delivered in Manchester in December 1954) and to clarify some of the exposition.

[1] As income per head rises, proportionately more is spent on manufactures, and proportionately less on food, if prices remain constant.

dependent on imports for its consumption of the other good; in Part II the countries are assumed to be incompletely specialized, producing domestically some of the imported good. In both Parts it is assumed that labour, capital, and technology are immobile between countries, and that only goods can move internationally. Both Parts are concerned with two general problems. The first is whether a particular type of economic expansion will increase a country's demand for imports less than or more than proportionately to the expansion of its output, the extreme cases occurring when expansion results in an absolute reduction of import demand, and when it increases absolute import demand more than total output (so that production for domestic consumption falls absolutely). The second is the conditions under which the adverse terms-of-trade movement required in certain cases of expansion to maintain equilibrium will outweigh the effects of expansion and lead to a reduction in aggregate real income. For reasons inherent in the difference of assumptions distinguishing the two Parts, the second problem is the main subject of Part I and the first of Part II. Part III relaxes the assumption of complete immobility of labour, capital, and technology common to the Parts I and II, and applies the results of those sections to the problem of the effects of international transmissions of productive power.

I.   ECONOMIC EXPANSION WITH COMPLETE SPECIALIZATION

In equilibrium, the volume and terms of trade must be such that each country's exports pay for its imports. Now suppose that Agraria's economy is static, but Mancunia's economy is growing. At unchanged terms of trade, Mancunia's demand for imports would increase by an amount, per period, determined by the amount of the increase in its output during the period and the magnitude of its marginal propensity to spend output on imports; the rate of increase in its demand for imports would be equal to the rate of growth of its output, multiplied by its output-elasticity of demand for imports.[2]

[2] In symbols, the increase in demand for imports is

$$(1) \qquad \frac{d(pM)}{dt} = \frac{d(pM)}{dY} \cdot \frac{dY}{dt} = m\frac{dY}{dt},$$

and the rate of increase of demand for imports is

$$(2) \qquad \frac{1}{pM}\frac{d(pM)}{dt} = \frac{Y}{pM} \cdot \frac{d(pM)}{dY} \cdot \frac{1}{Y} \cdot \frac{dY}{dt} = \epsilon R,$$

where p is the price of imports in terms of units of exports (assumed constant), M is the quantity of imports, t is time, Y is total output (income), m is the marginal

Since Agraria is assumed not to be expanding, Mancunia's increasing demand for imports of food will not be met at unchanged prices; to preserve international trading equilibrium the terms of trade must turn against Mancunia, in order to induce residents of both countries to divert their consumption from food to manufactures; thus part of the benefit of Mancunia's expansion accrues to Agraria through a cheapening of its imports of manufactures. Expansion in Mancunia also necessarily involves expansion of the volume of trade, measured in manufactured goods; the volume of trade, measured in foodstuffs, will increase so long as Agraria's demand for imports is elastic.

The division of the benefits of Mancunian expansion between the two countries depends on the extent to which the terms of trade must change to restore equilibrium. The conditions which determine this can be formulated in two alternative ways: in terms of international trade theory, it depends on the elasticities of the two countries' demands for imports; in terms of value theory, it depends on the elasticity of world (i.e. both countries') demand for manufactured goods.

To be formally precise, the proportional deterioration in a country's terms of trade which is required to improve its trade balance by a given proportion of the initial value of exports or imports is equal to the proportional improvement required, divided by the sum of the elasticities of demand for imports and for exports, minus one.[3] This

propensity to spend output on imports $\left(= \dfrac{d(pM)}{dY} \right)$, ϵ is the output-elasticity of demand for imports, and R is the rate of growth of output. The term 'output-elasticity' is used in preference to 'income-elasticity' to describe the behaviour of aggregate consumption as aggregate income rises, because this behaviour will depend on the specific cause of economic expansion and will not be determined solely by the individual citizen's income-elasticity of demand for imports: expansion due to population growth will tend to lower individual demand for imports by lowering output per head, but raise total demand by increasing numbers. It is assumed in this Part that m and ϵ are positive; the possibility that they may be negative is discussed briefly in the final paragraph.

[3] The effect of a deterioration of a country's terms of trade on its trade balance is given by

$$(3) \qquad dB = \frac{\delta B}{\delta p}\, dp = \frac{\delta(X - pM)}{\delta p}\, dp = \frac{X}{p}\,(\eta_x + \eta_m - 1)\, dp,$$

where B is the trade balance (initially zero), X and M are the initial exports and imports quantities, B is the initial price of imports in terms of exports, $\eta_x \left(= \dfrac{p}{X}\dfrac{\delta X}{\delta p} \right)$ is the elasticity of demand for the country's exports, and $\eta_m \left(= -\dfrac{p}{M}\dfrac{\delta M}{\delta p} \right)$ is the is in terms of international trade theory; in terms of value theory, the divisor is the elasticity of total world demand for the country's product, divided by the proportion of the total output of the good which is exported—or, by what is the same thing, the average propensity to spend on imports of the exporting country.[4] For brevity, this divisor will henceforth be described as 'the elasticity factor.'

Since Mancunia's expansion would worsen its trade balance (at unchanged terms of trade) in a proportion equal to the rate of growth of its import demand, which is equal to the product of its rate of growth and output-elasticity of demand for imports, the rate of deterioration of Mancunia's terms of trade which is required to maintain international equilibrium will be equal to this product, divided by the elasticity factor. More simply (using the value theory version of the elasticity factor), it will be equal to the product of Mancunia's rate of growth and marginal propensity to spend output on food imports, divided by the elasticity of world demand for manufactures.[5]

Given the rate of growth of Mancunia, the rate of deterioration of its terms of trade will be higher the higher its marginal propensity to spend on food, and the lower the elasticity of world demand for manufactures. The marginal propensity to spend on food may either rise or fall for a time, depending on the cause of expansion and the

elasticity of the country's demand for imports. Hence the proportional deterioration of the terms of trade $\left(\dfrac{dp}{p}\right)$ required to improve the trade balance by a given proportion $\left(\dfrac{dB}{X}\right)$ of the initial value of imports or exports is given by

(4) $$\frac{dp}{p} = \frac{dB}{X} \div (\eta_x + \eta_m - 1).$$

[4] Since the trade balance is the difference between national product and national expenditure, equation (3) of the previous footnote may be re-written as

(3)′ $$dB = \frac{\delta(Y - E)}{\delta p} dp = \frac{Y}{p} \eta_y dp,$$

where E represents national expenditure, which on the assumption of full employment will be unaffected by changes in the terms of trade, and $\eta_y \left(= \dfrac{p}{Y} \dfrac{\delta Y}{\delta p} \right)$ is the elasticity of world demand for the country's output. Hence in equation (4) the expression $(\eta_x + \eta_m - 1)$ can be replaced by

$$\frac{Y}{X} \eta_y = \eta_y \div \frac{X}{Y}.$$

[5] Since $\epsilon \div \dfrac{Y}{X} = m.$

nature of the demand for food, but eventually it will rise (assuming that there are limits to the extent to which income and price increases will reduce the marginal increment in the quantity of food consumed when output increases); the elasticity of world demand for manufactures is practically certain to fall over time, since as manufacturing output expands while food supply remains constant it will become increasingly difficult to induce people in both countries to consume manufactures rather than food. Consequently, at some stage continued growth of the Mancunian economy will begin to involve an increasingly rapid deterioration of Mancunia's terms of trade, and more and more of the benefit of Mancunian expansion will accrue to Agraria.

The rate of increase of Mancunia's real income will depend on the rate of growth of its output and the extent to which expansion turns its terms of trade against it. The loss of real income attributable to an adverse movement of the terms of trade may be approximated on the compensation principle, as being equal to the increased cost of imports resulting from the movement of the terms of trade; the rate of loss of real income due to this cause will be the product of the proportion of output spent on imports, and the rate of deterioration of the terms of trade. On this basis, the rate of increase of Mancunia's real income will fall short of the rate of increase of its output by a proportion equal to its marginal propensity to spend on food, divided by the elasticity factor.[6] As time goes on, the contribution which further growth makes to Mancunian real income will decrease, and eventually Mancunia would arrive at a point beyond which further growth would actually reduce its real income, the adverse effect on the terms of trade more than offsetting the increase in output. This would occur when the marginal propensity to spend on imports became equal to the elasticity factor.

---

[6] The rate of loss of real income due to deteriorating terms of trade R' which has to be weighed against the rate of increase of real income due to increasing output R, is

$$(5) \qquad R' = \frac{1}{Y} M \frac{dp}{dt}$$

which, using (4) with $\frac{dB}{X} = \epsilon R$, becomes

$$(6) \qquad R' = \frac{m}{\eta_x + \eta_m - 1} R.$$

For a more detailed exposition see H. G. Johnson, 'Equilibrium Growth in an International Economy', *Canadian Journal of Economics and Political Science*, XIX, no. 4, November 1953, 478–500, (Chapter V below), especially Part II.

If expansion were due to technical progress or capital accumulation, this could only occur after Agraria's demand for imported manufactures became inelastic, because the marginal propensity to spend on imports in this case is equal to the income term in Mancunia's elasticity of demand for imports, and therefore is less than that elasticity by the amount of the substitution elasticity. But in the case of expansion arising from population growth, the marginal propensity to spend on imports is likely to be substantially greater than the income-effect in the elasticity of demand for imports, so that Mancunia might begin to lose in terms of real income before Agrarian import demand became inelastic.[7] In either case, Mancunia will cease to benefit from growth long before the world is glutted with manufactured goods—a paradox more familiar in relation to agricultural production than industrial, and which qualifies the popular assumption that industrial expansion is a rapid and sure means of raising real income.

So far, it has been assumed that Mancunia's international trade is conducted competitively. Mancunia could avoid part of the loss from the deterioration of its terms of trade, and prevent itself from ever encountering a loss of real income from expansion, by imposing appropriate trade controls and adjusting them as it grew. The optimum degree of trade restriction at any moment would be that which equated the internal price of imports in terms of exports with their marginal cost to the country in terms of exports. This could be attained by levying an import duty at a rate equal to the reciprocal of the elasticity of supply of imports from Agraria, the elasticity being calculated at the optimum volume of trade.[8] As Mancunia expanded, its optimum trade volume would increase; whether the optimum degree of trade restriction would decrease or increase would depend on whether the elasticity of Agraria's demand for manufactures increased or decreased. Eventually, however, Agraria's

[7] Alternatively, Mancunia would begin to lose from growth when the elasticity of world demand for manufactures became equal to the product of Mancunia's average and marginal propensities to import; since both of these will be less than unity, except in an extreme case of population growth encountering diminishing returns in manufacturing, this result would generally occur only after world demand for manufactures became inelastic.

[8] According to the well-known formula, the marginal cost of imports is $\left(1 + \dfrac{1}{e}\right) q$, where q is the foreign price and e the elasticity of supply; with a tariff of $100t\%$, the internal price of imports is $(1 + t)q$, whence the optimum tariff is $t = \dfrac{1}{e}$.

demand for imports would become decreasingly elastic, and Mancunia would gain by increasing the degree of trade restriction as its output expanded; but it would never gain by increasing restrictions to the point of actually reducing its imports. On the other hand, it would never pay Mancunia to allow its exports to expand to the point at which Agrarian import demand became inelastic. Given appropriately restrictive trade policies, Mancunia would gain by growth so long as manufactured goods were useful to its citizens.

In the argument thus far, it has been assumed that Mancunia alone is growing; and it has been shown that in this case the gain from Mancunian expansion passes increasingly to Agraria through the deterioration of Mancunia's terms of trade, unless Mancunia follows an appropriate restrictive trade policy. One implication, which will not be pursued here, is that processes will be set in motion which will tend to restrain the rate of expansion in Mancunia. Another and more interesting implication is that Mancunia will benefit more from expansion if Agraria is also growing than it otherwise would; a corollary, excluded by assumption, is that Mancunia may benefit by investing labour, capital or technical skill in fostering the expansion of Agraria, even at the cost of reducing the rate of growth of Mancunian output.

If both economies are growing, the demand of each for the other's exports will increase at a rate determined by the product of its rate of growth and output-elasticity of demand for imports. The terms of trade will turn against the country for which this product is greater; this is not necessarily the country which is growing more rapidly, because a higher growth rate may be offset by a lower output-elasticity of demand for imports.

If conditions were such that growth proceeded at unchanged terms of trade, the rate of growth of real income in each country would be the same as its rate of growth of output. In a very limited sense, this situation could be described as 'balanced growth' of the world economy;[9] for it to occur the rates of growth of output in the two countries must be inversely proportional to their output-elasticities of demand for imports—the country for whose exports the output-elasticity of demand is relatively low must expand relatively less rapidly.

[9] The phrase has a limited meaning because it does not imply equality of the rates of increase of either aggregate or average real income in the two countries, nor does it imply that 'balanced growth' is in any sense superior to 'unbalanced growth'; it merely means that there is no international income-redistribution through changes in the terms of trade.

If economic expansion is due to capital accumulation or technical progress, real income per head will be rising; on the assumption that manufactures are a luxury good and food a necessity, the output-elasticity of Mancunia's demand for imports will be less than unity and that of Agraria's demand for imports will be greater than unity.[10] For balanced growth, Agraria must expand less rapidly than Mancunia. Agraria will not necessarily be worse off if it grows more rapidly than the requirement for balanced growth indicates—its real income will increase more rapidly the higher its growth rate so long as the elasticity factor exceeds its marginal propensity to spend on manufactures—but part of the benefits of more rapid growth will accrue to Mancunia. If the outputs of the two countries grow at the same rate, Mancunia's real income will grow more rapidly than Agraria's.

This conclusion provides a theoretical foundation for an argument sometimes advanced in favour of industrialization of backward countries, namely that in the long run world economic progress is biased against primary production. To derive an argument for industrialization from it, however, it is necessary to consider the relative costs of industrial as against agricultural expansion, and the relative rates of expansion which are in fact likely to be attained. The conclusion, moreover, is confined to cases of expansion due to capital accumulation or technical progress: if expansion is due to population growth and entails falling real income per head, the terms of trade will turn in favour of Agraria unless Mancunia is expanding relatively less rapidly, and the argument would provide a case for agriculturalization of Mancunia. This case might arise even if Mancunian expansion were due to other causes than population growth, so that the output-elasticity of demand for imports was less than unity in both countries.

Throughout the foregoing argument, it has been assumed that the output-elasticities of demand for imports will be positive. In concluding this section, three possible exceptions should be mentioned. First (though this is highly unlikely for such broad commodity groups as food and manufactures), one country's output may be inferior in the consumption of the other, so that if the latter's output expands due to capital accumulation or technical progress (raising real income per head) its demand for imports will fall. Second, if population growth in Agraria encounters strongly diminishing returns, the reduction in income per head may reduce individual

[10] In terms of concepts developed in Part II, economic expansion is anti-trade-biased in Mancunia and pro-trade-biased in Agraria in these cases.

demand for manufactures so much as to outweigh the effects of the increasing number of heads—this will occur if the individual income-elasticity of demand for manufactures is higher than the reciprocal of the elasticity of output per head with respect to population.[11] Third, if instead of foodstuffs Agraria produces industrial raw materials the demand for which is derived from the demand for manufactured goods, technical progress in Mancunia might operate so as to reduce the materials required per unit of output faster than total output increases. To make sense of this last case, however, it must be assumed that the materials are either directly consumable in Agraria or substitutable for factors of production in Mancunia—otherwise equilibrium could not be maintained by changes in the terms of trade. In all three cases, expansion of the country with the negative output-elasticity of demand for imports would reduce the volume of world trade and turn the terms of trade in its favour.

II. ECONOMIC EXPANSION WITH INCOMPLETE SPECIALIZATION

The argument of Part I assumed that each country was completely specialized on the production of its export good; this Part is concerned with the more realistic case in which each country produces domestically some of the goods which it imports.

For countries to be completely specialized in this way, and to remain so as expansion proceeds, it is necessary to assume that each country can only increase the relative amount of one of the goods which it produces at increasing relative cost. The increasing relative cost of production of a good as its relative production is increased may be due to either or both of two causes: diseconomies of scale in one or both lines of production; and differences in factor-intensities, which mean that, with constant factor supplies, diversion of production towards one of the goods reduces the demand for and relative price of the factor used relatively less in producing that good, thereby lowering the relative price of the other good. In what follows, it is

---

[11] Let total demand for manufactures in Agraria be $C = nc$, where n represents population and c represents consumption per head, determined by income per head y; then

$$\frac{dC}{dY} = c\,\frac{dn}{dY} + n\,\frac{dc}{dy}\,\frac{dy}{dn}\,\frac{dn}{dY} = \left(1 - \epsilon_c e_y\right) c\,\frac{dn}{dY}$$

where $\epsilon_c = \frac{y}{c}\frac{dc}{dy}$ and $e_y = -\frac{n}{y}\frac{dy}{dn}$; and $\frac{dC}{dY}$ will be negative if ϵ_c is greater than $\frac{1}{e_y}$.

F

assumed that agriculture is subject to diminishing returns as output expands, owing to the application of more labour and capital to a given supply of land, but that manufacturing makes negligible use of land and is subject to constant returns to scale. It is also assumed that agriculture is relatively labour-intensive, and manufacturing is relatively capital-intensive, in both countries.[12]

With incomplete specialization, a country's demand for imports is the difference between its total demand for and domestic supply of the good concerned. Economic expansion will increase the total demand, but it may increase the domestic supply still more, at constant relative prices; consequently, in contrast to the case of complete specialization, expansion may reduce a country's demand for imports and tend to turn the terms of trade in its favour. The country's marginal propensity to spend output on imports will be negative if its marginal propensity to spend output on consumption of importables falls short of what may be termed its marginal propensity to produce importables—the proportion of the increased value of output represented by increased production of the imported commodity, when output expands at constant prices—or, what is the same thing, when the ratio of the output-elasticity of the country's supply of importables to its output-elasticity of demand for them is greater than the ratio of its consumption to its production of them.[13]

If expansion increases a country's demand for imports (the other country not expanding), the terms of trade must turn against the expanding country; the volume of world trade will increase, and the other country will become more specialized on its export product, since the movement of the terms of trade in its favour will induce a reduction in its output of importable goods in favour of production

[12] This would imply that a shift of production from manufacturing to agriculture would tend to raise wages (and rent) and lower the earnings of capital; the effects of such redistributions of income on demand are ignored in the argument below.

[13] Let C represent consumption of importables and P domestic production of them; then the change in demand for imports with growth at constant prices is

$$(7) \quad \frac{d(pM)}{dt} = \frac{d(pC - pP)}{dt} = \left(\frac{d(pC)}{dY} - \frac{d(pP)}{dY} \right) \frac{dY}{dt} = (c - \pi) \frac{dY}{dt} = (\epsilon pC - \sigma pP)R$$

where c is the marginal propensity to spend output on consumption of importables, π is the marginal propensity to produce importables, $\epsilon \left(= \frac{Y}{pC} c \right)$ the output-elasticity of total demand for importables, and $\sigma \left(= \frac{Y}{pP} \pi \right)$ is the output-elasticity of domestic supply of importables.

of exportables. Conversely, if the expanding country's demand for imports decreases, the terms of trade must turn in its favour, the volume of world trade decrease, and the other country become less specialized on its export product. Whether the expanding country becomes more or less specialized cannot be definitely ascertained in either case, since this will depend on the net effect of the initial expansion and the subsequent change in the terms of trade.

Whether a country's expansion increases or reduces its demand for imports, the change in the terms of trade required to restore equilibrium will depend, as before, on the elasticity factor; but each country's elasticity of demand for imports will now depend on the elasticities of total demand for and domestic supply of the imported good, as well as the ratio of total consumption to domestic production of this good.[14] In terms of value theory, the elasticity factor is equal to the sum of the elasticities of world demand for and world supply of one of the goods, divided by the ratio of world trade in that good to world production or consumption.[15]

If a country's expansion reduces its demand for imports, the increase in its real income due to expansion of output will be augmented by the favourable effect of the associated improvement in the country's terms of trade. Conversely, if expansion increases its demand for imports, the growth of real income due to expansion of output will be reduced, and may be cancelled or outweighed, by a loss of real income due to deteriorating terms of trade. The condition for real income to be reduced by expansion is the same as that stated in Part I, that the marginal propensity to spend output on imports should exceed the elasticity factor, though the meanings of these terms are different in the case of incomplete specialization. It can be deduced from this condition that expansion can only lead to a reduction in aggregate real income in three cases: where the foreign demand for the country's exports is inelastic (the extreme case of which is that the country's exports are 'Giffen goods' abroad); where growth actually reduces domestic production of importables; or

[14] $$\eta_m = -\frac{p}{M}\frac{\delta M}{\delta p} = -\frac{C}{M}\frac{p}{C}\frac{\delta C}{\delta p} + \frac{P}{M}\frac{p}{P}\frac{\delta P}{\delta p} = \frac{C}{M}\eta_c + \frac{P}{M}\eta_s$$

where η_c and η_s are respectively the price-elasticities of total consumption and domestic production of importables.

[15] This follows from the fact that exports demanded are the difference between foreign consumption and production, and the value of imports demanded is the difference between domestic production and consumption of exportables; hence the balance of trade is the difference between world demand and supply of exportables (zero in equilibrium). Differentiation and definition of elasticities on the usual sign conventions yields the result stated.

when the aggregate marginal propensity to spend output on the consumption of importables exceeds the individual marginal propensity to spend on consumption of these goods (as would be the case if expansion were due to population growth which reduced output per head, and importables were agricultural products).[16]

The major question posed by economic expansion under conditions of incomplete specialization, which it was necessary to discuss only briefly on the simpler assumptions of Part I, is whether (given the type of economy and nature of expansion) a country's demand for imports will expand more than or less than proportionately to the expansion of its output—whether, that is, its expansion tends to increase or decrease its relative dependence on international trade. At the extremes, expansion may reduce the country's demand for imports, rendering it absolutely less dependent on trade, or increase its demand for imports by more than the total increment in output, rendering it absolutely more dependent on trade.

For analysis of this problem, it is convenient to distinguish initially between the effects of expansion on consumption and on production (at constant prices), and to classify these effects into three possible types—'pro-trade-biased', 'neutral', and 'anti-trade-biased'—[17]

---

[16] The condition for growth to reduce real income is $m(=c-\pi) > \eta_x + \eta_m - 1$ $\left(=\eta_x - 1 + \dfrac{C}{M}\eta_c + \dfrac{P}{M}\eta_s\right)$. Using the compensation-principle approximation for the effect of a price change on real income, η_c may be subdivided into income and substitution terms as follows:

$$(8) \qquad \eta_c = -\frac{p}{C}\frac{\delta C}{\delta Y'}(-M) - \frac{p}{C}\left\{\frac{\delta C}{\delta p}\right\} = \frac{M}{C}c' + x,$$

where $\left\{\dfrac{\delta C}{\delta p}\right\}$ is the compensated price-effect and x the corresponding (necessarily positive) elasticity, and c' is the marginal propensity to spend on importables when real income changes due to a price change (and may be identified with the individual marginal propensity to spend on importables). Hence the condition for falling real income is

$$(9) \qquad (1 - \eta_x) + (-\pi) + (c - c') > \frac{C}{M} x + \frac{P}{M}\eta_s;$$

since the terms on the right are positive, it is necessary for the fulfilment of the condition that at least one of the terms on the left be positive. (If exports are a 'Giffen good' abroad, η_x is negative.)

[17] This terminology replaces that of 'export-biased', 'neutral', and 'import-biased', employed in the original lectures and *Manchester School* article, which was taken over from J. R. Hicks ('An Inaugural Lecture', *Oxford Economic Papers*, N.S., V, no. 2, June 1953, 117–35 especially 127 ff). The generalization

according to whether they tend to increase the demand for imports (supply of exports) more than proportionally, proportionally, or less than proportionally to the expansion of output. On the consumption side, an expansion will be described as 'neutral' if it increases the total demand for importable goods in the same proportion as it increases the demand for exportable goods; biased against trade or 'anti-trade-biased' if it increases the demand for importable goods in lesser proportion than it increases the demand for exportable goods; and biased in favour of trade or 'pro-trade-biased' if it increases the demand for importable goods in greater proportion than it increases the demand for exportables. In formal terms, it will be 'pro-trade-biased', 'neutral', or 'anti-trade-biased' according as the output-elasticity of demand for importable goods is greater than, equal to, or less than unity. On the production side, an expansion will be described as 'neutral' if it increases the supply of exportable and importable goods in the same proportion, 'anti-trade-biased' if it increases the supply of importable goods in greater proportion than the supply of exportable goods, and 'pro-trade-biased' if it increases the supply of importable goods in lesser proportion than the supply of exportable goods. In formal terms, it will be 'pro-trade-biased', 'neutral', or 'anti-trade-biased', according as the output-elasticity of supply of importable goods is less than, equal to, or greater than unity. If expansion reduces the domestic supply of importable goods it will be described as 'ultra-pro-trade-biased'; and if it reduces the supply of exportable goods it will be described as 'ultra-anti-trade-biased'.[18] Formally, ultra-pro-trade-bias means a negative output-elasticity of supply of importables, and ultra-anti-trade-bias a negative output-elasticity of supply of exportables.

An expansion which is pro-trade-biased or anti-trade-biased on both sides will be pro-trade-biased or anti-trade-biased on balance. Likewise, an expansion which is neutral on both sides will be neutral on balance; but an expansion which is equally pro-trade-biased on one side and anti-trade-biased on the other will not be neutral, because consumption of imports exceeds domestic production—for neutrality, bias on the consumption side must be offset by a greater

of Hicks' terminology, which was developed to deal with the effects of technical progress on the production pattern, to the effects of expansion of other kinds, while perfectly straightforward, has proved a hindrance rather than a help to understanding.

[18] Parallel cases of ultra-bias on the consumption side are excluded for simplicity; possible causes have been mentioned in Part I.

opposite bias on the production side.[19] Ultra-anti-trade-bias on the production side implies ultra-anti-trade-bias on balance, because it means that domestic production of importables increases more than total output and therefore than demand for importables; ultra-pro-trade-bias on the production side excludes the possibility of ultra-anti-trade-bias on balance, for similar reasons, but it does not exclude the possibility of anti-trade-bias on balance.

The effects of different types of economic expansion in the two countries on their demands for imports may now be examined in detail. We shall begin with the effects of economic expansion in Mancunia, then consider the effects of expansion in Agraria, and finally consider the effects of expansion in both together.

If economic expansion in Mancunia is due to technical progress, it will be anti-trade-biased on the consumption side, since it will raise real income per head and (by assumption) increasing income per head will be spent relatively more on manufactures than on food. The effects on the production side will depend on whether technical progress proceeds more rapidly in one line of production than in the other, and whether it is capital-saving, labour-saving, or neutral in each case. For simplicity, it will be assumed that technical progress merely raises the output obtainable from a given combination of factors of production without making it advantageous to alter the combination employed, so that the effects will depend only on whether it proceeds at the same pace in both lines of production, or more rapidly in one or the other.[20]

If technical progress proceeds more rapidly in one sector, output in that sector (at constant prices) will increase more than proportionately to total output for two reasons: first, with unchanged

---

[19] The rate of growth of demand for imports is

$$(10) \qquad \frac{1}{pM} \frac{d(pM)}{dt} = \left(\epsilon \cdot \frac{C}{M} - \sigma \frac{P}{M} \right) R$$

$$= \left(\frac{C}{M} b_c + \frac{P}{M} b_p + 1 \right) R$$

where b_c ($= \epsilon - 1$) and b_p ($= 1 - \sigma$) are the degrees of bias (positive for pro-trade-bias, negative for anti-trade-bias) on the consumption and production sides respectively. Expansion is pro-trade-biased, neutral, or anti-trade-biased according as $b_c + \frac{P}{C} b_p \gtreqless 0$. Where the biases are of opposite sign, the consumption bias predominates unless the degree of production bias is sufficiently greater (absolutely) to offset the influence of its fractional coefficient.

[20] Technical progress which alters the optimum factor combination could be treated as a case of the type of progress discussed here, combined (notionally) with an increase in the supply of the 'saved' factor.

factor-employment in the two sectors, its output will rise more rapidly than output in the other sector: second, factors of production will shift into that sector until rising costs there and decreasing costs in the other sector equalize factor earnings in the two sectors. Whether output in the other sector actually declined would depend on the relative rates of progress in the two sectors, and the degree to which relative costs altered as factors shifted from one sector to another; but if progress occurred in one sector only, output in the other sector would necessarily fall.

The classical economists took the view that technical improvements in agriculture would be of negligible importance in the long run, as compared with improvements in industry; on that assumption, technical progress in Mancunia would be ultra-pro-trade-biased in production, and Mancunian demand for food imports would increase with expansion, though it might increase more or less than proportionately to the expansion of output. The classical view, however, has not proved a valid historical generalization; on the more tenable assumption that technical progress proceeds at approximately the same pace in both lines of production, expansion in Mancunia due to this cause would be anti-trade-biased on balance, and might be ultra-anti-trade-biased if the output-elasticity of demand for food were sufficiently low.

Expansion due to capital accumulation will also be anti-trade-biased on the consumption side, since it will raise income per head. On the assumptions stated earlier, that manufacturing is relatively capital-intensive and subject to constant returns while agriculture is relatively labour-intensive and subject to decreasing returns, capital accumulation will be ultra-pro-trade-biased on the production side: it will reduce agricultural output at constant prices. This rather unexpected conclusion may be established by the following argument, the general lines of which were originally developed by T. M. Rybczynski of the London School of Economics.[21]

If agricultural output were kept constant as capital accumulated, the ratio of capital to labour would have to increase in both agriculture and manufacturing, in order to absorb the extra capital. This in turn would imply a reduction in the earnings of capital, relative to wages. Since agriculture is assumed to be relatively more

[21] The writer first encountered the argument in a paper read by W. M. Corden to the Oxford-London-Cambridge Joint Seminar at Cambridge, in November 1954. For a geometrical exposition, see T. M. Rybczynski, 'Factor Endowment and Relative Commodity prices', *Economica*, N.S., XXII, no. 88, November 1955, 336–41.

labour-intensive than manufacturing, the cost of food would rise relatively to the cost of manufactures. To restore the ratio of relative costs to its initial level, agriculture would have to contract and manufacturing expand still further, reducing the relative cost of agricultural production by lowering the capital-to-labour ratio in both industries and by raising the combined marginal productivity of labour and capital in agriculture.

Capital accumulation will therefore be ultra-pro-trade-biased on the production side; and expansion due to this cause will necessarily increase Mancunia's demand for imported food, though the demand may increase more or less than proportionally to the expansion of Mancunia's total output.

Expansion due to population growth will be pro-trade-biased on the consumption side, since it will tend to reduce real income per head. On the production side, its effects will not necessarily be the reverse of those of capital accumulation, owing to the assumption of diminishing returns in agriculture. Population growth will tend to promote expansion of agricultural production. If agriculture, like industry, were subject to constant returns, the expansion of agricultural production would have to go far enough to reduce manufacturing output: maintenance of the initial relative cost ratio would require maintenance of the initial capital-to-labour ratios in the two sectors, which in turn would require sufficient contraction of manufacturing to release the capital needed to equip the additional labour for agricultural production. But with diminishing returns in agriculture raising the relative cost of food as production expands, expansion of both agriculture and manufacturing might be required to absorb the additional labour at unchanged relative prices of food and manufactures. Consequently population growth need not be ultra-anti-trade-import-biased on the production side; it might even be pro-trade-biased, if diminishing returns operated strongly in agriculture, though it could not be ultra-pro-trade-biased. On balance, expansion due to population growth in Mancunia may therefore be pro-trade-biased or anti-trade-biased, and even ultra-anti-trade-biased.

Having surveyed the effects of different kinds of expansion in Mancunia, let us consider the effects of expansion in Agraria. Expansion due to technical progress in Agraria will be pro-trade-biased on the consumption side, since rising real income will be spent proportionately more on manufactured goods. Unless technical progress proceeds more rapidly in manufacturing than in agriculture, expansion due to this cause will be pro-trade-biased on balance; if it proceeds more rapidly in manufacturing, expansion may be import-biased. In the classical case of negligible agricultural progress, expansion would be ultra-anti-trade-biased on balance, promoting self-sufficiency.

Expansion due to capital accumulation will also be pro-trade-biased on the consumption side; but it will be ultra-anti-trade-biased on the production side and therefore ultra-anti-trade-biased on balance, promoting self-sufficiency and tending to turn the terms of trade in Agraria's favour. Expansion arising from population growth will be anti-trade-biased on the consumption side. If returns diminish only gently in agriculture, population growth will be pro-trade-biased on the production side, and possibly ultra-pro-trade-biased if returns diminish sufficiently gently; in the latter case, expansion may, be anti-trade-biased or pro-trade-biased on balance, but not ultra-anti-trade-biased. On the other hand, if agricultural returns diminish strongly, population growth may be anti-trade-biased (though not ultra-anti-trade-biased) on the production side and therefore anti-trade-biased, possibly ultra-anti-trade-biased, on balance. The two extreme cases, of pro-trade-bias when agricultural returns diminish gently and ultra-anti-trade-bias when agricultural returns diminish strongly, have an obvious application to the problems of under-developed countries and the probable effects of population growth in certain parts of the world on the prospects for the terms of trade between manufactures and primary products.

This completes the examination of the effects of expansion of various types in the two countries on their demands for imports; the results are summarized in the accompanying table. It is now necessary to put the results together in an examination of the effects of expansion in both countries together. In doing so, it will be assumed that the cause of expansion is the same in both countries, though this is not necessarily the most interesting assumption to make.

If expansion is due to technical progress in both countries, and progress is equally rapid in both lines of production, its effects will be anti-trade-biased in Mancunia and pro-trade-biased in Agraria. Consequently, if progress is equally rapid in the two countries, the terms of trade will turn in Mancunia's favour and Mancunia's real income will rise more rapidly than Agraria's. If, on the other hand, Agraria is progressing relatively slowly as compared with Mancunia, Agraria will benefit from Mancunia's progress through a favourable movement of her terms of trade, though this may mean a much lower rate of increase of real income than Agraria would enjoy in the previous case. Moreover, as real income rises in Mancunia, a point may come at which Mancunia's expansion becomes ultra-anti-trade-biased, technical progress there raising food production more than enough to satisfy the growing demand for it; at that point Agraria would begin to lose in consequence of Mancunia's expansion.

SUMMARY OF EFFECTS OF EXPANSION

Type of Expansion	Mancunia			Agraria		
	Con-sumption	Pro-duction	Net Effect	Con-sumption	Pro-duction	Net Effect
I. Technical Progress						
(a) Classical Case	A	UP	A or P, not UA	P	UA	UA
(b) Equal rates	A	N	A, possibly UA	P	N	P
II. Capital Accumulation	A	UP	A or P, not UA	P	UA	UA
III. Population Increase						
(a) Slightly Diminishing Returns	P	UA	UA	A	UP	A or P, not UA
(b) Strongly Diminishing Returns	P	P, not UP	P	A	A, not UA	A, possibly UA

A = Anti-trade-biased   UA = Ultra-anti-trade-biased
P = Pro-trade-biased   UP = Ultra-pro-trade-biased
N = Neutral

If technical progress proceeds more rapidly in manufacturing than in agriculture, it will tend to be pro-trade-biased in Mancunia and anti-trade-biased in Agraria, so that the terms of trade would tend to turn against Mancunia unless Agraria was expanding relatively faster. In the extreme classical case expansion would be ultra-pro-trade-biased in Mancunia and ultra-anti-trade-biased in Agraria, and the terms of trade would turn in Agraria's favour regardless of the relative rates of progress in the two countries.

If world expansion is due to capital accumulation, it will be ultra-pro-trade-biased on the production side in Mancunia and ultra-anti-trade-biased on the production side in Agraria, so that Mancunia's demand for imports will increase and Agraria's decrease. Capital accumulation tends to increase manufacturing output and decrease food output in both countries, thereby turning the terms of trade in favour of Agraria. The volume of world trade may either rise or fall over time, depending on the relative ease of diverting production from industry to agriculture in the two countries; if this is relatively easier in Agraria, the volume of world trade will increase.

The effects of world population growth are more complicated than those of world capital accumulation, since they depend on the strength with which diminishing returns operate in the agricultural sectors of the two economies. If returns diminish very gently in both countries, population growth will be ultra-anti-trade-biased in Mancunia and pro-trade-biased in Agraria, and the terms of trade will turn in Mancunia's favour. At the other extreme of strongly diminishing returns in both countries, population growth will be pro-trade-biased in Mancunia and anti-trade-biased, possibly ultra-anti-trade-biased, in Agraria, since in both countries most of the increased population would tend to be forced into manufacturing; the terms of trade in this case would tend to turn in favour of Agraria. If diminishing returns operate strongly in Mancunia and gently in Agraria, population growth may be pro-trade-biased in both countries; in this case the volume of world trade will expand relatively to world production, but the terms of trade may turn in either country's favour. In the converse case, the terms of trade would seem likely to turn in favour of Mancunia.

The effects of the combination of different types of expansion in the two countries may be worked out in the same sort of way, with the aid of the summary table. Owing to the large number of possible cases, this is left to the interested reader. The conclusions which emerge from the analysis may be summarized in the general proposition that expansion will tend to increase Mancunia's demand for imports, and reduce Agraria's demand for imports, except possibly when *either* expansion is due to technical progress which is not proceeding much more rapidly in industry than in agriculture, *or* expansion is due to population growth and agriculture is subject to only gently diminishing returns. Apart from these last two cases, expansion in either country or in both will tend to turn the terms of trade against Mancunia and in favour of Agraria.

III. INTERNATIONAL TRANSMISSIONS OF PRODUCTIVE POWER

The argument of the preceding two Parts has started from the 'classical' assumption that labour, capital, and technology are internationally immobile, only goods being free to move between countries. Though this assumption is perhaps more justifiable nowadays than it used to be, it is clearly unduly restrictive; accordingly, this Part relaxes the assumption and considers certain effects of international movements of labour, capital, and technology. It does not, however, attempt to analyse the effects of economic expansion on the volume and terms of international trade, on the assumption of complete freedom of movement of these elements of productive power;[22] instead, it is concerned with the narrower problem of the effects of international transmission of productive power—that is, with the difference it would make to a country's (specifically, Mancunia's) international trade position if advances in technical knowledge in that country were communicated and applied to the other country as well, if capital were invested abroad instead of at home, or if labour emigrated instead of remaining at home. Posing the problem in this way avoids the complications which arise from allowing both countries to grow at the same time, while permitting the application of conclusions reached previously on the assumption of international immobility of knowledge, labour, and capital.

Before we proceed to analyse the effects on international trade of the different types of transmission of productive power, something should be said about a problem which they raise in common, namely that all three may give rise to both a short-run and a long-run transfer problem. In the short run, the transportation and establishment of migrant labour, the construction of capital equipment in one country rather than another, and the communication of technical knowledge may require the expenditure of a certain amount of current income in a different way than it otherwise would have been spent. In the long run, each may give rise to an international flow of income (migrants' remittances, interest and dividends, or royalties) from the receiving to the transmitting country, and consequently to

[22] For interesting recent attempts at such an analysis for the case of capital accumulation, see D. M. Bensusan-Butt, 'A Model of Trade and Accumulation', *The American Economic Review*, XLIV, no. 4, September 1954, 511–29, and W. A. Lewis, 'Economic Development with Unlimited Supplies of Labour', *The Manchester School of Economic and Social Studies*, XXII, no. 2, May 1954, 139–91, especially 176–89.

a different pattern of expenditure than would result if the income were retained in the country of origin. In both cases, the effect will be to make the terms of trade more favourable than they would be in the absence of the transfer, for the country for whose export good demand is increased as a result of the transfer. So far as the short-run problem is concerned, there is no presumption that the terms of trade will turn in favour of one country or the other;[23] but on the assumption that capital and technology are exported by the country with the higher income per head, and labour by the country with the lower income per head, it can be inferred that any resulting long-run international income flows would tend to improve Mancunia's terms of trade in the case of transmissions of capital and knowledge, and Agraria's terms of trade in the case of labour migration.

In what follows, transfer problems of both types will be ignored, except in the case of foreign investment, where the receipt of a flow of interest or dividends is generally the *sine qua non* of transmission. Thus the transmission of technical knowledge can be treated simply as an increase in technical knowledge abroad; migration as a combined decrease in home and increase in foreign population; and foreign capital investment as a combination of capital decumulation at home, capital accumulation abroad, and a transfer of income from foreigners to residents. It is simplest to consider the three cases in order of increasing difficulty.

The effect of the transmission of technical knowledge on Mancunia's trading position depends on two factors. The first is the relative rate of technical progress in manufacturing as compared with agriculture. The second is whether Mancunia can discriminate in the transmission of knowledge between the two lines of production, or whether the communication of knowledge is an all-or-nothing affair.

The communication of improvements in agricultural technique to Agraria will redound to the benefit of Mancunia, because its effects will be ultra-pro-trade-biased on the production side and pro-trade-biased on the consumption side, and therefore pro-trade-biased on balance; consequently, the terms of trade will tend to turn in favour

---

[23] Though a presumption that they will turn against the transmitting country can be created by introducing tariffs, transport costs incurred in the exportable good of the importing country, or non-traded goods which are more substitutable in production or consumption for exportable than for importable goods, all of which mean that expenditure tends to be biased towards the exportable goods of the country in which the spender is located, so that a transfer of spending power associated with a transmission of productive power tends to reduce the demand for the transmitting country's export good.

of Mancunia, and its real income will be higher than it otherwise would be. On the contrary, the communication of technical progress in manufacturing will be ultra-anti-trade-biased, since it will promote expansion of manufacturing in Agraria at the expense of agriculture, and will tend to turn the terms of trade against Mancunia.

Mancunia gains by the communication of agricultural progress to Agraria, and loses by the communication of manufacturing progress to Agraria. If it can do so, it will gain by withholding the communication of improvements in its manufacturing technique, and confining the transmission of progress to the communication of improvements in agricultural technique—a conclusion which has sometimes found practical expression in the colonial policies of imperial countries. If, on the other hand, the communication of technical progress is an all-or-nothing affair, Mancunia will benefit from the transmission if technical progress is proceeding equally rapidly in agriculture and manufacturing, since the effects of 'neutral' progress in Agraria will be pro-trade-biased on the consumption side; the benefits will be greater the more rapidly technical progress proceeds in agriculture as contrasted with industry, and the likelihood of loss greater the more rapidly progress proceeds in industry as compared with agriculture.

This analysis assumes that technical knowledge accumulates autonomously; this was probably true in the past, but in the modern age of organized research technical knowledge can be manufactured by investment in research. On that alternative assumption, it would follow (as a corollary of the optimum tariff argument) that Mancunia would gain by encouraging research into agricultural methods on a larger scale than would occur commercially, since agricultural progress would promote a favourable tendency of Mancunia's terms of trade; and it would also benefit Mancunia to subsidize agricultural research in Agraria, and to foster the diffusion of improved agricultural techniques in that country.

The second type of transmission of productive power, the migration of labour from Mancunia to Agraria, poses the same analytical problem as a simultaneous and equal reduction of population in Mancunia and increase of population in Agraria. On the simple Part I assumption of complete specialization, the effect of migration on international trade is straightforward: it would reduce Mancunia's demand for food imports below what it would otherwise be, and raise Agraria's demand for manufactures above what it would otherwise be, so that the terms of trade would necessarily turn in favour of Mancunia.[24] This conclusion may also be derived from the fact that migration will reduce the world supply of manufactures and increase that of food, while increasing the demand for both (Agraria's output must rise more than Mancunia's falls, since otherwise migration would be unattractive). Migration would reduce Mancunia's total output, though less than proportionally to the reduction in population (owing to diminishing returns, and assuming that migrants were representative of total population); total real income would fall less than output, owing to the favourable terms-of-trade movement, and might even increase if the elasticity of world demand for food were sufficiently low; for both reasons, real income per head in Mancunia would increase. The opposite effects would occur in Agraria.

In the general case of incomplete specialization, the problem is more complicated, since, as was shown in Part II, population growth will tend to have opposite effects on the two countries' demands for imports, so that the effects of migration on import demands will tend to be in the same direction in both countries. Consequently, while the direction of change of the volume of trade will be determinate, a migration of labour from Mancunia to Agraria tending to increase each country's demand for imports, the movement of the terms of trade will depend on the relative magnitudes of the changes in import demand in the two countries.

In certain cases, however—those in which diminishing returns operate with markedly different severity in the agricultural sectors of the two economies—the direction of change of the terms of trade resulting from migration can be established directly from the conclusions arrived at in Part II. If returns in Mancunian agriculture diminish strongly, population growth in Mancunia would be pro-trade-biased, and emigration would reduce Mancunia's demand for food imports; while if returns in Agrarian agriculture diminish rather gently, population growth in Agraria could not be ultra-

---

[24] The total improvement in Mancunia's balance of payments at unchanged relative prices would be the sum of the amount by which emigration reduced Mancunia's total output, multiplied by Mancunia's marginal propensity to import food, and the amount by which immigration increased Agraria's total output, multiplied by Agraria's marginal propensity to import manufactures. At the margin of migration, these changes in import demand would be equal to the value of the marginal product of labour, multiplied by the average propensity of labour to consume imports. For substantial migrations, the changes in total output would be larger in Mancunia, and smaller in Agraria, than shown by the pre-migration marginal productivities of labour in the two countries, because of the operation of diminishing marginal productivity.

anti-trade-biased, so that immigration would increase Agraria's demand for imports of manufactures; thus in this case migration would definitely improve Mancunia's balance of payments (at unchanged prices) and turn the terms of trade in her favour. Conversely, if returns diminished gently in Mancunian agriculture and strongly in Agrarian agriculture, population growth would be ultra-anti-trade-biased in both countries; and migration would increase Mancunian demand for imported food while reducing Agrarian demand for imported manufactures, so that the terms of trade would turn against Mancunia.

In the general case, the direction of change of the terms of trade will depend on the balance of the factors which determine the consumption and production shifts and the consequential changes in import demands in the two countries. The conditions which determine the movement of the terms of trade can, however, be stated more precisely, and the range of factors influencing the outcome can be narrowed down by introducing more restrictive assumptions than heretofore.

The simplest approach to a more precise analysis is to start from the effect of migration on world demand for and supply of manufactured goods: if world demand for manufactures increases more than or decreases less than world production of manufactures (at constant prices) the terms of trade will turn in Mancunia's favour, and vice versa.

On the consumption side, the effect of migration is likely to be favourable to Mancunia. At the margin, the changes in total output in the two countries due to migration may be identified with the marginal productivities of labour in the two countries; and the marginal propensities of the two countries to consume manufactures may be identified with the average propensities of labour to consume manufactures. Since the marginal labourer in Agraria is presumably better off than the marginal labourer in Mancunia (the motive for migration), both the change in output and the marginal propensity to consume manufactures from it will be greater in Agraria. Consequently, the net effect of migration will be to increase world demand for manufactures and so tend to turn the terms of trade in Mancunia's favour. This conclusion can also be inferred from the presumption that migration will raise world output.

On the production side, the problem is more complicated. Emigration must increase Mancunia's production of manufactures, by making labour scarcer and so promoting a movement of resources into manufacturing, which economizes on the use of labour; but immigration may either decrease or increase Agraria's output of manufactures, depending on whether diminishing returns operate gently or strongly in Agrarian agriculture. To say anything more specific about the net effect on world manufacturing output, it is necessary to make more specific assumptions about the production functions for the two industries in the two countries.

To begin with, we abstract from diminishing returns in agriculture, and assume constant returns to scale in the application of doses of capital and labour to land. On this assumption, migration will increase manufacturing output in Mancunia and reduce it in Agraria. The problem now is to investigate what determines which change will be the larger.

We begin by recapitulating the reasons why the outputs of manufactures in the two countries must change in the directions stated. To release a man from the Mancunian economy, while preserving the same relative prices of agricultural and manufacturing output, it is necessary to switch capital and labour from agriculture to manufacturing, in order to re-employ the capital released by the withdrawal of the man from agriculture. The amount of labour that must be diverted to manufacturing is equal to the capital-to-labour ratio in agriculture (which determines the amount of capital freed there by the withdrawal of one labourer) divided by the difference between the capital-to-labour ratios in manufacturing and agriculture (which determines the amount of capital which is re-employed by the movement of a unit of labour into manufacturing), and is in fact the reciprocal of the proportional excess of the capital-to-labour ratio in manufacturing over that in agriculture.[25] The larger this excess, the less labour needs to be shifted to re-employ the capital freed by migration, and vice versa. Similarly, to absorb extra labour in Agraria at constant relative commodity prices, capital must be released by a shift of labour from manufacturing into agriculture, the amount of labour which must be shifted varying inversely with the proportional excess of the capital-to-labour ratio in manufacturing over that in agriculture.

Consequently, the shift of labour into manufacturing in Mancunia will be greater or less than the shift of labour out of manufacturing in Agraria, according as the proportional difference between the

---

[25] Let the capital-to-labour ratios in manufactures and agriculture be respectively k and k'; then the shift of labour into manufactures required to absorb the capital released by withdrawal of one unit of labour from agriculture is $\frac{k'}{k - k'}$, which is the reciprocal of the proportional excess of k over k'.

G

capital-to-labour ratios employed in the manufacturing and agricultural sectors is less or greater in Mancunia than in Agraria. The amounts of the increase in manufacturing output in Mancunia and decrease in Agraria, however, depend not only on the changes in labour employed but also on the average productivities of labour in manufacturing. To proceed any further, it is necessary to establish a link of some kind between average productivity of labour in manufacturing, and proportional differences in capital-to-labour ratios in the two sectors; this requires the introduction of still more restrictive assumptions.

One such set of assumptions, which conforms closely to the conventions of contemporary international trade theory, is that manufacturing production functions are identical in the two countries, and that agricultural production functions are the same in both countries except that output in agriculture is higher in Agraria for any combination of labour and capital.[26] On these assumptions, the marginal productivity of labour and its average productivity in each industry will be higher in Agraria than in Mancunia when relative prices of food and manufactures are the same in both countries, and the capital-to-labour ratios will be higher in both sectors in Agraria than in Mancunia.[27] If the elasticity of substitution between capital and labour is greater in agriculture than in manufacturing, the proportional difference between the capital-to-labour ratios will be less in Agraria than in Mancunia, and more labour, with a higher average productivity, will shift out of manufacturing in Agraria than shifts into manufacturing in Mancunia. Consequently total world production of manufactures will fall. In conjunction with the increased demand for manufactures, this means that the terms of trade must shift in favour of Mancunia in this case. But if the elasticity of substitution between capital and labour is greater in manufacturing than in agriculture, the proportional difference between the capital-to-labour ratios will be greater in Agraria than in Mancunia, and

[26] If production functions were identical in agriculture also, manufactures were capital-intensive at all factor prices, and trade were taking place with incomplete specialization in both countries, equalization of labour's marginal productivity and of its average productivity in each industry as between the two countries would necessarily be implied; hence migration would not change world output of either good.

[27] If relative factor prices were the same in the two countries, food would be cheaper in Agraria (due to superior agricultural productivity); to offset this, the relative price of labour would have to be higher in Agraria, since a higher price of labour would raise the relative price of food, the labour-intensive good, as compared with manufactures, the capital-intensive good; a higher price of labour implies a higher capital-to-labour ratio in both industries.

the net effect of migration on world manufacturing output may be either an increase or a decrease, because of the opposing effects of a smaller labour shift and a higher average productivity of labour in Agraria.

The third type of transmission of productive power, the investment of Mancunian capital in Agraria, has the same effect analytically as a combination of capital accumulation in Agraria and decumulation in Mancunia, accompanied by a transfer of income from Agraria to Mancunia. As has already been argued, the income transfer by itself would tend to turn the terms of trade in favour of Mancunia (on the assumption that income per head, and hence the marginal propensity to consume manufactures, is higher in the investing country). The effect of capital decumulation in Mancunia would be to reduce Mancunia's demand for imports, since it would reduce the demand for food while increasing domestic production of it; similarly, capital accumulation in Agraria would reduce Agraria's demand for imports, since it would increase output of manufactures there by more than the increase in total output. Thus (apart from the effect of the income transfer) foreign investment by Mancunia would reduce the level of foreign trade below what it otherwise would be;[28] but because it would reduce both countries' demands for imports, its effects on the terms of trade might be either favourable or unfavourable to Mancunia.

As in the case of labour migration, the conditions which determine the effect of foreign investment on Mancunia's terms of trade can most readily be investigated by considering its effects on world demand for manufactures and on world supply of them (at constant prices).

At the margin, the decrease in output in Mancunia and increase in output in Agraria can be identified with the marginal productivities of capital in the two countries. Further, under competitive conditions the return payable on Mancunia's investment in Agraria will be equal to the marginal productivity of capital there, so that all the increase in output in Agraria due to Mancunia's investment will accrue as

[28] Payment of the transfer would necessarily reduce Agraria's demand for manufactured imports still more; receipt of the transfer might make Mancunia's demand for food imports greater than it would have been in the absence of foreign investment, though for this to happen the transfer would have to exceed the additional output that would have resulted from investing the capital at home by enough to raise demand for food more than the withdrawal of the capital from domestic investment increases Mancunia's food production. Thus, though the volume of trade in manufactures would fall, the volume of trade in food might conceivably rise.

income to Agraria. The total change in demand for manufactures due to the transmission of capital will therefore be determined entirely by the increase in Mancunia's income above what it otherwise would have been; and since part of the increase in income will increase Mancunia's demand for manufactures, the consumption effect of foreign investment will be favourable to Mancunia.

On the production side, the effect of foreign investment will be favourable or unfavourable to Mancunia according as the decrease in Mancunian manufacturing output is greater or less than the increase in Agrarian manufacturing production. The total supply of manufactures is more likely to decrease, turning the terms of trade in favour of Mancunia, the more gently returns in agriculture diminish in Mancunia and the more strongly they diminish in Agraria. A more precise statement of the conditions which determine the movement of the terms of trade would require, as in the case of labour migration, more restrictive assumptions about production conditions. If, for example, it is assumed that production functions in both lines of production are subject to constant returns and are the same in both countries except that output of food is less in Agraria than in Mancunia for any combination of labour and capital, it can be shown by an argument similar to that presented earlier that only if the elasticity of substitution is greater in agriculture than in manufacturing is it possible for the reduction in Mancunian manufacturing to exceed the increase in Agrarian manufacturing, making the production effect favourable to Mancunia.

CONCLUSION

In conclusion, something should be said in recognition of the limitations of the two-country assumption on which the argument of the preceding Parts has been based. One effect of this assumption is to exaggerate the magnitude of the influence of economic expansion on the terms of trade, and the resulting divergence of real income and output. This is perhaps not a serious defect, given the bias of economic theory towards thinking in closed-economy terms. But the assumption has a more serious drawback, in that it emphasizes the complementarity, as contrasted with the competitiveness, of relations between nations. Specifically, while an analysis of the relations between the two broad sectors of industry and agriculture in a growing world economy brings out some interesting conclusions, it cannot be applied directly to the effects and problems of growth in any one industrial or primary producing country. For that sort of problem, the two broad sectors, the nature and pace of whose expansion governs the terms of trade between food (including materials) and manufactures, should be conceived of each as consisting of a number of imperfectly competitive member countries. Expansion of any one country would influence the terms of trade of all members of its group, to an extent depending on the country's share in world trade and the elasticity of world demand for its group's exportable product; and would also influence its own terms of trade relatively more than those of other members of its group, depending on the extent to which its particular ranges of exports and imports were substitutable for the exports and imports of other countries in world consumption. Correspondingly, the evolution of the volume and terms of trade of any single country would be influenced, not only by the nature and pace of the expansion of the two groups as aggregates, but also by the nature and pace of its own expansion as compared with that of the rival members of its group; and the latter influence (which involves such difficult problems as competition *via* technical progress) might be more important than the former.

CHAPTER IV

Increasing Productivity, Income-Price Trends and the Trade Balance[*]

OF the many factors which have been discussed in the attempt to provide a theoretical explanation of chronic balance-of-payments disequilibria in general, and a meaningful concept of 'dollar shortage' in particular, those centring on the 'dynamic' problems associated with the high rate of increase of American productivity have tended to find increasing favour in recent years.[1] Such explanations of chronic disequilibrium are of two sorts.[2] On the one hand, there is the argument that American money income rises less rapidly than productivity, so that American prices fall and the outside world is obliged to choose between secular deflation and secular depreciation (or between periodic deflations and periodic devaluations); on this line of argument chronic disequilibrium is a problem of monetary adjustment. On the other hand, there is the argument, elegantly formulated on a recent occasion by Professor Hicks,[3] that technical progress in the United States is strongly biased in favour of import substitutes, so that, apart from monetary complications, economic

---

[*] *The Economic Journal*, LXIV, no. 255, September 1954, 462–85.

[1] The economists most notable for their early and sustained emphasis on this aspect of the dollar problem have been Thomas Balogh and John H. Williams. See Thomas Balogh, *The Dollar Crisis: Causes and Cure* (Oxford, 1949) and earlier articles mentioned therein; John H. Williams, *Postwar Monetary Plans* (Oxford, 1949) and *Economic Stability in the Modern World* (Stamp Memorial Lecture, November 1952).

[2] The high rate of increase of American productivity also plays a part in other explanations of dollar shortage, for example, that emphasizing the instability of the American economy; but the latter argument seems to depend essentially on the high absolute level of American productivity rather than on its rate of change.

[3] J. R. Hicks, 'An Inaugural Lecture', *Oxford Economic Papers*, N.S., V, no. 2, June 1953, 117–35. Hicks' argument is foreshadowed in Gottfried Haberler's contribution 'Dollar Shortage?', chap. 24 in S. E. Harris, ed., *Foreign Economic Policy for the United States* (Cambridge, 1948) and in Honor Croome, 'The Dollar Siege', *Lloyds Bank Review*, N.S., no. 17, July 1950, 25–46. See also Sir Dennis Robertson, *Britain in the World Economy* (London, 1954), chap. III.

progress there imposes a real loss on the outside world;[4] on this line of argument chronic disequilibrium is basically a problem of real adjustment.

The purpose of what follows is to throw some light on the logical implications of the first of these arguments, through an investigation of the relation between rates of increase of productivity and income-price trends or policies on the one hand, and the trend of the balance of trade on the other, in a highly-simplified two-country model of international trade.[5] Part I sets out the assumptions of the model and develops the basic equation required in the analysis; Part II analyses the effects of increasing productivity on the balance of trade, on the alternative assumptions that increasing productivity is reflected in proportionately rising money incomes or in proportionately falling prices; and Part III discusses the income-price policy necessary in one country to maintain equilibrium in its trade balance, given the income-price trend in the other country. Part IV sketches briefly the extension of the analysis required to deal with dynamic problems of balance-of-payments equilibrium. While the analysis employs mathematical techniques, these are of a type now familiar in this field, and their main use is to bring the relevant variables together in a systematic way. The more important conclusions bearing on the theory of dollar shortage are summarized in non-mathematical terms in Part V.

[4] For a real loss to the outside world to result, technical progress in the United States must not merely be biased in favour of import substitutes, but sufficiently so to offset the favourable effects of progress in American export industries. Moreover, such import-biased progress could scarcely affect *all* the countries of the outside world adversely, since those which produced substitutes for American exports would enjoy a favourable movement of their terms of trade. Finally, import-biased progress might well be the result of other factors, such as delays by the outside world in making the necessary monetary adjustments, or the protectionist character of American commercial policy, rather than an independent feature of the American economy. For these reasons the hypothesis that American progress is import-biased does not impress the writer as a satisfactory starting-point for analysis of the dollar problem.

[5] The use of a two-country model can be a legitimate tool of analysis in international trade theory, *provided* that it is clearly recognized that only one of the 'countries' can be actually identified, the other 'country' being the rest of the world; unfortunately there has been a tendency in the literature to apply the two-country model to the relations between the United Kingdom and the United States, a use for which it is clearly not appropriate. In the argument of this chapter, country 2 is taken to be the United States, and country 1 the rest of the world; some of the complications which arise in a many-country system are considered briefly in the Appendix.

I. THE MODEL

The analysis which follows is conducted in terms of a world of two countries, country 1 and country 2. In order to isolate the effects of increasing productivity, it is assumed that each country has a fixed supply of labour,[6] which is kept continuously employed[7] in the production of a single good.[8] The output of this good (denoted by Y) is assumed to be increasing at the continuous rate $R \left(= \frac{1}{Y} \frac{dY}{dt} \right)$ determined by technical progress and capital accumulation;[9] the price per unit of the good (denoted by p), measured in an international monetary unit common to the two countries, is assumed to change at the rate $r_p \left(= \frac{1}{p} \frac{dp}{dt} \right)$, which may be positive, negative or zero; and the level of money income per head (denoted by w) changes at the rate r_w. By definition, $r_w = r_p + R$.[10]

[6] To abstract from the effects of population growth.

[7] To abstract from problems of variations in effective demand, *inter alia*, variations induced by the changes in the balance of trade which are the object of study. The simplest assumption is that the government absorbs a quantity of domestic output which is varied so as to maintain equality between total demand for and supply of domestic output, and that private saving is sufficiently high so that this quantity is always positive. Implicit in this assumption is the difficulty that, strictly interpreted, it means that changes in the trade balance are accurately forecast and offset by the economic authorities, and therefore are in some sense 'planned'. Such difficulties are ignored in what follows.

[8] The assumption that a number of goods are produced, unless hedged about by enough other assumptions to reduce it to equivalence with a single-good case, either introduces problems of re-allocation of production at varying real cost, which make the change in productivity in part a dependent variable, or, on the assumption of constant relative cost of all products, introduces awkward problems of discontinuity in international adjustment. There is also the difficulty that technical progress and capital accumulation will have differential effects on the relative costs of different goods.

[9] In a single-good model capital accumulation must take the form of employing larger stocks of the good in the production process. Capital accumulation, unless 'neutral' in the Harrod sense, introduces problems of change in the proportion of current output devoted to investment, and both it and technical progress may involve changes in income-distribution, which may influence the demand for imports. Such complications are ignored here; for a discussion of some of the problems in a closed economy, see Joan Robinson, 'The Production Function and the Theory of Capital', *Review of Economic Studies*, XXI(2), no. 55, 81–106.

[10] By definition, $w = \frac{pY}{L}$ where L is the (fixed) quantity of labour. Hence

$$\frac{1}{w} \frac{dw}{dt} = \frac{1}{pY} \left(p \frac{dY}{dt} + Y \frac{dp}{dt} \right) = R + r_p.$$

Each country consumes a part of its output itself, and exports the remainder (denoted by X) to the other country in exchange for imports of the other country's product. Each country's demand for the other country's exports is assumed to be a function of two variables: its own output (which is identical with its income, valued in units of domestic product) and the price of its imports relative to the price of its own product. In symbols, $X_1 = f_2(\pi, Y_2)$ and $X_2 = f_1\left(\dfrac{1}{\pi}, Y_1\right)$, where $\pi\left(=\dfrac{p_1}{p_2}\right)$ is the price of country 1's good relative to the price of country 2's good. The income elasticity of a country's demand for imports is denoted in what follows by ϵ

$$\left(\epsilon_1 = \frac{Y_1}{X_2}\frac{\partial X_2}{\partial Y_1}, \qquad \epsilon_2 = \frac{Y_2}{X_1}\frac{\partial X_1}{\partial Y_2}\right)$$

and the price-elasticity of its demand for imports by η

$$\left(\eta_1 = \frac{\pi}{X_2}\frac{\partial X_2}{\partial \pi}, \qquad \eta_2 = -\frac{\pi}{X_1}\frac{\partial X_1}{\partial \pi}\right)^{11}.$$

We may now proceed to analyse the behaviour of the balance of trade between the two countries over time. Before doing so, however, it is necessary to define more precisely the problem in which we are interested, and in particular to choose a criterion for an improvement or deterioration in country 1's trade balance with country 2. Broadly speaking, there are two alternative criteria to be considered, each of which corresponds to a distinct conception of the dollar problem. On the one hand, in conformity with the practice of the modern theory of exchange adjustment, we may measure country 1's trade balance in terms of international currency, and define an improvement in its trade balance as a decrease in the (international currency) value of its trade deficit, or an increase in the value of its

[11] Although these elasticities are defined with reference to a change in the relative price of imports, they will be identical with elasticities defined with reference to a change in the absolute price of imports, the price of the home good remaining unchanged, since (on the usual assumption of homogenous demand functions of zero degree in prices) an equi-proportional change in both prices will leave the quantity demanded unchanged. For the same reason a rise in the price of the home good will have the opposite effect on quantity demanded to that of an equi-proportional rise in the price of imports, so that η_1 can be expressed in terms of π, as in the text. This footnote was suggested by a comment from I. F. Pearce.

trade surplus. This would involve conceiving of the dollar problem in terms of the current-account deficit of the rest of the world with the United States, measured in gold. On the other hand, we may measure country 1's trade balance as a fraction of its imports, and define an improvement in its trade balance as a decrease in the ratio of its import surplus to its imports, or an increase in the ratio of its export surplus to its imports.[12] This would imply conceiving of the dollar problem in terms of the proportion of the imports of the rest of the world from the United States not paid for by exports to the United States.

The first alternative provides a monetary criterion of improvement, and the second provides a 'real' criterion of improvement. Unfortunately, except in the case in which trade is initially balanced, an improvement or deterioration on one criterion may not be an improvement or deterioration on the other: a doubling of commodity prices, for example, would double the money value of a deficit or surplus but leave the 'real' deficit or surplus unchanged. Nor is there any compelling economic reason for preferring one criterion to the other, since in different contexts we may be interested in either the money balance or the 'real' balance, according, for example, to the assumptions made about the source of financing of the balance.

There are, however, two considerations which suggest the adoption of the second criterion in preference to the first.[13] One is that the 'real' balance is the more fundamental, and that changes in its money value arising from general movements in prices are more appropriately treated as gains or losses in purchasing power on capital account.[14] The other is that adoption of the second criterion both permits a more satisfactory dynamic formulation of the problem and greatly simplifies the argument. Consequently, the second criterion is adopted here, though the first criterion is developed at various points in footnotes.

The behaviour of a country's 'real' balance over time is most conveniently studied through the ratio of the value of its exports to the value of its imports. An increase in this ratio, which is referred to henceforward as 'the export ratio', means an improvement in the country's real balance, and vice versa.

---

[12] Alternatively, the trade balance could be measured as a fraction of the country's exports.

[13] The original draft of this chapter argued entirely in terms of the money balance. The present version owes much to comments from R. F. Harrod, Milton Friedman, M. R. Fisher and A. Asimakopulos.

[14] I am indebted for this argument to Milton Friedman.

Country 1's export ratio is defined as $T_1 = \dfrac{p_1 X_1}{p_2 X_2} = \dfrac{\pi X_1}{X_2}$. Differentiating this by t, and using the symbols defined above, we obtain

$$\frac{dT_1}{dt} = \frac{1}{X_2^2}\left[X_2\left(X_1 \frac{d\pi}{dt} + \pi \frac{\partial X_1}{\partial \pi}\frac{d\pi}{dt} + \pi \frac{\partial X_1}{\partial Y_2}\frac{dY_2}{dt} \right) \right.$$

$$\left. - \pi X_1 \left(\frac{\partial X_2}{\partial \pi}\frac{d\pi}{dt} + \frac{\partial X_2}{\partial Y_1}\frac{dY_1}{dt} \right) \right]$$

$$= \frac{\pi X_1}{X_2}\left(r_\pi - \eta_2 r_\pi + \epsilon_2 R_2 - \eta_1 r_\pi - \epsilon_1 R_1 \right)$$

where $r_\pi = \dfrac{1}{\pi}\dfrac{d\pi}{dt}$. Substituting for r_π $(= r_{p_1} - r_{p_2})$, and defining $R_{T_1} = \dfrac{1}{T_1}\dfrac{dT_1}{dt}$, this becomes

(1) $$R_{T_1} = (\eta_1 + \eta_2 - 1)(r_{p_2} - r_{p_1}) + \epsilon_2 R_2 - \epsilon_1 R_1.$$

This last expression is our basic analytical equation:[15] it expresses the rate of change of country 1's export ratio, as a function of the

[15] Country 1's trade balance, measured in international currency units, is $B_1 = p_1 X_1 - p_2 X_2$. The equation for its change over time, found by differentiation of B_1 by t, may be expressed as

(1)' $$R_{B_1} = \left(\frac{1}{p_1 X_1}\frac{dB_1}{dt} \right) = b_1 r_{p_2} + \left(\frac{\eta_1}{T_1} + \eta_2 - 1 \right)(r_{p_2} - r_{p_1}) + \left(\epsilon_2 R_2 - \frac{\epsilon_1 R_1}{T_1} \right)$$

where $b_1 = \dfrac{B_1}{p_1 X_1}$. It should be noted that in contrast to the definitions of rates of change employed in the text, the definition of R_{B_1} here is merely a convention employed to simplify the right-hand side of the equation.

The equation is most easily understood as follows. The first term on the right-hand side expresses the fact that an equi-proportional change in both prices would alter the money value of a given real deficit or surplus proportionally. The coefficient of the second term is an analogue of the Hirschmann condition for devaluation to improve the trade balance when trade is initially unbalanced (see A. O. Hirschmann, 'Devaluation and the Trade Balance: A Note', *Review of Economics and Statistics*, XXXI, no. 1, February 1949, 50–3), and reflects the fact that, with initially unbalanced trade, the criterion for a price reduction (devaluation) by country 1 to improve its (foreign) balance involves a *weighted* sum of the elasticities of international demand. The third term expresses the fact that, if trade is initially unbalanced, an equi-proportional expansion of each country's imports would alter the money balance.

When trade is initially balanced, the equation for the change in the money balance reduces to the equation given in the text for the real balance. The simplification achieved by consideration of the real rather than the money trade balance might usefully be extended to the whole theory of exchange adjustment.

rates of change of prices and the rates of change of productivity in the two countries.[16]

As a guide to the subsequent argument, it may be noted that the right-hand side of the equation falls naturally into two parts. The first expresses the influence of the price-trends, which depends on their relative magnitudes and on whether the sum of the two elasticities of demand for imports is greater or less than unity. The second expresses the influence of the productivity trends, which depends on their relative magnitudes and on the income-elasticities of demand for imports.

II. INCOME AND PRICE STABILITY AND THE TRADE BALANCE

The equation derived in the previous part expresses the general relation between the trade balance (in the form of the export ratio) and price and productivity trends. In this section we deal with the four particular cases which are suggested by the consideration that, either as a matter of policy or as a consequence of the working of economic forces, increasing productivity may result in a proportionately falling price level, aggregate money income remaining constant, or in proportionately rising money income, the price level remaining constant.

(a) Constant Price Level in Both Countries

On the assumption that the price level remains constant in both countries and money incomes rise proportionately to increasing productivity, $r_{p1} = r_{p2} = 0$, and the basic equation becomes

$$(2) \qquad R_{T_1} = \epsilon_2 R_2 - \epsilon_1 R_1.$$

Country 1's trade balance turns more favourable or less favourable according to whether $\epsilon_2 R_2$ is greater or less than $\epsilon_1 R_1$; it will remain unchanged if these two expressions are equal.

A number of implications of this result are of interest. If productivity is not increasing in country 1, but is increasing in country 2, country 1's trade balance is bound to improve unless the commodity it produces is an inferior good in the consumption of country 2 (i.e. unless ϵ_2 is negative); conversely, if country 1's productivity is

---

[16] The equation could be cast in terms of the rates of change of money income per head, rather than of prices, by use of the relationship $r_w = r_p + R$; but the resulting expression is much more cumbersome, and consequently is not introduced until the argument requires it.

increasing but country 2's productivity is not, country 1's trade balance is bound to deteriorate unless its consumers regard country 2's product as an inferior good.[17]

It does not necessarily follow, however, that when productivity in both countries is increasing the trade balance turns in favour of the country whose productivity is increasing at the slower rate, since the effect of a country's growth on its demand for imports depends on both its rate of increase of productivity and its income elasticity of demand for imports. Thus productivity may be increasing less rapidly in country 1 than in country 2, and the trade balance may turn against country 1, because country 1's income-elasticity of demand for country 2's goods is sufficiently greater than country 2's income-elasticity of demand for country 1's goods to offset the favourable influence of country 1's lower rate of growth.[18]

In terms of the dollar problem, this result would imply that if productivity increased faster in the United States than it did elsewhere, and if the United States (and the outside world) followed the policy of inflating money incomes proportionately to increases in productivity, a chronic dollar shortage would still be a possibility in consequence of an income-elasticity of foreign demand for American goods sufficiently higher than the American income-elasticity of demand for imports.[19] Such a dollar problem, however, would imply that the rate of increase of productivity in the United States was too low, not too high, relative to that in the rest of the world.

[17] Cf. Hicks, loc. cit., 124. Henceforward the argument neglects the possibility of one country's product being inferior in consumption in the other country, and proceeds on the assumption of positive income-elasticities of demand for imports.

[18] In this case the change in the money balance is given by

$$(2)' \qquad R_{B_1} = \epsilon_2 R_2 - \frac{1}{T_1} \epsilon_1 R_1.$$

If initially country 1 has a deficit ($T_1 < 1$) its money trade balance may turn against it, even though its demand for imports is growing less rapidly than country 2's demand for its exports ($\epsilon_1 R_1 < \epsilon_2 R_2$).

[19] Purely as an illustration, and without any commitment to their relevance or meaningfulness, we may refer to Chang's estimates of the income-elasticities of American demand for imports, 1·27, and of world demand for American exports, 2·917 (T. C. Chang, Cyclical Movements in the Balance of Payments (Cambridge, 1951), 148). These would imply a dollar problem of the kind described above, unless the United States grew 2·3 times as fast as the rest of the world; but both the estimates and their application here are so dubious that the exercise should not be taken seriously.

(b) Price Constant in One Country, Money Income Constant in the Other

Since the two cases in which price is constant in one country and money income constant in the other are symmetrical, only one of them need be analysed. We shall consider the case in which price is constant in country 1, and money income constant in country 2. In this case $r_{p_1} = 0$ and $r_{p_2} = -R_2$, and the basic equation becomes[20]

$$(3) \qquad R_{T_1} = (1 + \epsilon_2 - \eta_1 - \eta_2)R_2 - \epsilon_1 R_1.$$

This equation indicates that country 1's trade balance is certain to turn adverse if $(1 + \epsilon_2 - \eta_1 - \eta_2)$ is negative; that is, if the sum of the two elasticities of international demand is greater than one plus country 2's income-elasticity of demand for imports. But country 1's trade balance may improve if the sum of the two price-elasticities is less than this critical sum; and it will improve if this condition is satisfied *and* R_2 is greater than

$$\frac{\epsilon_1 R_1}{\epsilon_2 + 1 - \eta_1 - \eta_2}.$$

The explanation of these results becomes very simple if we neglect the effects of increasing productivity in country 1 and consider the effects of increasing productivity in country 2, accompanied by proportionately falling prices, on country 1's trade balance. These effects are of two kinds. First, increasing productivity in country 2 increases country 2's income, and therefore its demand for imports, through the income-elasticity of demand for imports; this effect tends to improve country 1's trade balance. Second, increasing productivity in country 2 by assumption lowers the price of country 2's goods, and so affects both countries' demands for imports. This effect may work either way: if the sum of the elasticities of international demand is less than unity, the trade balance turns in favour

[20] The corresponding equation for the behaviour of the money balance is

$$(3)' \qquad R_{B_1} = \left(\epsilon_2 + \frac{1}{T_1} - \frac{\eta_1}{T_1} - \eta_2 \right) R_2 - \frac{\epsilon_1 R_1}{T_1},$$

and the condition for an improvement in country 1's money balance to be possible is that $\frac{\eta_1}{T_1} + \eta_2$ should be less than $\epsilon_2 + \frac{1}{T_1}$. From the formula it follows that if country 1's demand for imports is inelastic ($\eta_1 < 1$) increasing productivity in country 2 accompanied by falling prices is more likely to improve country 1's money balance the larger is country's 1's initial deficit or the smaller is its initial surplus (the smaller is T_1); but if country 1's demand for imports is elastic ($\eta_1 > 1$) the opposite conclusion follows.

of country 1; if the sum of the elasticities is greater than unity, it turns in favour of country 2. For increasing productivity in country 2 to turn the trade balance against country 1, the sum of the elasticities of demand must be sufficiently greater than unity to outweigh country 2's income-elasticity of demand for imports. If productivity in country 1 is also increasing, and the price level there is constant, there is an unfavourable effect on country 1's trade balance through its increasing demand for imports which must also be considered.

The assumption that the price level is constant in country 1 and income constant in country 2 yields a model analogous to that assumed in the monetary explanation of chronic dollar shortage mentioned in the introduction to this chapter, if we identify country 2 with the United States and country 1 with the outside world; and the results just stated have some bearing on the theoretical arguments used to demonstrate the reality of 'dollar shortage'. In the first place, as we have shown, it is not necessarily true that if increasing productivity in the United States resulted entirely in falling prices, and increasing productivity elsewhere resulted entirely in rising money incomes, the trade balance of the United States would turn in its favour. In the second place, a favourable movement of the American trade balance arising from productivity-induced reductions in the prices of American goods would necessarily imply that the responsiveness of world demand to changes in relative prices was sufficiently high for monetary or exchange-rate adjustments by the outside world to remedy the situation.[21]

This analysis points to a certain inconsistency between the argument that there is a persistent tendency towards dollar shortage because the United States does not inflate incomes sufficiently to keep pace with rising productivity, and the assertion sometimes found in close association with it that the elasticities of international demand are too low for devaluation against the dollar to have a favourable effect on the trade balance of the rest of the world with the United States. The latter assertion ought logically to carry with it the view that the greater the rate of increase in productivity and the

---

[21] While this argument relates to the real balance, it applies *a fortiori* to the money balance, if the United States is assumed to have an initial export surplus ($T_1 < 1$). Devaluation or deflation by the outside world would improve the outside world's dollar balance if $\frac{\eta_1}{T_1} + \eta_2 > 1$, whereas increasing American productivity with falling prices would worsen the outside world's dollar balance only if $\frac{\eta_1}{T_1} + \eta_2 > \epsilon_1 + \frac{1}{T_1}$.

less the accompanying inflation of incomes in the United States, the less serious will be the dollar problem of the outside world. The former argument, in so far as it stresses the rapidity of American progress, assumes that the elasticities of international demand are sufficiently high for devaluation against the dollar to be a successful policy.[22]

(c) Money Income Constant in Both Countries

On the assumption that money income remains constant in both countries and prices fall proportionately to the rate of increase of productivity, $r_{p_1} = -R_1$ and $r_{p_2} = -R_2$, and the basic equation becomes[23]

$$(4) \qquad R_{T_1} = (\eta_1 + \eta_2 - \epsilon_1 - 1)R_1 - (\eta_1 + \eta_2 - \epsilon_2 - 1)R_2.$$

If both coefficients of the rates of growth are positive—that is, if the sum of the elasticities of international demand is greater than unity plus the higher income-elasticity of demand for imports—the trade balance turns towards or against country 1 according to whether R_1 is greater or less than $\dfrac{\eta_1 + \eta_2 - \epsilon_2 - 1}{\eta_1 + \eta_2 - \epsilon_1 - 1}R_2$. In this case, if country 1's income-elasticity of demand for imports is greater than country 2's, the trade balance must turn against it unless it is growing, and reducing its price level, more rapidly than country 2. If both coefficients are negative (the sum of the elasticities is less than one plus the lower income-elasticity of demand for imports) the trade balance turns towards or against country 1 according to whether R_1 is less than or greater than $\dfrac{\eta_1 + \eta_2 - \epsilon_2 - 1}{\eta_1 + \eta_2 - \epsilon_1 - 1}R_2$. In this case, if country 1's income-elasticity of demand for imports is greater than country 2's, its trade balance must turn against it unless it is growing less rapidly than country 2.

Finally, if one coefficient is positive and the other negative (the sum of the elasticities lies between one plus the lower and one

---

[22] A dollar shortage could emerge under the postulated circumstances, even if the sum of the elasticities of international demand were less than unity; but it would be the result of increasing productivity in the rest of the world.

[23] The corresponding equation for the behaviour of the money balance is

$$(4)' \qquad R_{B_1} = \left(\frac{\eta_1}{T_1} + \eta_2 - \frac{\epsilon_1}{T_1} - 1\right)R_1 - \left(\frac{\eta_1}{T_1} + \eta_2 - \epsilon_2 - \frac{1}{T_1}\right)R_2.$$

This gives the same qualitative possibilities as below, but the conditions demarcating the cases are more complicated.

plus the higher income-elasticity of demand for imports) the trade balance turns in favour of the country with the lower income-elasticity of demand for imports, regardless of the rates of growth. In this case if country 1 has the higher income-elasticity of demand for imports its trade balance is bound to turn against it.

The complications of this analysis result from the fact that, by assumption, each country's growth has two effects on the trade balance, one operating through income and the other through relative prices. The effect of increasing productivity in lowering the price of its output may tend either to worsen or to improve its trade balance: if it tends to improve the trade balance, it may or may not do so sufficiently to offset the adverse effect through increasing income.

This case also has some relevance to the monetary version of the increasing-productivity explanation of chronic dollar shortage commented on in previous sections. One might reasonably argue that under modern conditions the most that a restrictive fiscal and monetary policy can be expected to do is to prevent an increase in money income, since an attempt to bring about an actual deflation of incomes would produce unacceptable political and economic strains; and that the alternative of devaluation or depreciation, if it becomes the long-run trend, has seriously adverse effects in the destruction of confidence in and generation of speculation against the currency.[24]

The argument presented in this section indicates that, even on the assumption that productivity rises faster in the United States than it does elsewhere, and that the whole of the impact of rising American productivity falls on prices, it does not necessarily follow that the rest of the world would be forced up against these politico-economic limits of monetary policy. This general problem is pursued further in the next part of the argument.

III. CONSISTENT INCOME-PRICE TRENDS

The analysis presented in Part II was concerned with the behaviour of the balance of trade under alternative assumptions as to the response of prices and money incomes to the increase of productivity

[24] These are admittedly Anglo-centric considerations. Also it should be emphasized that they are judgments about the limitations of monetary techniques of adjustment, the first of which implies an assumption of money illusion with respect to income. A deflation of money income does not necessarily entail a reduction of real income, under the posited circumstances, since productivity is assumed to be rising in both countries. The real income adjustment required by the preservation of the balance of trade is discussed in the next part of this chapter.

in the two countries. In this part we shall be concerned with a different problem, the trend of price and money income required in one country to prevent a change in its balance of trade, given the trend of price and money income in the other country as a datum.[25, 26]

Since the price and income trends in each country are related by the identity $r_w = r_p + R$, the essential problem can be solved by finding the price trend in country 1 required to prevent a change in its trade balance, given the price trend in country 2. This is accomplished by setting $R_{T_1} = 0$ in the basic equation, and solving for r_{p_1} as a function of r_{p_2}: the resulting equation is[27]

$$(5a) \qquad r_{p_1} - r_{p_2} = \frac{\epsilon_2 R_2 - \epsilon_1 R_1}{\eta_1 + \eta_2 - 1}.$$

It is useful, however, to set out explicitly the alternative versions of the required relation between income-price trends in the two countries, which are:

$$(5b) \qquad r_{p_1} - r_{w_2} = \frac{\epsilon_2 R_2 - \epsilon_1 R_1}{\eta_1 + \eta_2 - 1} - R_2.$$

$$(5c) \qquad r_{w_1} - r_{p_2} = \frac{\epsilon_2 R_2 - \epsilon_1 R_1}{\eta_1 + \eta_2 - 1} + R_1.$$

$$(5d) \qquad r_{w_1} - r_{w_2} = \frac{\epsilon_2 R_2 - \epsilon_1 R_1}{\eta_1 + \eta_2 - 1} + R_1 - R_2.$$

These equations can be interpreted and applied in several ways, and a full investigation of their implications is ruled out by considerations of space. The analysis which follows is confined to

[25] A datum, in the sense either of the outcome of economic forces, or of an objective of economic policy; the distinction is illustrated in the ensuing argument.

[26] The analysis which follows assumes that the critical factor $\eta_1 + \eta_2 - 1$, which determines the direction of the effect of a change in relative prices on the trade balance, does not change sign over the relevant range of relative-price change. This assumption seems legitimate in the present context, though it might not be valid for problems involving a very large change in the trade balance, e.g. the correction of a structural imbalance after a war; and the implication of the present section, that there is always *some* monetary adjustment which will preserve trade balance, should not be extended without further examination to such cases.

[27] The corresponding equation for the behaviour of the money balance is

$$(5a') \qquad r_{p_1} - r_{p2} = \frac{b_1 r_{p_2} + \epsilon_2 R_2 - \epsilon_1 R_1 / T_1}{\eta_1 / T_1 + \eta_2 - 1}.$$

distinguishing various ways in which the central problem can be posed, and illustrating the ways in which the equations can be applied.[28]

In the first place, it may be of interest to determine the relative rate of change of price or money income in country 1, as compared with that in country 2, which is required to prevent a change in the trade balance. Equations (5a) to (5d) have been set out in the form most convenient for answering this question: the required rate of change of the country 1 trend-variable (price or income) will be (algebraically) greater or less than the rate of change of the country 2 variable shown on the left-hand side in each, according to whether the expression on the right-hand side is positive or negative. Thus [by equation (5a)] the preservation of an unchanged trade balance requires that price in country 1 should rise more rapidly or fall less rapidly than price in country 2,[29] if $\dfrac{\epsilon_2 R_2 - \epsilon_1 R_1}{\eta_1 + \eta_2 - 1}$ is positive, and rise less rapidly or fall more rapidly than price in country 2[30] if this latter expression is negative.

Secondly (and with more relevance to the dollar problem), it may be of interest to determine whether the preservation of the balance of trade requires an absolute deflation (negative rate of change) of price or income in country 1, given the rate of change of price or income in country 2. This sort of question is answered by transferring the country 2 trend-variable to the right-hand side of the relevant equation and substituting its assumed actual value; if the resulting expression is negative, then an absolute deflation (of price or money income, as the case may be) is required of country 1. For example [equation (5d)], an absolute deflation of money income in country 1 will be required if $R_2 - R_1 + \dfrac{\epsilon_1 R_1 - \epsilon_2 R_2}{\eta_1 + \eta_2 - 1}$ is (algebraically) greater than the assumed rate of change of money income in country 2. This condition, it may be noted, will not necessarily be fulfilled, even if money income is actually falling in country 2

[28] The analysis can be extended to determine the rate of change of the exchange rate of either country which is required to prevent a change in the balance of trade, on the assumption that the rate of change of price or money income in terms of local currency is given in both countries, by making use of the relation $r_p = r_p' - r_q$, where r_p' is the rate of change of domestic currency price and r_q is the rate of change of the country's exchange rate, defined as the number of units of local currency required to buy a unit of international currency.

[29] Or perhaps rise while price in country 2 is falling.

[30] Or perhaps fall while price in country 2 is rising.

(r_{w_2} negative) and the rate of increase of productivity in country 2 is greater than in country 1, so that price is falling more rapidly relative to money income in country 2 than it is in country 1. In such circumstances, as equation (5b) indicates, it may not even be necessary for country 1 to deflate its price level, let alone its money income, to preserve an unchanged trade balance. On the other hand, in the opposite circumstances—a rising price-trend and a higher rate of increase of productivity in country 2 than in country 1—the preservation of the trade balance might require country 1 to deflate its money income [equation (5c)].

Thirdly, it may be of interest to determine the minimum rate of increase of money income or price in country 2 which is necessary to permit the trade balance to be preserved without country 1 being obliged to undertake a (secular) deflation of income or price.[31] This is simply another version of the previous type of question, and may be answered by setting the country 1 trend-variable equal to zero and solving for the country 2 trend-variable in the relevant equation. For example [equation (5b)], the minimum rate of increase of money income in country 2 required to enable country 1 to preserve the trade balance without a price deflation is

$$r_{w_2} = \frac{\epsilon_1 R_1 - \epsilon_2 R_2}{\eta_1 + \eta_2 - 1} + R_2.$$

Since the right-hand expression can be negative, it may not be necessary for country 2 to inflate its income for country 1 to avoid a price deflation.

Finally, although the problem lies outside the scope of this chapter, equations (5a) to (5d) can be used to throw light on the behaviour of country 1's real income over time, assuming that it follows whatever policy is required to prevent any change in its balance of trade.[32] Equation (5a) determines the trend of country 1's commodity terms of trade: if its right-hand side is positive, country 1's terms of trade will move in its favour over time, and its real income will increase more rapidly than its productivity; if the

---

[31] The obligation here is to preserve the trade balance, not necessarily to prevent a deterioration of the balance; see the remarks below on the application to the dollar problem.

[32] In the following argument 'real income' is identified with the purchasing power of money income; this means that, where trade is unbalanced, changes in the purchasing power of the associated 'invisible' transfer are ignored. The terms of trade concepts employed are 'net', not 'gross'. Strictly speaking, the argument here should be confined to the case of balanced trade.

right-hand side of the equation is negative, country 1's terms of trade will move against it over time, and its real income will increase less rapidly than its productivity. Equation (5c) determines the trend of the real value of country 1's income in terms of country 2's product—country 1's single-factoral terms of trade; if the right-hand side of the equation is positive, country 1's real income is necessarily increasing, since its money income will buy an increasing quantity of either good. If the right-hand side of the equation is negative, however, country 1's real income may be either increasing or decreasing, depending on whether or not the decreasing cost of producing its own good outweighs the increasing cost of obtaining country 2's good through exchange. The determination of the conditions under which country 1's real income falls absolutely involves an index-number problem which is beyond the scope of the present analysis.[33] Equation (5d) determines the movement of country 1's double-factoral terms of trade: if the right-hand side of this equation is positive, country 1's real income will rise more rapidly than country 2's. From this equation it is evident that the country with the higher rate of increase of productivity does not necessarily enjoy the higher rate of increase of real income.[34]

The application of results arrived at under the second and third heads above to the theoretical dollar-shortage problem requires a certain caution, since the equations do not distinguish between cases in which the elasticities of international demand are high enough for deflation (or devaluation) to improve the trade balance and those in which they are not, while the meaning of the solution of the equation is different in the two cases. If the sum of the elasticities is greater than unity, a value of the country 1 trend-variable higher than that indicated by the relevant equation would turn the trade balance against country 1: the solution of the equation is an upper limit, and the restriction it imposes on the country 1 trend is necessary to prevent an adverse movement in country 1's balance of trade. But if the sum of the elasticities is less than one, a value of the country 1 trend-variable higher than that indicated by the relevant equation would turn country 1's trade balance in its favour: the solution of the equation is a lower limit, and the restriction it

[33] See H. G. Johnson, 'Equilibrium Growth in an International Economy', *Canadian Journal of Economics and Political Science*, XIX, no. 4, November 1953, 478–500, especially 495–6 (chap. IV below, especially 142–4) for a criterion in the case of balanced trade.

[34] Real income being defined as in the last footnote but one; psychic comparisons are, of course, impossible without a value judgment precluded by the anonymity of countries 1 and 2.

imposes on the country 1 trend is necessary to prevent an adverse movement in country 2's balance of trade.

The implication of these considerations for the theory of dollar shortage is that only on the assumption that the price-elasticities of American demand for imports and world demand for American exports are sufficiently high for devaluation against the dollar to improve the trade balance of the rest of the world with the United States can it be maintained that falling American prices resulting from rapidly increasing productivity force the rest of the world to choose between secular deflation and secular exchange depreciation. On the assumption of adverse elasticities, no price-income trend in the United States could force the latter choice, since any 'dollar shortage' could be cured by sufficient inflation or appreciation against the dollar, and a deflationary trend in the United States would necessarily contribute to the cure.[35]

This explanation of dollar shortage therefore requires the assumption of sufficiently high elasticities of international demand for traditional monetary policies to be effective. But even on that assumption, the proposition that American incomes lag behind productivity and American prices tend to fall does not necessarily imply chronic dollar shortage. The analysis presented above and in Part II shows that the outside world would not necessarily have to deflate money incomes, or even prices, even if the whole increase in American productivity were absorbed in price reduction. On the other hand, however, the rest of the world might be obliged to follow policies of secular deflation of prices, and perhaps of incomes, even if money incomes in the United States grew faster than productivity, so that American prices rose.[36]

IV. INCOME-PRICE TRENDS AND THE BALANCE OF PAYMENTS

Throughout the argument of the preceding three sections, we have been concerned with various aspects of the relationship between

[35] The argument could, of course, be rescued by drawing a sharp distinction between short-run and long-run elasticities of international demand; or it could be stood on its head, and chronic dollar shortage be attributed to the failure of the United States to pursue a monetary policy sufficiently deflationary to enable the rest of the world to close its dollar gap without an intolerable rate of domestic inflation. Elements of the latter argument may be found in the literature of the post-war dollar problem, but not in a consistently developed form.

[36] Contrast Lionel Robbins, 'The International Economic Problem', *Lloyds Bank Review*, N.S., no. 27, January 1953, 1–24 especially 2–7, where this possibility is denied by implication.

income-price trends and rates of increase of productivity on the one hand and the behaviour of the balance of trade on the other. Since balance-of-payments equilibrium or disequilibrium depends on the behaviour of the net balance of capital transactions as well as on the behaviour of the trade balance, it may be useful to indicate briefly how the analysis may be extended to consider the effects of increasing productivity and income-price trends on the overall balance of payments, exclusive of balancing items.

To do so, we introduce the symbol $C_1 = \left(\dfrac{G_2}{p_2 X_2}\right)$ to represent the ratio of the net flow (G_2, which may be positive or negative) of autonomous payments on capital account from country 2 to country 1 measured in international currency units, to country 1's purchases of imports from country 2—'the transfers ratio'; and we define $T'_1 = T_1 + C_1$ as the ratio of the value of country 1's receipts from country 2 to the value of its purchases from country 2—'the receipts ratio'. If $T'_1 = 1$, country 1's balance of payments is in equilibrium, and if T'_1 increases over time, country 1's balance of payments is improving.

The behaviour of country 1's receipts ratio over time is given by the equation[37]

(6)
$$R_{T'_1} = \frac{T_1}{T_1 + C_1} R_{T_1} + \frac{C_1}{T_1 + C_1} R_{C_1},$$

where R in each case stands for the proportional rate of change over time of the subscripted variable. Unlike equation (1), this equation contains the initial values of exports, imports and capital movements, and can therefore, in general, be employed only with reference to a given initial position.

If the value of net capital transfers increases at the same rate as country 1's imports, $R_{C_1} = 0$ and $R_{T'_1} = \dfrac{T_1}{T_1 + C_1} R_{T_1}$; if it increases at the same rate as country 2's imports, $R_{C_1} = R_{T_1}$ and $R_{T'_1} = R_{T_1}$. In both these cases, which correspond to the assumption that one of the countries lends or gives to the other a constant

[37] The corresponding equation for the behaviour of the money balance is

$$R_{B^*_1} = R_{B_1} + \frac{G_2}{p_1 X_1} R_{G_2},$$

where $B^*_1 = B_1 + G_2$, $R_{B^*_1} = \dfrac{1}{p_1 X_1} \dfrac{dB^*_1}{dt}$, $R_{G_2} = \dfrac{1}{G_2} \dfrac{dG_2}{dt}$ and R_{B_1} is as defined in Part I.

fraction of its exports or imports, the receipts ratio changes in the same direction as the export ratio, and the analysis of the previous sections applies to the behaviour of country 1's balance of payments as well as its balance of trade. In other cases, the previous analysis can be extended to describe the behaviour of the balance of payments, or the relation between income-price trends required to maintain an unchanged balance of payments, by making use of equation (6).

The simplest way of doing this is to start from the alternative version of (6),

$$R_{T_1'} = \frac{T_1}{T_1 + C_1} \left(R_{T_1} + \frac{G_2}{p_1 X_1} R_{C_1} \right).$$
(7)

Since we have been interested either in the direction of change, or in the conditions for no change to occur, only the bracketed term on the right-hand side is relevant. From it can be deduced, for example, that the relation between the price-trends of the two countries required to preserve an unchanged balance of payments between them is

$$
(8) \qquad r_{p_1} - r_{p_2} = \frac{\epsilon_2 R_2 - \epsilon_1 R_1 + \frac{G_2}{p_1 X_1} R_{C_1}}{\eta_1 + \eta_2 - 1}.
$$

For certain problems the analysis can be carried further by substituting expressions in the rates of change of prices and productivity for R_{C_1}. For example, international loans or gifts might be assumed to increase at the same rate as money income in the lending country. On this assumption, $R_{C_1} = (\eta_1 - 1)(r_{p_2} - r_{p_1}) + (1 - \epsilon_1)R_1$ if country 1 is the lending country, and $R_{C_1} = \eta_1(r_{p_2} - r_{p_1}) + R_2 - \epsilon_1 R_1$ if country 2 is the lending country.[38] Alternatively, in the case of reparations payments of constant amount in international currency per unit of time,

$$R_{C_1} = \eta_1(r_{p_2} - r_{p_1}) - r_{p_2} - \epsilon_1 R_1.[39]$$

The introduction of the variable R_{C_1} makes it possible to consider explicitly[40] another type of problem, the rate of increase of inter-

---

[38] In the first case $C_1 = \dfrac{a p_1 Y_1}{p_2 X_2}$, and in the second case $C_1 = \dfrac{b p_2 Y_2}{p_2 X_2}$, where a is a negative and b a positive constant. $\dfrac{1}{p_1 Y_1} \dfrac{d(p_1 Y_1)}{dt} = r_{p_1} + R_1$ and $\dfrac{1}{p_2 X_2} \dfrac{d(p_2 X_2)}{dt} = r_{p_2} + \epsilon_1 R_1 - \eta_1 (r_{p_2} - r_{p_1})$.

[39] In this case $C_1 = \dfrac{\overline{G}_2}{p_2 X_2}$ where $\overline{G}_2$ is the fixed rate of reparations.

[40] The argument is, of course, implicit in the analysis of Parts II and III.

national capital movements relative to the value of trade which is necessary to maintain balance-of-payments equilibrium under various assumptions about income-price trends in the two countries. By setting $R_{T_1'} = 0$, in equation (6), we obtain the intuitively obvious result that, to maintain an unchanged balance of payments, the transfers ratio must change in the opposite direction to the export ratio if country 1 is a capital importer (C_1 positive) and in the same direction as the export ratio if country 1 is a capital exporter (C_1 negative). By substituting for R_{T_1} in this equation according to the assumed income-price trends, we obtain the rate of change of the transfers ratio required to maintain an unchanged balance of payments under the assumed conditions. On the assumption that initially the balance of payments is in equilibrium ($T_1' = 1$) this rate of change of the transfers ratio will maintain equilibrium. For example, the rate of increase of the transfers ratio required to maintain equilibrium with prices constant in both countries is

$$(9) \qquad R_{C_1} = \frac{T_1}{C_1}(\epsilon_1 R_1 - \epsilon_2 R_2) = \frac{1}{-b_1}(\epsilon_1 R_1 - \epsilon_2 R_2),$$

where b_1 is the initial ratio of country 1's export surplus to its exports.[41] In the case in which country 1 is initially running a trade deficit (b_1 negative), this equation indicates, as one would expect, that the higher is the rate of increase of productivity in country 2 relative to country 1 the lower is the rate of increase of the transfers ratio required to maintain balance-of-payments equilibrium without a change in the terms of trade between the two countries. However, even with a higher rate of growth of productivity in country 2 than in country 1, an increase in the transfers ratio might be required if country 2's income-elasticity of demand for imports were sufficiently lower than country 1's.

These conclusions are obviously relevant to another aspect of the theory of dollar shortage, the contention that the maintenance of international equilibrium requires the United States to lend abroad on an increasing scale, and that the United States has a chronic tendency not to lend abroad on a sufficient scale to cover its structural export surplus. This contention obviously demands a judgment as

---

[41] On the assumption of initial equilibrium, $G_2 = -b_1 . p_1 X_1$. The corresponding equation for the required rate of change of the (international) money value of transfers is:

$$R_{G_2} = \frac{1}{-b_1} [(1 - b_1)\epsilon_1 R_1 - \epsilon_2 R_2].$$

to the degree of monetary or real adjustment which the rest of the world can or should be expected to make, and the assumptions selected in the above illustration are only one of the possibilities; but the argument of the preceding section suggests the general conclusion that the need for increasing American foreign lending or gifts cannot be deduced from productivity and income-price trends alone.

More detailed investigation of problems of international lending lies outside the scope of this chapter. In any case, it would be advisable to approach them with the aid of a rather different model, both because the concept of the transfers ratio ignores problems of amortization and interest payments and because allowance for interest payments would require a distinction between output and income which is not made in the model employed here.[42]

V. CONCLUSION

This chapter has considered the relation between productivity and income-price trends on the one hand, and the balance of trade on the other, from a variety of points of view. In the process, a number of observations have been made about one theoretical explanation of dollar shortage, that which attributes dollar shortage to the effects of the rapid increase in American productivity in lowering the money prices of American goods relative to the prices of goods produced elsewhere. In concluding, it may be useful to restate the main points of our analysis which bear on this theory.

In the first place, it is necessary to recognize that increasing productivity in the United States affects the American trade balance in two ways, and not just one as this theory implies. In addition to its effect on relative prices of American and foreign goods, increasing American productivity raises American real income and therefore—unless American imports are inferior goods in American consumption—increases American demand for imports. By itself (that is, apart from its effects on relative prices) rapidly increasing American productivity is a factor working against and not towards the emergence of a dollar shortage of the kind described, and could only contribute to the creation of dollar shortage by increasing too slowly to offset the influence of increasing productivity in the rest of the world on the demand for American exports. Consequently, in so far as proponents of this theory emphasize the high rate of increase

---

[42] *Cf.* H. G. Johnson, *loc. cit.*, Part I, which deals with some of the latter complications in connection with a related problem.

of American productivity *per se*, rather than its alleged effects on relative prices, their analysis is misleading or wrong.

Secondly, with regard to the effect of increasing American productivity on the relative prices of American and foreign goods, the assumption that relatively falling American prices turn the trade balance of the United States in its favour necessarily implies that elasticities of international demand are high enough for devaluation against the dollar to improve the trade balance of the rest of the world with the United States.[43] Logically, a decrease in American prices relatively to prices in the rest of the world is equivalent to appreciation of other currencies against the dollar,[44] and if appreciation against the dollar worsens the trade balance of the outside world with the United States, depreciation against the dollar must improve it.

Nothing in the argument presented here, however, contradicts the proposition that productivity and price trends in the world economy may lead to a chronic dollar shortage of the type described. Indeed, our analysis points to a number of factors which might contribute to this result. Further, it should be emphasized that our argument has been concerned only with this one theory of dollar shortage, to the exclusion of other possible explanations. We have, for example, abstracted from problems of cyclical instability and chronic stagnation by proceeding on the assumption of the maintenance of full employment.

Finally, a general conclusion implicit in the analysis presented in the preceding sections should perhaps be stated explicitly. It has sometimes been suggested or implied that all would be well in the world economy if each country stabilized prices by allowing money incomes to expand proportionally to increases in productivity. Our analysis shows that there is no such simple rule which defines the long-run monetary policies required to maintain balance-of-payments equilibrium between growing economies under a régime of fixed exchange rates.

[43] This conclusion is strengthened by the consideration that the theory assumes not merely that a relative decrease in American prices improves the American trade balance, but that it improves it by more than is required to offset the income-effect of the increase in productivity which is assumed to bring about the fall in prices.

[44] This is true of the 'money' balance only on the assumption of initially balanced trade; but on the assumption of an initial American export surplus, a decrease in American prices has a less favourable effect than an increase in foreign prices on the American 'money' trade balance, so that the conclusion just stated is strengthened.

Appendix to Chapter IV:

The n-Country Case[1]

THE foregoing argument has been conducted in terms of a two-country model and its application is restricted to consideration of relations between one country and the rest of the world taken as a whole. In this appendix we shall discuss briefly the extension of the model to a world of n countries, each of which is assumed to produce a single good, the output of which is increasing at a given rate, and to consume its own and other countries' products in quantities determined by its own output (income) and the relative prices of the various goods.

On these assumptions, the export ratio of country i is

$$(1) \qquad T_i = \frac{\sum\limits_{j \neq i} p_i X_{ji}}{\sum\limits_{j \neq i} p_j X_{ij}},$$

where X_{ji} is the quantity of exports from country i to country j and p_i is the price of country i's output in international currency units; and the basic equation for the behaviour of country i's trade balance over time is

$$(2) \qquad R_{T_i} = \sum_j \left(\frac{p_j}{T_i} \frac{\delta T_i}{\delta p_j} r_j + \frac{Y_j}{T_i} \frac{\delta T_i}{\delta Y_j} R_j \right),$$

where r_j and R_j are respectively the price and productivity trends in country j.

On differentiation and re-arrangement of terms this becomes

$$(3) \qquad R_{T_i} = \sum_{j \neq i} (x_{ji} \eta_{ji.i} + x_{ji} - m_{ij} \eta_{ij.i}) \, r_i - \sum_{j \neq i} m_{ij} \, \epsilon_{ij} \, R_i$$

$$+ \sum_{k \neq i} \sum_{j \neq i} (x_{ji} \eta_{ji.k} - m_{ij} \eta_{ij.k} - m_{ik}) \, r_k + \sum_{k \neq i} x_{ki} \, \epsilon_{ki} \, R_k,$$

[1] The argument of this Appendix owes much to a paper read by J. J. Polak and Ta-Chung Liu at the 1952 meeting of the Econometric Society on 'The Stability of the Exchange Rate Mechanism in a Multi-Country System', and to the comments on it made by N. Georgescu-Roegen. The discussion is reported in *Econometrica*, 21, no. 3, July 1953, 468–70, and a revised version of the paper published in *Econometrica*, 22, no. 3, July 1954, 360–89.

where $\eta_{ji.k} \left(= \dfrac{p_k}{X_{ji}} \dfrac{\delta X_{ji}}{\delta p_k} \right)$ is the elasticity of j's demand for i's good

with respect to a change in the price of k's good; $\epsilon_{ki} \left(= \dfrac{Y_k}{X_{ki}} \dfrac{\delta X_{ki}}{\delta Y_k} \right)$

is the income-elasticity of k's demand for i's good; and $x_{ji} \left(= \dfrac{p_i X_{ji}}{\sum\limits_{j \neq i} p_i X_{ji}} \right)$

and $m_{ij} \left(= \dfrac{p_j X_{ij}}{\sum\limits_{j \neq i} p_j X_{ij}} \right)$ are the proportional shares of i's exports to

and imports from j in i's total exports and total imports. This equation can be re-written more simply as

$$(4) \qquad R_{T_i} = (1 - \bar{\eta}_{w.i} - \bar{\eta}_{i.w})\, r_i + \sum_{k \neq i} (\eta_{w.k} - \bar{\eta}_{i.k} - m_{ik})\, r_k \\ - \bar{\epsilon}_i R_i + \sum_{k \neq i} x_{ki}\, \epsilon_{ki} R_k,$$

where $\eta_{w.i} \left(= -\sum\limits_{j \neq i} x_{ji}\, \eta_{ji.i} \right)$ is the elasticity of the rest of the world's

demand for i's exports with respect to a change in i's price and $\bar{\eta}_{i.w} \left(= \sum\limits_{j \neq i} m_{ij}\, \eta_{ij.i} \right)$ is the elasticity of i's demand for imports with

respect to an equi-proportional change in their prices,[2] both defined with the conventional change of sign; $\bar{\eta}_{w.k} \left(= \sum\limits_{j \neq i} x_{ji}\, \eta_{ji.k} \right)$ is the

elasticity of the rest of the world's demand for i's exports, and $\bar{\eta}_{i.k} \left(= \sum\limits_{j \neq i} m_{ij}\, \eta_{ij.k} \right)$ is the elasticity of i's demand for imports, with

respect to a change in the price of k's good; and $\bar{\epsilon}_i \left(= \sum\limits_{j \neq i} m_{ij}\, \epsilon_{ij} \right)$ is

the income-elasticity of i's demand for imports.

Equations (3) and (4) express the behaviour of country i's export ratio over time, as a function of price trends (operating through own-price and cross elasticities of demand) and productivity trends (operating through income-elasticities of demand) in the world economy. For brevity, we shall ignore the influence of productivity trends and consider only the influence of price trends, leaving the interested reader to pursue the analysis along the lines indicated for the two-country case.

On the usual assumption that an equi-proportional change in all prices would leave quantities demanded unchanged, equal price trends in all countries would leave each country's export ratio

[2] On the assumption that a rise in i's price has the same effect on i's demand for imports as an equi-proportional fall in all other prices.

unaltered: consequently, on this assumption the sum of the co-efficients of the price-trend terms in equations (2)–(4) will be zero. Making use of this relationship, and ignoring productivity changes, equation (4) may be re-written

$$(5) \quad R_{T_i} = (\bar{\eta}_{i.w} + \bar{\eta}_{w.i} - 1)(r_a - r_i) + \sum_{k \neq i} (\bar{\eta}_{w.k} - \bar{\eta}_{i.k} - m_{ik})(r_k - r_a).$$

The term r_a can represent anything at all; but it can most usefully be employed either to represent the price trend in any one of the n countries, so that one of the price-trend terms can be eliminated,[3] or to represent any sort of average of price trends in the various countries. For our purpose, the latter is the more interesting.

On the assumption that r_a represents the average trend of prices in the world economy, equation (5) exhibits the influence of price trends on country i's export ratio as the sum of two terms. The first is the effect on i's export ratio of the movement of country i's price level relative to the general level of world prices, which will be favourable if the sum of the elasticities of demand for its exports and its demand for imports is greater than one and its price level is falling relative to the world price level, or if the sum of the elasticities is less than one and its price level is rising relative to the world price level. The second term is the sum of the effects on the export ratio of the deviations of the price trends of other countries from the world trend: the net effect will be favourable if the goods whose prices increase relatively to the world price level are close substitutes for the product of country i in world consumption, so that a rise in their prices improves i's export ratio, and the products whose prices fall relatively to the world price ratio are remote substitutes for or complements to i's product in world consumption,[4] so that a rise in their prices would worsen i's export ratio; and vice versa.

This second term introduces complications not allowed for in the two-country model. To illustrate, assume that the sum of the elasticities of demand for country i's imports and exports is greater than unity; then, according to the two-country model, i's trade balance would necessarily improve if prices in the rest of the world

---

[3] For example, in a two-country world, equation (5) reduces to

$$R_{T_1} = (\eta_1 + \eta_2 - 1)(r_2 - r_1)$$

(the price-trend term employed in the main argument of the chapter).

[4] The terms 'substitute' and 'complement' are employed here in the loose sense, and not in the technical sense defined by demand theory; nor is the argument intended to be rigorous.

rose relatively to the price of i's good. In the n-country model, however, this result need not hold if prices in the other countries, though increasing relatively to the price of i's good, are rising at different rates; and country i may have to deflate or devalue in order to preserve its trade balance, even though its price level is rising less rapidly than that of any other country. Conversely, if the sum of the elasticities is less than unity, and i's price level is rising faster than that of any other country, its trade balance may nevertheless turn adverse; but in this case deflation or devaluation would further worsen the situation.

CHAPTER V

Equilibrium Growth in an International Economy[*][1]

IN recent years Keynesian theory has been extended to the analysis of economic growth by the introduction of a relation between investment and productive capacity to supplement the Keynesian relation between investment and effective demand. Combination of the two relations permits the specification of an equilibrium rate of growth, defined as that rate of growth which maintains full employment of capacity.[2] So far, however, except for some rather brief comments by R. F. Harrod,[3] the development of this model has been largely confined to a closed economy. It is the purpose of this chapter to extend the model to a two-country international economy, and to deduce certain conclusions about equilibrium growth in such an economy. The analysis proceeds from consideration of an open economy, the rate of expansion of demand for whose exports is given, to consideration of a two-country closed system; and from the assumption that balance-of-payments equilibrium is preserved by international lending and borrowing (Part I) to the assumption that it is preserved by exchange rate adjustment (Part II). No attempt is made to deal with the stability of growth equilibrium and the results of departures from it; because of this, and because of the extremely simple assumptions on which the analysis is conducted, the conclusions derived are of limited practical application. Nevertheless,

* *The Canadian Journal of Economics and Political Science*, XIX, no. 4, November 1953, 478–500.

[1] Preparation of this material began in the autumn of 1950 with an unpublished study which appears here as the 'pure lending' case which concludes Part I. Further work on the problem was carried on during my tenure of a Visiting Professorship in the Graduate School of Economics, University of Toronto. I should like to express my gratitude to colleagues there, particularly G. A. Elliott and Wm. C. Hood, for their advice and encouragement.

[2] Alternatively, the model can be used to specify the rate of growth which maintains a 'normal' degree of excess capacity.

[3] R. F. Harrod, *Towards a Dynamic Economics* (London, 1948) Lecture 4, Section (a), 101–15.

it is hoped that they may have some usefulness as a logical frame of reference for discussion of international growth problems.

PART I

The basic growth model developed by Harrod and Domar comprises two relations:

i. The investment required to employ existing capital fully is equal to the fraction (assumed to be constant) of income saved multiplied by the capacity output of existing equipment, i.e.

$$(1) \qquad\qquad I_t = s\, Y_t,$$

where I_t is the required rate of investment, s is the savings ratio, and Y_t is the capacity rate of output at time t.

ii. The increment to capacity output resulting from this investment is

$$(2) \qquad\qquad \frac{dY_t}{dt} = \frac{I_t}{k} = aI_t,$$

where k is the capital coefficient or ratio (assumed to be constant) of capital to output and a is its reciprocal, the output coefficient or ratio of output to capital.

From these two relations it follows that the rate of growth of investment, capacity, and income which keeps productive capacity continuously fully employed is

$$(3) \qquad\qquad r = \frac{1}{Y_t}\frac{dY_t}{dt} = \frac{s}{k} = as.$$

It should be observed that for consistency the model must assume either that the working population is growing at least at the rate r, or that technical progress of a type which leaves the capital coefficient unchanged is going on rapidly and steadily enough to prevent the capital stock from outgrowing the labour required to work it. One of these alternatives is assumed in the argument which follows. For mathematical convenience in dealing with the international aspects of the model, it is also assumed that the price level is constant, that output is measured in units such that the price of a unit of output is one unit of currency, and that units of currency are so defined that exchange rates are initially equal to unity.[4]

[4] These simplifications, and part of the argument of Part II, are derived from Arnold C. Harberger, 'Currency Depreciation, Income, and the Balance of Trade', *Journal of Political Economy*, LVIII, no. 1, February 1950, 47–60.

The Harrod-Domar model applies to a closed economy, in which the only outlet for saving is investment. In an open economy, however, imports as well as savings constitute leakages from effective demand, while exports as well as investment may fill the gap between domestic demand for and supply of home production at capacity output. Equation (1) then becomes

(4) $$(s + m)Y_t = I_t + X_t,$$

where m represents the fraction of income spent on imports (assumed constant) and X_t the current rate of exports; and equation (3) becomes

(5a) $$r_t = a \left(s + m - \frac{X_t}{Y_t}\right),$$

which may be re-written as

(5b) $$r_t = a(s - b_t),$$

where b_t is the country's current export surplus expressed as a fraction of its production. From these equations it is possible, following Harrod, to derive such conclusions as: if the proportional export surplus is falling over time, the equilibrium rate of growth rises over time; and if the rate of growth of exports exceeds the equilibrium rate of growth, the latter is falling over time.[5] This second conclusion follows from differentiation of (5a) with respect to t, which yields

(6) $$\frac{dr}{dt} = -a\frac{X_t}{Y_t}(x - r_t)$$

where x is the rate of growth of exports. The conclusion assumes that Y_t is positive; throughout the chapter it is assumed that only that part of the future in which equilibrium output is positive is of economic interest.

From the formulae it may also be inferred that the equilibrium rate of growth will be higher the higher the output coefficient, the savings ratio, the import ratio, and the level of production capacity, and the lower the level of exports and their rate of growth; alternatively, that the equilibrium rate of growth will be higher the higher the output coefficient and the savings ratio and the lower the export surplus (or the higher the import surplus) as a fraction of total output.

Analysis in these terms is suggestive, but possibly misleading, since

[5] *Cf.* Harrod, op. cit.

production, exports, the equilibrium rate of growth, and the proportional export surplus are not constants but variables dependent on the constants of the system—the output coefficient, the savings ratio, the import ratio and the rate of growth of exports, and the initial levels of exports and productive capacity—and on the passage of time. In order to be certain of our results, it is necessary to solve the differential equation in Y implicit in the equation[6] defining r. The solution is

$$(7) \qquad Y_t = Y_0 \, e^{a(s+m)t} + \frac{aX_0}{x - a(s + m)} \left(e^{a(s+m)t} - e^{xt} \right)$$

where Y_0 and X_0 are the initial levels of productive capacity and exports. After manipulating we obtain the following results:

(i) Let

$$(8) \qquad r_0 = a\left(s + m - \frac{X_0}{Y_0}\right) = a\,(s - b_0)$$

be the initial equilibrium rate of growth. If x is less than r_0, r is greater than x and rises over time, approaching the asymptote $r_\infty = a(s + m)$. If x is equal to r_0, r is constant and equal to x. If x is greater than r_0, r is less than x and falls continually over time, implying an eventual reversal of the growth of output. In short, the equilibrium rate of growth rises, is constant, or falls over time according to whether the rate of growth of exports is less than, equal to, or greater than the country's initial equilibrium growth rate.

The economic meaning of this result (bearing in mind the extreme simplicity of the model) is that if a country's equilibrium growth rate is higher than the rate of growth of demand for its exports, it must grow at an increasing rate if effective demand is to keep pace with capacity to produce. If its equilibrium growth rate is lower than the rate of growth of demand for its exports, it must grow at a decreasing rate if effective demand is not to outrun capacity to produce. Only if its equilibrium growth rate is equal to the rate of growth of demand for its exports will it be able to maintain equilibrium between effective demand and capacity by growing at a constant rate.

(ii) If x is less than r_0, the ratio of the export surplus (import surplus) to total production will fall (rise) over time; if there is an initial export surplus it will turn into an import surplus. To put it another way, the proportional trade balance will fall (algebraically)

---

[6] The time subscripts of the variables are omitted in the remainder of the argument.

over time, approaching the asymptote $b_\infty = -m$. Conversely, if x is greater than r_0, the ratio of the trade balance to total production will rise (algebraically) over time; if there is an initial trade deficit it will turn into a surplus. If x is equal to r_0, the initial export or import surplus will grow at the same rate as exports and equilibrium output, that is, at the rate $r = x = a(s - b_0)$.

The economic meaning of this is that if a country's equilibrium growth rate is higher than the rate of growth of demand for its exports, it must not only grow at an increasing rate to keep its productive capacity fully employed, but will also find its trade deficit increasing, or its surplus decreasing, as time passes. The converse holds true if its equilibrium growth rate is lower than the rate of growth of demand for its exports.

(iii) The equilibrium level of output and the equilibrium rate of growth will be higher at any point in the future, the higher the initial level of productive capacity and the lower the initial level of exports; the higher the savings ratio and the imports ratio; and the lower the rate of growth of exports. At any date in the future at which equilibrium output is increasing, the equilibrium output and rate of growth will be higher the higher the output coefficient (the lower the capital coefficient); but after equilibrium output begins to decrease, as it will eventually if the rate of growth of exports is greater than the initial equilibrium rate of growth, a higher output coefficient may lower the equilibrium output and rate of growth.[7]

The results arrived at so far have depended on three simplifying assumptions, common in international trade multiplier theory, which are implicit in equation (4). The first of these is that investment utilizes only domestic output. If the creation of new productive capacity requires a certain proportion of imported goods, the equation for the equilibrium growth rate becomes

$$(9) \qquad r = \frac{a}{1 - m'}\left(s + m - \frac{X}{Y}\right)$$

where m' is the fraction of investment expenditure spent on imported goods, assumed to be constant. If a is re-defined as the ratio of output to the domestically produced fraction of capital, all the preceding results apply, with the extension that the output coefficient varies with both output per unit of total capital and the proportion of investment goods imported.

[7] For example, in the special case $Y_0 = 1000$, $X_0 = 100$, $a = 0.4$, $s + m = 0.12$, $x = 0.16$, an increase in a to 0.5 reduces Y at $t = 10$ from 423.16 to 256.65.

The second assumption is that domestic production has no import content: imports are required only for consumption. If production has an import content, income is no longer identical with production, but is less to the extent of the import content; and, to maintain full-capacity production, investment must be large enough to offset the gap between exports on the one hand, and the sum of (1) expenditure on the import content of domestic production and (2) saving and expenditure on imports from domestically earned income, on the other hand. On the assumption of a constant fractional import content of domestic output q, equations (4) and (5a) become

$$(10) \qquad (s + m)(1 - q) Y + qY = I + X$$

and

$$(11) \qquad r = a\left(s + m + qc - \frac{X}{Y}\right),$$

where $c(=1 - s - m)$ is the fraction of income spent on home-produced goods. All the conclusions previously arrived at still stand, with the difference that now

$$(12) \qquad r_0 = a\left(s + m + qc - \frac{X_0}{Y_0}\right) = a(s - sq - b_0);$$

and the further conclusion follows that the equilibrium level of income and equilibrium rate of growth will be higher, the higher is the fractional import content of domestic production.

The third assumption is that trade surpluses or deficits are financed in a way that does not give rise to international interest payments—for example by unilateral transfers or by movements of international reserves. This assumption, while defensible in short-period multiplier theory, is questionable in the context of economic growth, and it would seem more appropriate to assume that trade deficits or surpluses are financed by transfers of interest-bearing assets.[8] On the latter assumption, however, the problem becomes much more complicated, since income is no longer determined exclusively by current output: income arising from current production will be augmented or reduced by interest receipts from, or payments to, the outside world, the magnitude of which will in turn depend on the past history of the balance of payments. Leakages from domestically

[8] This term is used to include the creation of new assets and the redemption of existing assets.

earned income may be offset by consumption of domestic goods out of interest earned on foreign investments, as well as by exports and investment in new capacity; or such leakages may be augmented by the payment of interest to foreigners.

For simplicity, we may assume that differences between receipts and payments on current account (including both the trade balance and interest payments on past debts) are financed by transfers of perpetual[9] securities bearing a constant rate of interest i. On this assumption (and ignoring the first and second qualifications discussed above) equations (4) and (5a) become[10]

(13) $$(s + m) Y = cZ + I + X$$

and

(14a) $$r = a\left(s + m - \frac{cZ}{Y} - \frac{X}{Y}\right),$$

where Z is interest income, or the negative of interest payments, determined by the equation

(15a) $$\frac{dZ}{dt} = i (X + Z - mY - mZ).$$

Equations (14a) and (15a) may be re-written

(14b) $$r = a\left(s + s\frac{Z}{Y} - b\right)$$

and

(15b) $$\frac{dZ}{dt} = ibY,$$

[9] Since we are continuing to assume that capital movements are entirely accommodating, there is no need to enter into the complications entailed by the amortization of dated securities. These should not affect the conclusions, if behaviour is governed entirely by income and financial arrangements have no autonomous influence. For an investigation of such problems, however, see Evsey Domar, 'The Effect of Foreign Investment on the Balance of Payments', *American Economic Review*, XL, no. 5, December 1950, 805–26.

[10] This formulation assumes that interest receipts are spent (and interest payments not spent) in the same ratios as home-produced income. It will be observed that, on the assumption that all income from foreign investment is either saved or spent on imports, and that all interest payments are made at the expense of forgone saving and imports, the introduction of interest payments and receipts makes no difference to the conclusions about equilibrium growth arrived at above.

where b is now the current account surplus expressed as a fraction of domestic production.

Equations (14) suggest that the equilibrium rate of growth will be higher the lower the ratio of foreign investment income (or the higher the ratio of foreign interest payments) to domestic production—as well as the higher the output coefficient and the savings and import ratios, and the lower the ratio of exports to output.

Since a rate of growth of exports greater than the equilibrium growth rate implies the eventual emergence of an export surplus and net foreign lending, one might also be tempted to conclude that allowance for interest payments reinforces the previous conclusion that if the rate of growth of exports exceeds the equilibrium growth rate the latter must fall over time. The equations just presented, however, provide no warrant for this conclusion. By differentiation of (14a) we have

$$(16) \qquad \frac{dr}{dt} = -\frac{acZ}{Y}(z - r) - \frac{aX}{Y}(x - r)$$

where

$$z = \frac{1}{Z}\frac{dZ}{dt}.$$

Thus the behaviour of the equilibrium growth rate over time depends on its relation to the rate of growth of interest payments as well as on its relation to the rate of growth of exports, and there is no presumption that if the equilibrium growth rate is initially below the rate of growth of exports it will remain there. This problem must therefore be investigated by explicit reference to the equations for Y and Z implicit in the differential equations (14) and (15). Unfortunately, these equations

$$(17) \quad Y_t = \left[\frac{a(s+m)-N}{M-N}Y_0 - \frac{acZ_0}{M-N} - \frac{a(is-M)}{(M-N)(x-M)}X_0\right]e^{Mt}$$

$$- \left[\frac{a(s+m)-M}{M-N}Y_0 - \frac{acZ_0}{M-N} - \frac{a(is-N)}{(M-N)(x-N)}X_0\right]e^{Nt}$$

$$- \frac{a(x-is)}{(x-M)(x-N)}X_0 e^{xt}$$

(18)

$$Z_t = \left[\frac{im}{M - N} Y_0 + \frac{a(s + m) - N}{M - N} Z_0 - \frac{i(as - N)}{(M - N)(x - N)} X_0 \right] e^{Nt}$$

$$- \left[\frac{im}{M - N} Y_0 + \frac{a(s + m) - M}{M - N} Z_0 - \frac{i(as - M)}{(M - N)(x - N)} X_0 \right] e^{Mt}$$

$$+ \frac{i(x - as)}{(x - M)(x - N)} X_0 e^{xt}$$

where

(19)

$$M = \tfrac{1}{2} \left\{ a(s + m) + i(1 - m) + \sqrt{[a(s + m) + i(1 - m)]^2 - 4ais} \right\}$$

$$N = \tfrac{1}{2} \left\{ a(s + m) + i(1 - m) - \sqrt{[a(s + m) + i(1 - m)]^2 - 4ais} \right\}$$

turn out to be too complex for the ready derivation of simple relations between the constants of the system and the behaviour of the equilibrium growth rate.

One conclusion that can be easily established, however, is that only in certain circumstances does there exist a rate of growth of exports which would permit the economy to maintain equilibrium between effective demand and productive capacity by growing at a steady rate. An obvious case is that in which initially trade is balanced and there are no interest receipts or payments: in these circumstances a rate of growth of exports $x = as$ would allow equilibrium growth at the constant rate $r = as$. More generally, a rate of growth of exports permitting equilibrium growth at a constant rate exists only in those cases in which the initial equilibrium rate of growth of output is equal to the initial rate of growth of interest income or interest payments. Such cases are described by the quadratic equation

(20)
$$\frac{X_0 + Z_0}{Y_0 + Z_0} = \frac{a(s + m) Z_0 + imY_0}{iY_0 + aZ_0}.$$

One special case is that in which trade is initially balanced and $a(1 - s)Z_0 = (as - i)Y_0$; here equilibrium growth at a constant rate i is possible if exports are expanding at the rate $x = i$. It may be noted also that if the current account is initially in balance but there is a difference between exports and imports made up by interest receipts or payments, no rate of growth of exports exists which would permit equilibrium growth at a constant rate.

All of the preceding argument has been concerned with the requirements of equilibrium growth in a single economy, the rate of growth of whose exports is given. Except when confined to the case of a relatively small country, analysis in these terms is unsatisfactory, for two reasons. In the first place, it does not consider the requirements of equilibrium growth in the rest of the world. Second, it does not allow for the repercussions of variations in a country's imports on incomes abroad, and through them on its own exports. This is the familiar problem of the foreign trade multiplier; in the present context, however, the problem is that, if each country grows in such a way as to maintain full employment of its productive capacity, it may, by so doing, alter the requirements of equilibrium growth for other countries and therefore for itself. The requirements of equilibrium growth in the components of the world economy are interdependent, and cannot be studied for each economy in isolation.

In order to investigate this problem, let us consider a closed system of two countries, country 1 and country 2, trading exclusively with one another. To simplify the problem, we again abstract from the foreign content of investment expenditure the import content of domestic production, and the payment of interest on international loans. A simple extension of the preceding analysis yields the following (simultaneous differential) equations for the equilibrium growth rates of the two countries:

$$(21a) \qquad r_1 = a_1\left(s_1 + m_1 - m_2 \frac{Y_2}{Y_1}\right)$$

and

$$(21b) \qquad r_2 = a_2\left(s_2 + m_2 - m_1 \frac{Y_1}{Y_2}\right).$$

Differentiation of these equations with respect to time yields

$$(22a) \qquad \frac{dr_1}{dt} = \frac{a_1 m_2 Y_2}{Y_1}(r_1 - r_2)$$

and

$$(22b) \qquad \frac{dr_2}{dt} = \frac{a_2 m_1 Y_1}{Y_2}(r_2 - r_1)$$

and hence the conclusion that, if the equilibrium growth rate for country 1 is higher than that for country 2, the former must rise and the latter fall continually over time. For this there is a dual explanation: in the first place, if country 2 were to continue to grow at the same rate, country 1's exports would be a decreasing fraction of its total production, and an increasing proportion of its output would have to be absorbed by investment; in the second place, country 2 could not continue to grow at the same rate, since its exports (country 1's imports) would be an increasing proportion of its total output, so that a decreasing fraction of its output would be available for investment.

This conclusion can be translated into terms of the constants of the system as follows. Let $r_{10} = a_1(s_1 - b_{10})$ and $r_{20} = a_2(s_2 - b_{20})$ be the initial equilibrium growth rates of the two countries, where the b's represent the initial trade balances of the countries, expressed as fractions of their initial capacity levels of output, i.e.

$$(23) \qquad b_{10} Y_{10} = m_2 Y_{20} - m_1 Y_{10} = - b_{20} Y_{20}.$$

Then if r_{10} is greater than r_{20}, the equilibrium growth rate of country 1 will rise and that of country 2 fall continually over time, and vice versa if r_{10} is less than r_{20}. Only if r_{10} is equal to r_{20} can effective demand be kept in line with capacity to produce in the two countries together by each of them growing at a constant (and the same) rate; otherwise their equilibrium growth rates will diverge over time. It will be observed that in the case of initially balanced trade, the course of the two countries' equilibrium growth rates over time depends on the relative magnitudes of their 'closed-economy equilibrium growth rates', $a_1 s_1$ and $a_2 s_2$; in other cases it depends also on the initial balance of trade between them and on the relative sizes of their initial productive capacities.

Equations (21a) and (21b) also suggest a variety of conclusions about the relation between the equilibrium growth rates for the two countries and the constants of the system—the output coefficients, the savings and import ratios, and the initial productive capacities of the two countries. Unfortunately the solutions

$$(24a) \quad Y_1 = \frac{1}{M - N} \Big(\{[a_1(s_1 + m_1) - N]Y_{10} - a_1 m_2 Y_{20}\}e^{Mt}$$

$$- \{[a_1(s_1 + m_1) - M]Y_{10} - a_1 m_2 Y_{20}\}e^{Nt} \Big)$$

$$(24b) \quad Y_2 = \frac{1}{M - N} \Big(\{a_2 m_1 Y_{10} + [a_1(s_1 + m_1) - N]Y_{20}\}e^{Nt}$$

$$- \{a_2 m_1 Y_{10} + [a_1(s_1 + m_1) - M]Y_{20}\}e^{Mt} \Big)$$

where

$$M = \tfrac{1}{2}\Big\{ a_1(s_1 + m_1) + a_2(s_2 + m_2)$$
$$+ \sqrt{[a_1(s_1 + m_1) - a_2(s_2 + m_2)]^2 + 4a_1a_2m_1m_2}\Big\}$$

$$N = \tfrac{1}{2}\Big\{ a_1(s_1 + m_1) + a_2(s_2 + m_2)$$
$$- \sqrt{[a_1(s_1 + m_1) - a_2(s_2 + m_2)]^2 + 4a_1a_2m_1m_2}\Big\}$$

of the simultaneous differential equations are too complex to permit easy verification of such conclusions. However, it can easily be shown that at any future date the equilibrium output and equilibrium growth rate in country 1 will be higher, and in country 2 lower, the higher the initial productive capacity of country 1 and the lower the initial productive capacity of country 2.

As before, it is possible to extend the analysis to take account of the assumptions that part of investment expenditure is spent on imported goods, that domestic production has an import content, and that interest is paid on international loans. The assumption that domestic production has an import content is the easiest to deal with, since it merely requires re-writing equations (21) as

(25a) $$r_1 = a_1 (s_1 - s_1q_1 - b_1)$$

and

(25b) $$r_2 = a_2 (s_2 - s_2q_2 - b_2),$$

where the q's stand for fractional import contents of domestic production and $b_1Y_1 = (m_2 - m_2q_2 + q_2)Y_2 - (m_1 - m_1q_1 + q_1)Y_1 = - b_2Y_2$. With the appropriate re-definition of r_{10} and r_{20}, the behaviour of the two countries' equilibrium growth rates over time will depend as before on the relative magnitudes of their initial equilibrium growth rates.

Introduction of the assumption that part of investment expenditure is spent on imported goods is more difficult, since this assumption implies that the equilibrium growth rate in each country depends partly on the current equilibrium growth rate for the other. Both r_1 and r_2 now appear in each of the equations corresponding to (21a) and (21b); solving for them separately yields the (simultaneous differential) equations

$$(26a) \quad r_1 = \frac{a_1}{1 - m_1' - m_2'} \left[(1 - m_2')(s_1 + m_1) + m_1 - (m_2 + m_2's_2)\frac{Y_2}{Y_1} \right],$$

$$(26b) \quad r_2 = \frac{a_2}{1 - m_1' - m_2'} \left[(1 - m_1')(s_2 + m_2) + m_2 - (m_1 + m_1's_1)\frac{Y_1}{Y_2} \right],$$

where the m''s are the fractions of investment expenditure spent on imports. Differentiation of these equations with respect to time yields

$$(27a) \qquad \frac{dr_1}{dt} = \frac{a_1(m_2 + m_2's_2)}{1 - m_1' - m_2'} \frac{Y_2}{Y_1} (r_1 - r_2)$$

and

$$(27b) \qquad \frac{dr_2}{dt} = \frac{a_2(m_1 + m_1's_1)}{1 - m_1' - m_2'} \frac{Y_1}{Y_2} (r_2 - r_1)$$

from which it is seen that the behaviour of the equilibrium growth rates over time will depend on two things: the relative magnitudes of the two growth rates (as before) and the sum of the two foreign content fractions of investment expenditure. Three cases may be distinguished:

(i) If the sum of the two fractional foreign contents of investment is less than unity: the equilibrium growth rate in country 1 will rise and that in country 2 will fall if the former is higher than the latter, and vice versa. Unless the equilibrium growth rates are the same in the two countries, they will diverge over time.

(ii) If the sum of the two fractional foreign contents of investment is greater than unity: the equilibrium growth rate in country 1 will *fall* and that in country 2 will *rise* if the former is higher than the latter, and vice versa. In this case, if the equilibrium growth rates are not the same in the two countries, they will converge over time. The explanation of this result is that, if the fractional foreign contents of investment sum to more than unity, the effect of a simultaneous increase in investment in country 1 and equal decrease in investment in country 2 is to decrease effective demand for country 1's output and increase effective demand for country 2's output. If country 1's output is growing less rapidly than country 2's, the preservation of equilibrium between effective demand and capacity in both countries requires a relative increase in investment in country 1 and decrease in country 2, to reduce the rate of increase of demand for country 1's output and increase that for country 2's output.

(iii) In the limiting case in which the fractional foreign contents of investment sum to exactly unity, the equilibrium growth rates of the two countries are completely undetermined. Equations (26a) and (26b) reduce to a single equation stating that aggregate investment must be equal to aggregate saving. This is because, in this case, a given total of investment has the same effect on effective demand for the output of each of the two countries; regardless of how it is distributed between them.

These conclusions may be expressed in terms of the constants of the system as before. Again, the complexity of the implicit equations for equilibrium outputs as functions of time precludes ready verification of the relations between the magnitudes of the constants and the equilibrium growth rates suggested by equations (26a) and (26b).

It may be noted in passing that there are no grounds in theory for selecting either case (i) or case (ii) above as more 'realistic'. If allowance is made for the influence of transport costs and trade restrictions in the real world, case (i) is likely to be the more relevant,[11] though case (ii) might have some bearing on growth problems in primary producing areas.

Allowance for interest payments on international lending alters the equations for the equilibrium growth rates to

(28a) $$r_1 = a_1 \left[s_1 + m_1 - \frac{(c_1 - m_2)Z}{Y_1} - \frac{m_2 Y_2}{Y_1} \right],$$

(28b) $$r_2 = a_2 \left[s_2 + m_2 + \frac{(c_2 - m_1)Z}{Y_2} - \frac{m_1 Y_1}{Y_2} \right],$$

where Z stands for interest payments (which may be negative) received by country 1 from country 2, determined by the equation

(29) $$\frac{dZ}{dt} = i[Z + m_2(Y_2 - Z) - m_1(Y_1 + Z)].$$

The introduction of interest payments makes it impossible to deduce the future course of the equilibrium growth rates from their initial magnitudes—although it is clear that only in certain cases will an initial equality of equilibrium growth rates continue. Equations

---

[11] Cf. P. A. Samuelson, 'The Transfer Problem and Transport Costs: The Terms of Trade When Impediments Are Absent', *Economic Journal*, LXII, no. 246, 278–304, especially 289–99.

(28a) and (28b) do, however, suggest some conclusions about the influence of interest payments and receipts on the equilibrium growth rates at any particular moment.[12] Specifically, receipt of interest by one country from the other may tend either to raise or to lower its equilibrium growth rate, depending on whether the fraction of interest receipts it spends on its own goods is less or greater than the fraction of interest payments by which the paying country reduces its imports from the receiving country; and conversely for the payment of interest by one country to the other. In the limiting case in which the fraction of interest income spent by the receiving country on its own product is equal to the fraction of interest payments made at the expense of imports by the paying country, and the fraction of interest income spent on imports by the paying country is equal to the fraction of interest payments made at the expense of consumption of home goods by the paying country, interest payments and receipts would have no influence on the equilibrium growth rates. If no part of interest receipts were saved or of payments dissaved, the effect of interest transfers on the equilibrium growth rates would depend on whether the sum of the fractions of interest receipts spent on (payments made at the expense of) imports were less than or greater than unity. The effects of interest payments are therefore analogous to, though more complicated than, the effects of foreign contents of investment expenditure.

To complete the analysis of the two-country case in which current account surpluses or deficits are covered by international lending or borrowing, let us consider another possible problem of international economic growth. In all of the cases discussed so far, it has been assumed that imports are different from, and complementary to, home-produced goods. Let us now assume instead that the international economy consists of two countries, each producing the same product, and that one of these countries is growing at a constant rate different from its closed-economy equilibrium growth rate, and maintaining equilibrium between capacity production and effective demand by either borrowing from or lending to the other country the difference between its domestic savings from capacity output and the volume of output required for investment by its rate of growth. What conditions are imposed on the rate of growth of the other

---

[12] The argument of the rest of this paragraph departs from the assumption that interest income is spent exactly like other income; fuller investigation of the subject would involve amendment of equations (28) and (29). It is of course obvious that if interest payments and receipts affect only saving, the equilibrium growth rates will be unaffected.

country, if equilibrium between productive capacity and effective demand is to be maintained there?

On the assumption that country 2 is the country which is growing at a constant rate ($= r_2$), the equation for the equilibrium growth rate in country 1 is

(30) $$r_1 = a_1\left(s_1 - \frac{r_2 - a_2 s_2}{a_2}\frac{Y_2}{Y_1}\right).$$

If r_2 is greater than $a_2 s_2$, country 2 is growing faster than its own saving would permit and country 1 is obliged to grow in such a way as to make available to country 2 (through an excess of saving over domestic investment) the extra goods required to maintain this rate of growth. Conversely, if r_2 is less than $a_2 s_2$, country 2 is growing less rapidly than is required to employ its saving at capacity output and country 1 is obliged to grow in such a way as to absorb the excess of saving over investment in country 2. In the first case country 1 is a lender, adjusting to the requirements of the borrowing country, in the second case it is a borrower, adjusting to the requirements of the lending country. The implications of this adjustment for the equilibrium growth rate of country 1 are different in the two cases. On differentiating equation (30) we obtain

(31) $$\frac{dr_1}{dt} = \frac{a_1 Y_2}{a_2 Y_1}(r_2 - a_2 s_2)(r_1 - r_2).$$

The interpretation of this result depends on whether country 2 is a borrower ($r_2 > a_2 s_2$) or a lender ($r_2 < a_2 s_2$).

In the case in which country 1 is a lender, its equilibrium rate of growth will rise, be constant, or fall over time according to whether r_2 is less than, equal to, or greater than r_{10}. By substitution for r_{10} and rearrangement of terms, this result can be translated into the conclusion that r_1 will rise, be constant, or fall over time according to whether r_2 is less than, equal to, or greater than s_A/k_A, where s_A and k_A are averages of the savings ratios and capital coefficients of the two countries, weighted by their initial capacity levels of output. This last expression may be replaced by r_A, which may be described as the equilibrium growth rate for the world economy as a whole; and the equilibrium growth rate of the lending country will be higher or lower than that of the borrowing country and will rise or fall over time according to whether the rate of growth of the borrowing country is less than or greater than the world equilibrium growth rate. In the former case, the lender's equilibrium growth rate will approach its closed-economy equilibrium growth rate (a_1s_1) asymptotically; in the latter case its equilibrium output must eventually cease growing and begin to fall.

In the case in which country 1 is a borrower, its equilibrium growth rate will rise, be constant, or fall, according to whether the rate of growth of country 2 is greater than, equal to, or less than country 1's initial equilibrium growth rate; alternatively, according to whether country 2's growth rate is greater than, equal to, or less than the equilibrium growth rate for the international economy as a whole. The rate of growth of country 1 will converge on that of country 2: if r_2 exceeds r_A, r_1 will rise, approaching r_2 asymptotically; and the ratio of the output of country 1 to the output of country 2 will approach $a_1(a_2s_2 - r_2)/a_2(r_2 - a_1s_1)$ in the course of time. If r_2 is less than r_A, r_1 will fall over time, approaching asymptotically either r_2 or a_1s_1, whichever is the greater. In this case, of course, the equilibrium output of country 1 is always rising.

The equation

$$(32) \quad Y_1 = \left(Y_{10} + \frac{a_1(r_2 - a_2s_2)}{a_2(r_2 - a_1s_1)} Y_{20} \right) e^{a_1s_1t} - \frac{a_1(r_2 - a_2s_2)}{a_2(r_2 - a_1s_1)} Y_{20} \, e^{r_2 t}$$

for the equilibrium output of country 1 implicit in equation (30) permits the verification of the following conclusions about the influence of the constants of the system on the equilibrium output and equilibrium rate of growth of country 1:

(i) If country 1 is a lender, its equilibrium output and equilibrium growth rate at any future date will be higher the higher are its initial productive capacity and its savings ratio, and the lower the initial productive capacity and rate of growth and the higher the savings ratio and output coefficient of country 2. The equilibrium output and equilibrium rate of growth of country 1 will be higher the higher country 1's output coefficient so long as its equilibrium output is rising; but this may not be so after equilibrium output begins to fall, in those cases in which it does.

(ii) If country 1 is a borrower, its equilibrium output will be higher at any future date the higher its own and the higher country 2's initial capacity output; its equilibrium growth rate will be higher the lower its initial capacity output and the higher the initial capacity output of country 2. Its equilibrium output and equilibrium growth rate will both be higher, the higher the savings ratio and the higher the output coefficient of either country. The influence of the rate of growth of country 2, however, is rather more complicated. The higher the rate of growth of country 2, the lower will be the equilibrium level of output for country 1 in the early future, but the higher will it become eventually—except when the rate of growth of country 2 is less than a_1s_1, in which case country 1's equilibrium output is reduced at all future dates. The higher the rate of growth of country 2, the lower will be the equilibrium growth rate for country 1 in the early future, and the higher will it eventually become, without exception.

The analysis of this case may be extended to take account of interest on international loans, in the same way as the cases previously discussed. Allowing for interest payments, the equation for country 1's equilibrium growth rate becomes

$$(33) \qquad r_1 = a_1 \left[s_1 + (s_1 - s_2) \frac{Z}{Y_1} - \frac{r_2 - a_2 s_2}{a_2} \frac{Y_2}{Y_1} \right],$$

where Z represents interest paid by country 2 to country 1 (negative if country 1 is a borrower) determined by the equation

$$(34) \qquad \frac{dZ}{dt} = i \left(\frac{r_2 - a_2 s_2}{a_2} Y_2 + s_2 Z \right).$$

Equation (33) suggests that, in the case in which country 1 is a lender, the effect of interest receipts will be to raise or lower its equilibrium growth rate according to whether the proportion of its interest income it saves is greater or less than the proportion of interest payments dissaved by country 2; and conversely for the case in which country 1 is a borrower. If the fractions of interest payments or receipts saved or dissaved are the same in the two countries, the introduction of interest on international loans makes no difference to the conclusions about equilibrium growth stated above.

As in previous cases, it is no longer possible to obtain simple conclusions about the course of the equilibrium growth rate of country 1 over time, because this depends in part on the rate of growth of interest payments (or receipts), which may differ from the rate of growth of output of country 2. It is possible, however, to carry the analysis further than in previous cases involving interest payments, because the evolution of interest payments over time in this case does not depend on the evolution of the equilibrium output of country 1, but only on that of country 2, whose rate of growth is assumed to be given.

In particular, if the rate of interest on international loans i is less

K

than r_2/s_2 and if country 1 is initially receiving interest payments if it is a lender, or making interest payments if it is a borrower, the rate of growth of interest transfers will converge on the rate of growth of output in country 2, and the ratio of interest payments to output in country 2 will converge on $i(r_2 - a_2s_2)/a_2(r_2 - is_2)$. From equation (34),

$$(35) \qquad \frac{dz}{dt} = \frac{i(r_2 - a_2s_2)Y_2}{a_2Z}(r_2 - z).$$

If $(r_2 - a_2s_2)$ and Z have the same sign, z will converge on r_2 and Z will approach

$$\frac{i}{a_2}\left(\frac{r_2 - a_2s_2}{r_2 - is_2}\right)Y_2.$$

But unless $(r_2 - is_2)$ is positive, the latter implies Z and $(r_2 - a_2s_2)$ of opposite sign, which would be a contradiction. In an economically sensible model the rate of interest on capital must be less than the output coefficient—otherwise labour would receive no reward for its participation in production—and therefore the first condition stated above must be fulfilled if country 1 is a lender, and will be fulfilled if it is a borrower unless r_2 is substantially less than a_2s_2.

On the assumption that both of these requirements are fulfilled and that the international economy has been functioning for a long period of time, interest transfers may be approximated by their asymptotic value as given above, and equation (33) becomes

$$(36) \qquad r_1 = a_1s_1 - \frac{a_1r_2 - is_1}{a_2r_2 - is_2}(r_2 - a_2s_2)\frac{Y_2}{Y_1},$$

where for example in the general case

$$(37) \quad Y_1 = Y_{10}\, e^{a_1s_1t} + \frac{a_1r_2 - a_2s_2}{a_2r_2 - a_1s_1}Y_{20}\left[\frac{s_1(a_1 - i)}{a_1s_1 - is_2}e^{a_1s_1t} - \frac{r_2 - is_1}{r_2 - is_2}e^{r_2t}\right]$$
$$+ \frac{a_1r_2 - a_2s_2}{a_2r_2 - is_2}\frac{i(s_2 - s_1)}{is_2 - a_1s_1}Y_{20}\, e^{is_2t}$$

and in this special case,

$$(38) \quad Y_1 = Y_{10}\, e^{a_1s_1t} - \frac{a_1r_2 - is_1}{a_2r_2 - is_2}\frac{r_2 - a_2s_2}{a_1s_1 - r_2}(e^{a_1s_1t} - e^{r_2t})Y_{20}.$$

With the appropriate re-definition of r_{10}, the behaviour of country 1's equilibrium rate of growth over time will depend on the relation between r_2 and r_{10}, in the same way as when interest payments were excluded from consideration. It can also be established that, if country 1 is a lender, a higher rate of interest would raise or lower its equilibrium growth rate according to whether its savings ratio is greater or less than that of country 2; and that, if it is a borrower, a higher rate of interest would raise or lower its equilibrium growth rate according to whether its savings ratio is less or greater than that of country 2. Further propositions about the influence of the constants of the system on the equilibrium output and rate of growth of country 1 are left to the interested reader to determine.

PART II

In all of the problems of equilibrium growth discussed in Part I, it has been assumed that exchange rates were fixed, and that any deficits or surpluses which emerged in the course of international trade were covered by international lending or borrowing: accommodating capital movements have been taken to be the means of adjustment of current account disequilibria. In Part II we consider the problem of equilibrium growth on an alternative assumption, namely, that there are no capital movements or interest transfers between countries, and that each country's export earnings are kept equal to its expenditure on imports by appropriate changes in exchange rates. Again, for simplicity, the argument is confined to an international economy of two countries.

Initially, we ignore the problem of equilibrium growth, and consider the relationship between the growth rates of the two countries and the exchange rate adjustment necessary to keep trade between them in balance.

It is, of course, obvious that an initial equality of export and import values can only be preserved without a change in the exchange rate between the two countries' currencies if each country's expenditure on imports increases by the same amount in any period of time. Remembering that commodity and currency units have been chosen to make prices and exchange rates equal to unity, this requirement may be expressed as[13]

$$(39) \qquad m_1 \frac{dY_1}{dt} = m_2 \frac{dY_2}{dt},$$

[13] As in Part I, it is assumed, to begin with, that imports are demanded only for direct consumption.

where m_1 and m_2 are now the *marginal* propensities to import of the two countries. In terms of growth rates, this requirement is that

$$(40) \qquad \qquad \epsilon_1 R_1 = \epsilon_2 R_2,$$

where R stands for the rate of growth of output, and ϵ for the income elasticity of demand for imports.[14] Equality of exports and imports will only be preserved at an unchanged exchange rate if the two countries' growth rates are inversely proportional to their income elasticities of demand for imports. This conclusion may be re-phrased in a way more relevant to economic policy: the country with the lower income elasticity of demand for imports must grow at a higher rate, if it is not to impose on the other the necessity of an exchange rate adjustment.

The argument just presented indicates the conditions under which a zero trade balance between the countries can be maintained without exchange rate adjustments, but does not indicate the extent or direction of exchange adjustment required to preserve equality of export and import values if these conditions are not fulfilled. In considering the more general problem, it is convenient to define the exchange rate between the two countries' currencies as the number of units of country 1's currency which are required to buy a unit of country 2's currency (denoted below by p), so that a *rise* in the exchange rate corresponds to a depreciation of country 1's currency and an appreciation of country 2's currency. It is also convenient to measure imports in the physical units of their country of origin, rather than their value in the importing country.[15] Both of these conventions are employed in the remainder of the argument of Part II.

With the simplification permitted by our choice of commodity units, country 1's initial balance of trade, expressed in domestic currency, is

$$(41) \qquad \qquad B_1 = M_2 - pM_1 = 0,$$

where M_1 and M_2 are the initial quantities imported by the two

---

[14] This condition generalizes readily to any number of countries and is independent of the choice of units. If it is assumed, as in the previous section, that imports are a constant fraction of income, the condition reduces to $R_1 = R_2$, since in this case the income elasticities of demand for imports would be unity. This result is used in the later discussion of equilibrium growth.

[15] The significance of this is that consideration of changes in the exchange rate imposes the necessity of choosing between physical and monetary concepts of the propensity to import.

countries and p is initially equal to unity. Differentiation of this expression yields

$$(42) \quad \frac{dB_1}{dt} = \frac{\delta M_2}{\delta p}\frac{dp}{dt} + m_2\frac{dY_2}{dt} - M_1\frac{dp}{dt} - p\frac{\delta M_1}{\delta p}\frac{dp}{dt} - pm_1\frac{dY_1}{dt}.$$

By setting dB_1/dt equal to zero we obtain the change in country 1's exchange rate necessary to keep trade between the two countries in balance,

$$(43) \quad \frac{dp}{dt} = \left(pm_1\frac{dY_1}{dt} - m_2\frac{dY_2}{dt}\right) \bigg/ \left(\frac{\delta M_2}{\delta p} - p\frac{\delta M_1}{\delta p} - M_1\right).$$

By defining

$$(44a) \qquad\qquad \eta_1 = -\frac{p}{M_1}\frac{\delta M_1}{\delta p}$$

as the elasticity of country 1's (consumption) demand for imports from country 2, and

$$(44b) \qquad\qquad \eta_2 = \frac{p}{M_2}\frac{\delta M_2}{\delta p}$$

as the elasticity of country 2's (consumption) demand for imports from country 1, and remembering that initially $M_2 = pM_1$, this may be re-written[16] as

$$(45) \qquad R_p = \frac{1}{p}\frac{dp}{dt} = (\epsilon_1 R_1 - \epsilon_2 R_2)/(\eta_1 + \eta_2 - 1),$$

where R_p is the proportional change in the exchange rate required to preserve trade equilibrium between the two countries.

The denominator of this last expression is the familiar criterion for exchange stability, on the assumption that trade is initially balanced and output in both countries is kept constant. Equation (45) therefore indicates that if the exchange market is stable, country 1's currency must depreciate if

$$(46) \qquad\qquad \epsilon_1 R_1 > \epsilon_2 R_2$$

and appreciate if

$$(47) \qquad\qquad \epsilon_1 R_1 < \epsilon_2 R_2$$

[16] Supply elasticities do not enter into the analysis because they are precluded by the assumptions of the problem—each country's product is homogeneous and its quantity at any moment is fixed. It may be noted that the expression for R_p is independent of the units in which currencies and outputs are measured.

to preserve trade balance between the two countries; but if the exchange market is unstable, the opposite change in country 1's exchange rate is required in the two cases. This conclusion, of course, is not surprising.

The introduction of changes in the exchange rate as the means of preserving balance-of-payments equilibrium implies that real income can no longer be identified with output, and suggests the possibility that a country may suffer a loss of real income even though its output is growing. Specifically, economic expansion accompanied by depreciation required to keep the country's foreign trade balanced involves a gain in real income arising from higher output, and a loss in real income associated with the adverse movement of the terms of trade. Under what conditions, if any, may the loss outweigh the gain?

The loss of real income consequent on an adverse movement of the terms of trade can be approximated by use of the compensation principle: it will be approximately equal[17] to the increased output that would be necessary to enable the country to buy the same quantity of imports as before, without reducing its consumption of home-produced goods. Applying this approximation, the total change in country 1's real income consequent on growth is

$$(48) \quad \frac{dY_1^*}{dt} = -M_1\frac{dp}{dt} + \frac{dY_1}{dt}$$

$$= \left[(\eta_1 + \eta_2 - pm_1 - 1)\frac{dY_1}{dt} + m_2\frac{dY_2}{dt}\right] \Big/ (\eta_1 + \eta_2 - 1)$$

and the proportional change is

$$(49) \quad R_1^* = \frac{1}{Y_1}\frac{dY_1^*}{dt}$$

$$= \left[(\eta_1 + \eta_2 - pm_1 - 1)R_1 + m_2 R_2\frac{Y_2}{Y_1}\right] \Big/ (\eta_1 + \eta_2 - 1).$$

The latter equation indicates that if the exchange market is stable in the sense described above ($\eta_1 + \eta_2 > 1$) country 1 may suffer a loss of real income by growing too rapidly; this will be the case if

$$(50) \quad (pm_1 + 1 - \eta_1 - \eta_2)R_1 > m_2 R_2\frac{Y_2}{Y_1},$$

which is only possible if the sum of the two elasticities of international

---

[17] Actually something less, owing to the substitution effect.

demand, though greater than unity, is less than one plus the marginal propensity to spend on imports[18] of country 1. If the exchange market is unstable in the described sense $(\eta_1 + \eta_2 < 1)$ country 1 may suffer a loss of real income by growing too slowly;[19] this will be the case if

$$(51) \qquad (pm_1 + 1 - \eta_1 - \eta_2)R_1 < m_2 R_2 \frac{Y_2}{Y_1}.$$

This analysis can be readily extended to the problem of equilibrium growth. Since trade between the two countries is assumed to be kept in balance by changes in the exchange rate, the equilibrium growth rate in each country is its 'closed-economy equilibrium growth rate': $r_1 = a_1 s_1$ and $r_2 = a_2 s_2$, it being assumed as before that (at a given exchange rate) a constant fraction of income (output) is saved. On the related assumption that, at an unchanged exchange rate, a constant fraction of income would be spent on imports, the income elasticities of demand for imports become unity, and the equilibrium rate of change of the exchange rate becomes

$$(52) \qquad r_p = \frac{a_1 s_1 - a_2 s_2}{\eta_1 + \eta_2 - 1}.$$

From this it may be concluded that if the exchange market is stable,

[18] The marginal propensity to spend on imports is equal to the marginal propensity to import multiplied by the relative price of imports as compared with home goods (here, pm_1). The condition $\eta_1 + \eta_2 > pm_1 + 1$ is the condition for exchange stability when country 2's output is constant but country 1's output is allowed to vary in response to change in its balance of trade (cf. Harberger, loc. cit.). Country 1 can therefore suffer a loss of real income in the case in which the exchange market is stable when both countries stabilize output, only if the market would be unstable if country 1 did not stabilize its output.

[19] This assumes that, knowing the exchange market to be unstable, country 1 depreciates its currency (or country 2 appreciates its currency) in order to forestall the favourable balance of trade for country 1 that would otherwise emerge. Presumably, since capital movements have been excluded from consideration, continued depreciation of country 2's exchange rate would in 'realistic' cases eventually bring the exchange rate into a range in which country 2's demand for country 1's product would become sufficiently elastic for trade balance to be attained. If, in such cases, country 2 followed normal market criteria and depreciated its currency in order to preserve trade balance, country 1 could not lose by growing too slowly. However, as P. A. Samuelson has pointed out ['Disparity in Postwar Exchange Rates', chap. 22 in S. E. Harris, ed., *Foreign Economic Policy for the United States* (Cambridge, 1948), especially 409, n. 14], there is no theoretical reason why, even in the absence of capital movements, depreciation in an unstable market should eventually lead to a stable exchange equilibrium. An example in which no degree of depreciation leads to a stable equilibrium is provided below equation (57) *et seq.*

country 1's exchange rate must depreciate if its equilibrium growth rate $a_1 s_1$ is greater than $a_2 s_2$, the equilibrium growth rate of country 2; and conversely if the exchange market is unstable. Further, using the assumption that $m_2 Y_2 = p m_1 Y_1$, it follows from equation (49) that the (approximate) proportional change in country 1's equilibrium real income is

$$(53) \qquad r^* = \frac{a_1 s_1 (\eta_1 + \eta_2 - p m_1 - 1) + a_2 s_2 p m_1}{\eta_1 + \eta_2 - 1}.$$

From this equation it may be deduced that if the exchange market is stable, country 1's real income will be falling if

$$(54) \qquad a_1 s_1 - a_2 s_2 > \frac{\eta_1 + \eta_2 - 1}{p m_1}$$

—a result which is only possible if $\eta_1 + \eta_2$ is less than $1 + p m_1$ though greater than unity. If, on the other hand, the exchange market is unstable, country 1's real income will be falling if

$$(55) \qquad a_2 s_2 - a_1 s_1 > \frac{1 - \eta_1 - \eta_2}{p m_1}.$$

The foregoing analysis relates to equilibrium growth at a particular point in time; as in Part I, the more interesting problem is what happens to the equilibrium growth rates of the two countries over time. As we have seen, the equilibrium growth rate in each country depends only on its output coefficient and the fraction of its output which it saves. Since the output coefficient is assumed to be technologically determined, the course of the equilibrium growth rates over time will depend on the behaviour of the savings ratios.

On the assumption that a constant fraction of output is saved in each country, the equilibrium growth rates would be constant over time. To make this assumption, however, would be to assume a peculiar kind of 'money illusion', since unless the equilibrium growth rate is the same in each country the exchange rate will have to be changing in order to preserve trade balance, and constancy of the savings ratio in such conditions would imply that saving is not affected by changes in the terms of trade and the associated changes in the purchasing power of domestic output.[20] It would seem more logical to assume that saving is a constant fraction of real income

---

[20] *Cf.* H. G. Johnson, 'The Taxonomic Approach to Economic Policy', *Economic Journal*, LXI, no. 244, December 1951, 812–32, especially 816–17.

rather than of domestic output, and that the savings ratio consequently varies with the exchange rate: specifically, that a rise in the
exchange rate will reduce country 1's real income and lower its
savings ratio, and increase country 2's real income and raise its
savings ratio. Employing the compensation-principle approximation
for the effect of a change in the exchange rate on real income, and
the assumption that at an unchanged exchange rate imports would
be a constant fraction of output, we obtain

$$(56a) \qquad \frac{dr_1}{dt} = -a_1 s_1 m_1 \frac{dp}{dt},$$

$$(56b) \qquad \frac{dr_2}{dt} = +a_2 s_2 m_2 \frac{dp}{dt}.$$

(Here both s and m are variables, but by assumption are always
positive.)

From the above assumption that the savings ratio varies with the
exchange rate it may be concluded that if the exchange market is
stable, the equilibrium growth rates of the two countries will converge on one another over time: the currency of the country growing
at the higher rate must depreciate over time, lowering that country's
savings ratio and equilibrium growth rate and raising the savings
ratio and equilibrium growth rate of the other country until the two
equilibrium growth rates become equal. If, on the other hand, the
exchange market is unstable, the equilibrium growth rates of the
two countries will diverge over time: the currency of the faster
growing country must appreciate, raising that country's savings ratio
and equilibrium growth rate and lowering the savings ratio and
equilibrium growth rate of the other country.

This conclusion assumes that the exchange market is either stable
or unstable whatever the exchange rate, and ignores the possibility
that, as the exchange rate changes over time, the elasticities of
demand for imports may alter and a stable market become unstable,
or vice versa.[21] Detailed investigation of this problem, and of the
influence of the parameters of the system on the magnitudes of the
equilibrium growth rates at future dates, would require specification
of the form of the equations of demand for imports, which does not
seem worth while at the level of abstraction of this study.

One special case which merits further consideration—though more
for its consistency with the general conceptions of the Harrod-Domar

---

[21] It is changes in the sum of the two elasticities, and not in their individual
magnitudes, which are relevant here.

model than for its practical relevance—is that in which consumers in each country spend their incomes so as to maintain a fixed ratio between saving (measured in domestic output, since by assumption only domestic output is used for investment), consumption of home goods, and quantity of imports consumed. In this case, real income is exactly measurable, and saving and imports are constant fractions of real income.

The real incomes of the two countries will be

$$(57a) \qquad Y^*_1 = \frac{Y_1}{1 - m^*_1 + m^*_1 p}$$

and

$$(57b) \qquad Y^*_2 = \frac{Y_2}{1 - m^*_2 + m^*_2/p}$$

respectively; their savings ratios will be

$$(58a) \qquad s_1 = \frac{s^*_1}{1 - m^*_1 + m^*_1 p}$$

and

$$(58b) \qquad s_2 = \frac{s^*_2}{1 - m^*_2 + m^*_2/p}$$

respectively; and the quantities of each others' goods they import will be

$$(59a) \qquad M_1 = \frac{m^*_1 Y_1}{1 - m^*_1 + m^*_1 p}$$

and

$$(59b) \qquad M_2 = \frac{m^*_2 Y_2}{1 - m^*_2 + m^*_2/p}$$

where s^* and m^* stand for the ratios of saving and quantities imported to real income (and are equal to the proportions of income initially saved and spent on imports, since initially $p = 1$). The exchange rate can be determined directly from equation (41), as a function of the two equilibrium outputs and the import ratios, and substitution for the exchange rate in the savings ratio gives the two equilibrium growth rates as

$$(60a) \qquad r_1 = \frac{a_1 s^*_1}{1 - m^*_1 - m^*_2}\left(1 - m^*_2 - m^*_2 \frac{Y_2}{Y_1}\right),$$

$$(60b) \qquad r_2 = \frac{a_2 s^*_2}{1 - m^*_1 - m^*_2}\left(1 - m^*_1 - m^*_1 \frac{Y_1}{Y_2}\right).$$

From these equations the following conclusions may be derived:

(i) If $m_1^* + m_2^*$ is less than unity, and $a_1 s_1^*$ is greater (less) than $a_2 s_2^*$, the equilibrium growth rate of country 1 will rise (fall) continually over time, and that of country 2 will fall (rise) continually over time. The equilibrium growth rates will diverge, if they are not initially equal.

(ii) If $m_1^* + m_2^*$ is greater than unity, and $a_1 s_1^*$ is greater (less) than $a_2 s_2^*$, the equilibrium growth rate of country 1 will fall (rise) continually over time, and that of country 2 will rise (fall) continually over time. If the equilibrium growth rates are not initially equal, they will converge.

(iii) In the limiting case in which $m_1^* + m_2^*$ is equal to unity, the model breaks down if $a_1 s_1^*$ is not equal to $a_2 s_2^*$.

In short, the behaviour of the equilibrium growth rates in this case depends on the magnitude of $m_1^* + m_2^*$: the growth rates will converge or diverge according to whether the proportion of its income which each country initially spends on imports is on the average greater or less than one-half. The explanation of this result is that in this special case the elasticity of demand for imports is equal to the proportion of income spent on them and varies between the limits zero and unity; and that, if the sum of the elasticities is greater or less than unity at one exchange rate (price of one good in terms of the other) it will be so for all exchange rates. This may be seen from

$$(61) \qquad \eta_1 + \eta_2 - 1 = \frac{m_1^* + m_2^* - 1}{(1 - m_1^* + m_1^* p)(1 - m_2^* + m_2^*/p)}.$$

The denominator of the right-hand side of this equation is always positive, so that the exchange market will be stable or unstable at all exchange rates, depending on whether $m_1^* + m_2^*$ is greater or less than unity.[22] Consequently the direction of change of the exchange rate and the savings ratios (if the two equilibrium growth rates are unequal) depends on the sum of the fractions of income initially spent on imports. In the limiting case in which these fractions sum to unity, the exchange market is in neutral equilibrium, and no exchange rate adjustment can remedy a trade unbalance; consequently in this case the model breaks down if the growth rates are unequal.

Throughout Part II of our study of equilibrium growth, the analysis has proceeded on the basis of two assumptions which were relaxed early in the argument of Part I, namely that investment utilizes only home-produced goods and that domestic production

[22] *Cf.* n. 19, above.

has no import content; to conclude Part II, we shall deal briefly with the corrections to the preceding analysis required by relaxation of these assumptions. In both cases the necessary corrections are slight, amounting mainly to a re-definition of symbols, since the assumption that trade balance is maintained by exchange rate adjustment leaves the requirement of equilibrium growth the same as that for a closed economy (equality of full-capacity saving with investment), and the corrections chiefly relate to the elasticities on which the rate of change of the exchange rate depends.

The assumption that investment has a constant fractional component of imported goods m' (measured in real terms, using physical units defined to make prices and exchange rates initially equal to unity) does not alter the equilibrium growth rates for the two countries, which remain $r_1 = a_1 s_1$ and $r_2 = a_2 s_2$; and it strengthens our conclusions about their behaviour over time, since depreciation now lowers the output coefficient by reducing the purchasing power of investment expenditure. It does, however, alter the elasticities of demand for imports, since part of a country's imports are now required for current investment activity, not for current consumption, and are insensitive to changes in the exchange rate. Consequently the equilibrium rate of change of the exchange rate given in equation (52) becomes

$$(62) \quad r_p = \frac{a_1 s_1 - a_2 s_2}{e_1 + e_2 - 1} = \frac{a_1 s_1 - a_2 s_2}{\dfrac{m_1}{m_1 + m_1' s_1} \eta_1 + \dfrac{m_2}{m_2 + m_2' s_2} \eta_2 - 1},$$

where the e's stand for the total elasticities of demand for imports and the η's, as before, for the elasticity of demand for imports for consumption. The total elasticity of demand for imports here is the elasticity of consumption demand for imports, multiplied by the ratio of consumption imports to total imports.

The assumption that domestic production has a fixed proportional import content q does alter the equilibrium growth rates, since the income from which savings are made is less than the total output by the cost of the import content. In this case the equilibrium growth rates become[23]

$$(63a) \quad r_1 = a_1 s_1 (1 - pq_1),$$

$$(63b) \quad r_2 = a_2 s_2 \left(1 - \frac{q_2}{p}\right).$$

[23] If p is greater than $1/q_1$ (less than q_2), country 1's output (country 2's output) will be contracting, since the imports required for capacity production will

It may be noted that, even on the assumption of 'money illusion' described earlier (a constant fraction of income saved, regardless of the terms of trade) the equilibrium growth rates will vary with the exchange rate, since the latter will determine the cost of the import content of output and therefore the net disposable income of the country and the proportion of output saved. There is therefore a double reason for concluding that the equilibrium growth rates will converge or diverge according to whether the exchange market is stable or unstable. Allowance for the import content of production also affects the elasticities of demand for imports; and the equilibrium rate of change of the exchange rate becomes:

$$(64) \quad r_p = \frac{a_1 s_1 (1 - p q_1) - a_2 s_2 (1 - q_2/p)}{e_1 + e_2 - 1}$$

$$= \frac{a_1 s_1 (1 - p q_1) - a_2 s_2 (1 - q_2/p)}{\dfrac{m_1(1 - p q_1)\eta_1 + p m_1 q_1}{m_1(1 - p q_1) + q_1} + \dfrac{m_2(1 - q_2/p)\eta_2 + m_2 q_2/p}{m_2(1 - q_2/p) + q_2}} - 1.$$

The total elasticity of demand for imports in this case is the sum of two terms: the elasticity of consumption demand for imports, weighted by the ratio of consumption imports to total imports; and the proportion of income spent on imports (the imports ratio multiplied by the exchange rate) weighted by the ratio of production imports to total imports.[24] The latter term represents the effect on expenditure on consumption imports of the change in net disposable income resulting from the altered cost of the import content of production.

cost more than its total output, the difference having to be made up by disinvestment. Consideration of equation (64) shows that this can only occur if the exchange market is unstable.

[24] The appearance of this term implies that the import content of domestic production does not necessarily reduce the elasticity of demand for imports. Differentiation of e with respect to q shows that a higher import content ratio would increase the total elasticity of demand for imports, if the elasticity of consumption demand for imports is smaller than the proportion of (net disposable) income spent on consumption imports (e.g. if η_1 is less than $p m_1$).

PART THREE
THE BALANCE OF PAYMENTS

CHAPTER VI

Towards a General Theory of the Balance of Payments [*][1]

THE theory of the balance of payments is concerned with the economic determinants of the balance of payments, and specifically with the analysis of policies for preserving balance-of-payments equilibrium. So defined, the theory of the balance of payments is essentially a post-war development. Prior to the Keynesian Revolution, problems of international disequilibrium were discussed within the classical conceptual framework of 'the mechanism of adjustment'—the way in which the balance of payments adjusts to equilibrium under alternative systems of international monetary relations—the actions of the monetary and other policy-making authorities being subsumed in the system under consideration. While the Keynesian Revolution introduced the notion of chronic disequilibrium into the analysis of international adjustment, early Keynesian writing on the subject tended to remain within the classical framework of analysis in terms of international monetary systems—the gold standard, the inconvertible paper standard—and to be concerned with the role and adequacy in the adjustment process of automatic variations in income and employment through the foreign trade multiplier. Moreover, the applicability of the analysis to policy problems was severely restricted by its assumption of general under-employment, which implied an elastic supply of aggregate output, and allowed the domestic-currency wage or price level to be treated as *given*, independently of the balance of payments and variations in it.

The pre-war approach to international monetary theory reflected

* To be published in French by the Institut de Science Économique Appliquée.

[1] This chapter embodies ideas developed in lecture courses at Cambridge and elsewhere; part of the argument is reproduced from an earlier paper, 'Sketch of a Generalization of Keynesian Balance-of-Payments Theory', *The Indian Journal of Economics*, XXXVII, no. 144, July 1956, 49–56. The writer is grateful to the Institut de Science Économique Appliquée for providing him with both the opportunity and the incentive to attempt a more extensive exposition of these ideas.

L

the way in which balance-of-payments problems tended to appear at the time, namely as problems of international monetary adjustment. Since the war, for reasons which need not be elaborated here, the balance of payments has come to be a major problem for economic policy in many countries. Correspondingly, a new (though still Keynesian) theoretical approach to balance-of-payments theory has been emerging, an approach which is better adapted to postwar conditions than the 'foreign trade multiplier theory' and 'elasticity analysis' of the pre-war period in two major respects: it poses the problems of balance-of-payments adjustment in a way which highlights their policy implications, and it allows for conditions of full employment and inflation.

The essence of this approach, which has been termed 'the absorption approach,' is to view the balance of payments as a relation between the aggregate receipts and expenditures of the economy, rather than as a relation between the country's credits and debits on international account. This approach has been implicit to an important extent in the thinking of practical policy-makers concerned with balance-of-payments problems in post-war conditions. Its main formal development is to be found in the works of Meade, Tinbergen and Alexander, though many others have contributed.[2] The purpose of this chapter is to synthesize and generalize the work of these writers, and to use their approach to clarify certain aspects of the balance-of-payments policy problem.

Let us first summarize the traditional approach to balance-of-payments theory. The balance of payments must necessarily balance,

[2] See in particular J. E. Meade, *The Theory of International Economic Policy. Vol. I: The Balance of Payments* (London, 1951); J. Tinbergen, *On the Theory of Economic Policy* (Amsterdam, 1952); S. Alexander, 'The Effects of a Devaluation on a Trade Balance', *International Monetary Fund Staff Papers*, II, no. 2, April 1952, 263–78; also G. Stuvel, *The Exchange Stability Problem* (Oxford, 1951); A. C. Harberger, 'Currency Depreciation, Income, and the Balance of Trade', *Journal of Political Economy*, LVIII, no. 1, February 1950, 47–60; S. Laursen and L. A. Metzler, 'Flexible Exchange Rates and the Theory of Employment', *Review of Economics and Statistics*, XXXII, no. 4, November 1950, 281–99; R. F. Harrod, 'Currency Depreciation as an Anti-Inflationary Device: Comment', *Quarterly Journal of Economics*, LXVI, no. 1, February 1952, 102–16. The terminology of 'absorption' was initiated by Alexander; Machlup's criticisms of Alexander's argument (F. Machlup, 'The Analysis of Devaluation', *American Economic Review*, XLV, no. 3, June 1955, 255–78), though valid in detail, miss the main point of Alexander's contribution, a point obscured by Alexander's own emphasis on the contrast between the 'elasticity' and the 'absorption' approaches to devaluation and his attack on the former. The later argument of this paper attempts a reconciliation of the two approaches in a broader framework of analysis.

when all international transactions are taken into account; for imbalance or disequilibrium to be possible, it is necessary to distinguish between 'autonomous' international transactions—those which are the result of the free and voluntary choices of individual transactors, within whatever restrictions are imposed by economic variables or policy on their behaviour—and 'induced' or 'accommodating' international transactions—those which are undertaken by the foreign exchange authorities to reconcile the free choices of the individual transactors—and to define the 'balance of payments' to include only autonomous transactions. To put the point another way, balance-of-payments problems presuppose the presence of an official foreign exchange authority which is prepared to operate in the foreign exchange market by the use of official reserves so as to influence the exchange rate; and 'disequilibrium' is defined by changes in the official reserves, associated with imbalance between the foreign receipts and foreign payments of residents of the country, where 'resident' is defined to include all economic units domiciled in the country *except* the foreign exchange authority.[3]

The 'balance of payments' appropriate to economic analysis may then be defined as

$$(1) \qquad\qquad B = R_f - P_f$$

where R_f represents aggregate receipts by residents from foreigners, and P_f represents aggregate payments by residents to foreigners. The difference between the two constitutes a surplus (if positive) or a deficit (if negative); a surplus is accompanied by sales of foreign currency to the exchange authority by residents or foreigners in exchange for domestic currency, and conversely a deficit is financed by sales of domestic currency by residents or foreigners to the authority in exchange for foreign currency. To remedy a deficit, some action must be taken to increase receipts from foreigners and reduce payments to foreigners, or increase receipts more than payments, or reduce payments more than receipts; and conversely with a surplus (though the rectification of a surplus is not generally regarded as a 'balance-of-payments problem').

The 'balance of payments' can, however, be defined in another way, by making use of the fact that all payments by residents to

---

[3] Where the central bank or other monetary authority also holds the foreign exchange reserves, it is necessary for the purposes of this paper to separate its functions conceptually into two parts, and to class its transactions as monetary authority (including those with itself as exchange authority) among transactions of residents.

residents are simultaneously receipts by residents from residents; in symbols $R_r \equiv P_r$. Hence the balance of payments may be written

$$(2) \qquad B = R_f + R_r - P_f - P_r = R - P.$$

That is, the balance of payments is the difference between aggregate receipts by residents and aggregate payments by residents. A deficit implies an excess of payments over receipts, and its rectification requires that receipts be increased and payments decreased, or that receipts increase more than payments, or that receipts decrease less than payments; and conversely with a surplus. In what follows, however, surpluses will be ignored, and the argument will be concerned only with deficits.

The formulation of a balance-of-payments deficit in terms of an excess of aggregate payments by residents over aggregate receipts by residents constitutes the starting point for the generalization of the 'absorption approach' to balance-of-payments theory—what might be termed a 'payments approach'—which is the purpose of this chapter. It directs attention to two important aspects of a deficit —its monetary implications, and its relation with the aggregate activity of the economy—from which attention tends to be diverted by the traditional sectoral approach, and neglect of which can lead to fallacious analysis. These two aspects will be discussed in turn, beginning with the monetary implications of a deficit.

The excess of payments by residents over receipts by residents inherent in a balance-of-payments deficit necessarily implies one or other of two alternatives. The first is that cash balances of residents are running down, as domestic money is transferred to the foreign exchange authority.[4] This can, obviously, only continue for a limited period, as eventually cash balances would approach the minimum that the community wished to hold and in the process the disequilibrium would cure itself, through the mechanism of rising interest rates, tighter credit conditions, reduction of aggregate expenditure and possibly an increase in aggregate receipts. In this case, where the deficit is financed by dishoarding, it would be self-correcting in time; but the economic policy authorities may well be unable to allow the self-correcting process to run its course, since the international reserves of the country may be such a small fraction of the domestic money supply that they would be exhausted well before the running down of money balances had any significant corrective

[4] Where monetary authority and exchange authority are one and the same institution, domestic monetary liabilities may simply be extinguished by sales of foreign exchange.

effect. The authorities might therefore have to take action of some kind to reinforce and accelerate the effects of diminishing money balances.

This last consideration provides the chief valid argument for larger international reserves. The case for larger international reserves is usually argued on the ground that larger reserves provide more time for the economic policy authorities to make adjustments to correct a balance-of-payments disequilibrium. But, as Friedman has argued in criticism of Meade,[5] there is no presumption that adjustment spread over a longer period is to be preferred—the argument could indeed be inverted into the proposition that, the larger reserves, the more power the authorities have to resist desirable adjustments. The acceptable argument would seem to be that, the larger the international reserves in relation to the domestic money supply, the less the probability that the profit- or utility-maximizing decisions of individuals to move out of cash into commodities or securities will have to be frustrated by the monetary authorities for fear of a balance-of-payments crisis.

The second alternative is that the cash balances of residents are being replenished by open market purchases of securities by the monetary or foreign exchange authority, as would happen automatically if the monetary authority followed a policy of pegging interest rates or the exchange authority (as in the British case) automatically re-lent to residents any domestic currency it received from residents or foreigners in return for sales of foreign exchange. In this case, the money supply in domestic circulation is being maintained by credit creation, so that the excess of payments over receipts by residents could continue indefinitely without generating any corrective process—until dwindling reserves forced the economic policy authorities to change their policy in some respect.

To summarize the argument so far, a balance-of-payments deficit implies *either* dishoarding by residents, *or* credit creation by the monetary authorities—either an increase in V, or the maintenance of M. Further, since a deficit associated with increasing velocity of circulation will tend to be self-correcting (though the authorities may be unable to rely on this alone), a continuing balance-of-payments deficit of the type usually discussed in balance-of-payments theory ultimately requires credit creation to keep it going. This in turn implies that balance-of-payments deficits and difficulties are essentially monetary phenomena, traceable to either of two causes:

[5] Milton Friedman, 'The Case for Flexible Exchange Rates', 157–203 in *Essays in Positive Economics* (Chicago, 1953), especially 186, n. 11.

too low a ratio of international reserves relative to the domestic money supply, so that the economic policy authorities cannot rely on the natural self-correcting process; or the pursuit of governmental policies which oblige the authorities to feed the deficit by credit creation. In both cases, the problem is associated fundamentally with the power of national banking systems to create money which has no internationally acceptable backing.

To conclude that balance of payments problems are essentially monetary is not, of course, to assert that they are attributable to monetary mismanagement—they may be, or they may be the result of 'real' forces in the face of which the monetary authorities play a passive role. The conclusion does mean, however, that the distinctions which have sometimes been drawn between monetary and real disequilibria, for example by concepts of 'structural disequilibrium', are not logically valid—though such concepts, carefully used, may be helpful in isolating the initiating causes of disequilibrium or the most appropriate type of remedial policy to follow.

Formulation of the balance of payments as the difference between aggregate payments and aggregate receipts thus illuminates the monetary aspects of balance-of-payments disequilibrium, and emphasizes its essentially monetary nature. More important and interesting is the light which this approach sheds on the policy problem of correcting a deficit, by relating the balance of payments to the overall operation of the economy rather than treating it as one sector of the economy to be analysed by itself.

An excess of aggregate payments by residents over aggregate receipts by residents is the net outcome of economic decisions taken by all the individual economic units composing the economy. These decisions may usefully be analysed in terms of an 'aggregate decision' taken by the community of residents considered as a group (excluding, as always, the foreign exchange authority), though it must be recognized that this technique ignores many of the complications that would have to be investigated in a more detailed analysis.

Two sorts of aggregate decision leading to a balance-of-payments deficit may be distinguished in principle, corresponding to the distinction drawn in monetary theory between 'stock' decisions and 'flow' decisions: a (stock) decision to alter the composition of the community's assets by substituting other assets for domestic money,[6] and a (flow) decision to spend currently in excess of current receipts.

[6] With the community defined to include the monetary authority, a substitution of securities for domestic money can only be effected by drawing securities from abroad in exchange for international reserves.

Since both real goods and securities are alternative assets to domestic money, and current expenditure may consist in the purchase of either goods or securities, the balance-of-payments deficit resulting from either type of aggregate decision may show itself on either current or capital account. That is, a current account deficit may reflect either a community decision to shift out of cash balances into stocks of goods, or a decision to use goods in excess of the community's current rate of production, while a capital account deficit may reflect either a decision to shift out of domestic money into securities or a decision to lend in excess of the current rate of saving.

The distinction between 'stock' and 'flow' balance-of-payments deficits is important for both theory and practical policy, though refined theoretical analysis has generally been concerned with 'flow' deficits, without making the distinction explicit. The importance of the distinction stems from the fact that a 'stock' deficit is inherently temporary and implies no real worsening of the country's economic position, whereas a 'flow' deficit is not inherently temporary and may imply a worsening of the country's economic position.

Since a stock decision entails a once-for-all change in the composition of a given aggregate of capital assets, a 'stock' deficit must necessarily be a temporary affair;[7] and in itself it implies no deterioration (but rather the reverse) in the country's economic position and prospects.[8] Nevertheless, if the country's international reserves are small, the economic policy authorities may be obliged to check such a deficit by a change in economic policy. The policy methods available are familiar, but it may be useful to review them briefly in relation to the framework of analysis developed here.

To discourage the substitution of stocks of goods for domestic currency, the economic policy authorities may either raise the cost of stock-holding by credit restriction or reduce its attractiveness by

[7] A temporary deficit of this kind must be distinguished from a deficit which is 'temporary' in the sense that the causal factors behind it will reverse themselves, leading to a later compensating surplus: e.g. a deficit due to a bad harvest.

[8] The deficit involves the replacement of international reserves by stocks of exportable or importable goods and/or by holdings of internationally marketable securities, the change being motivated by private profit considerations. For this to constitute a deterioration from the national point of view, the alternatives facing private asset-holders must be assumed not to reflect true social alternative opportunities, or private asset-holders must be assumed to act less rationally than the economic policy authorities, or the national interest must be defined so as to exclude their welfare from counting. If any of these assumptions is valid, it indicates the need for a remedial policy, but not one conditional on the existence of a deficit or to be applied through the balance of payments. This point is argued more fully below, in connection with import restrictions.

currency depreciation.[9] Under both policies, the magnitude of the effect is uncertain—depreciation, by stimulating de-stabilizing expectations, may even promote stock accumulation—while unavoidable repercussions on the flow equilibrium of the economy are set up. These considerations provide a strong argument for the use of the alternative method of direct controls on stock-holding, an indirect and partial form of which is quantitative import restriction.

To discourage the substitution of securities for domestic currency, the same broad alternatives are available: credit restriction, which amounts to the monetary authority substituting domestic currency for securities to offset substitution of securities for domestic currency by the rest of the community; devaluation, which affects the relative attractiveness of securities only through expectations and may work either way; and exchange controls restricting the acquisition of securities from abroad. Considerations similar to those of the previous paragraph would seem to argue in favour of the use of controls on international capital movements as against the alternative methods available.

In both cases, evaluation of the policy alternatives suggests the use of control rather than price system methods. It should be recalled, though, that the problem is created by the assumed inadequacy of the country's international reserves. In the longer run, the choice for economic policy lies, not between the three alternatives discussed, but between the necessity of having to choose between them and the cost of investing in the accumulation of reserves large enough to finance potential 'stock' deficits. Also, nothing has been said about the practical difficulties of maintaining effective control over international transactions, especially capital movements.

In contrast to a 'stock' deficit, a 'flow' deficit is not inherently of limited duration. It will be so if the monetary authority is not prepared to create credit, but this is because its existence will then set up monetary repercussions which will eventually alter the collective decision responsible for it, not because the initial decision implied a temporary deficit. If the decision not to create credit is regarded as a specific act of policy equivalent to a decision to raise interest rates,[10] it follows that the termination of a 'flow' deficit

[9] Stocks are built up by witholding goods from export or by increasing imports; depreciation makes both of these less attractive. A third policy might be increased taxation, either of stocks or of home-market sales of goods.

[10] This assumption, which is slightly inconsistent with the argument above concerning the monetary implications of a deficit, is made here to avoid the necessity of repeating the analysis for the case where limited reserves prevent the authorities from allowing a deficit to solve itself.

requires a deliberate change of economic policy. Further, a 'flow' deficit may imply a worsening of the country's capital position, providing an economic as well as a monetary incentive to terminate the disequilibrium.[11]

In analysing the policy problems posed by 'flow' deficits, it is convenient to begin by abstracting altogether from international capital movements (other than reserve transactions between foreign exchange authorities) and considering the case of a current account deficit. In this case, if intermediate transactions are excluded, the balance of payments becomes the difference between the value of the country's output (its national income) and its total expenditure, i.e.

$$B = Y - E.$$

To facilitate analysis by avoiding certain complications associated with the possibility of changes in the domestic price level, income and expenditure are conceived of as being valued in units of domestic output. A deficit then consists in an excess of real expenditure over real income, and the problem of correcting a deficit is to bring real national income (output) and real national expenditure into equality.

This formulation suggests that policies for correcting current-account deficits can be classified broadly into two types: those which aim at (or rely on) increasing output, and those which aim at reducing expenditure. The distinction must, of course, relate to the initial impact of the policy, since income and expenditure are interdependent: expenditure depends on and varies with income, and income depends on and varies with expenditure (because part of expenditure is devoted to home-produced goods). Consequently any change in either income or expenditure will initiate multiplier changes in both. It can, however, readily be shown that, so long as an increase in income induces a smaller change in aggregate expenditure, the multiplier repercussions will not be large enough to offset the impact effect of a change, so that an impact increase in output or decrease in expenditure will always improve the balance on current account.[12]

[11] Whether this is so depends on the use to which the finance provided by the deficit is put, which involves comparison with what would have happened in the absence of the deficit. If the deficit finances additional investment in productive domestic capital or income-yielding foreign assets the net effect on the capital position may be favourable; if it finances additional consumption it is likely to be unfavourable, though even additional consumption may sometimes increase productive capacity.

[12] Differentiating the equation in the text, we obtain $dB = (1 - e)dY + dE$, where e is the marginal propensity to spend out of income, dY is the total *increase*

The distinction between output-increasing and expenditure-reducing policies may usefully be put in another way. Since output is governed by the demand for it, a change in output can only be brought about by a change in the demand for it; a policy of increasing domestic output can only be effected by operating on expenditure (either foreign or domestic) on that output. Given the level of expenditure, this in turn involves effecting a switch of expenditure (by residents and foreigners) from foreign output to domestic output. The distinction between output-increasing and expenditure-decreasing policies, which rests on the *effects* of the policies, may therefore be replaced by a distinction between expenditure-switching policies and expenditure-reducing policies, which rests on the *method* by which the effects are achieved.

A policy of expenditure-reduction may be applied through a variety of means—monetary restriction, budgetary policy, or even a sufficiently comprehensive battery of direct controls. Since any such policy will tend to reduce income and employment, it will have an additional attraction if the country is suffering from inflationary pressure as well as a balance-of-payments deficit, but a corresponding disadvantage if the country is suffering from unemployment. Moreover, since the impact reduction in expenditure and the total reduction in income and output required to correct a given deficit are larger the larger the proportion of the expenditure reduction falling on home-produced goods, and since different methods of expenditure-reduction may differ in this respect, the choice between alternative methods may depend on the inflationary-deflationary situation of the economy. Finally, since the accompanying reduction in income

in output (including multiplier effects) and dE is the autonomous *decrease* in expenditure. If multiplier effects through foreign incomes are ignored,

$$dY = \frac{1}{1-e(1-m)} \, dA,$$

where dA is an autonomous change in demand for domestic output and m is the proportion of marginal expenditure leaking into imports. Splitting dA into two components, dO for output-increasing policies and $-hdE$ for expenditure-reducing policies (where h is the proportion of expenditure reduction falling on domestic output), gives the result

$$dB = \frac{1-e}{1-e+em} \, dO + \left(1 - \frac{(1-e)h}{1-e+em}\right) dE.$$

Hence either an output-increasing or an expenditure-reducing policy will improve the balance, so long as e is less than unity. (Alexander has argued that since e includes induced investment it may well exceed unity; this possibility is ignored in the argument of the text). Expenditure reduction will in fact improve the balance so long as multiplier stability is present.

may lead to some reduction in the domestic price level, and/or a greater eagerness of domestic producers to compete with foreign producers both at home and abroad, expenditure-reducing policies may have incidental expenditure-switching effects.

Expenditure-switching policies may be divided into two types, according to whether the policy instrument employed is general or selective: devaluation (which may be taken to include the case of a deflation-induced reduction of the domestic price level under fixed exchange rates), and trade controls (including both tariffs and subsidies and quantitative restrictions). Devaluation aims at switching both domestic and foreign expenditure towards domestic output; controls are usually imposed on imports, and aim at (or have the effect of) switching domestic expenditure away from imports towards home goods, though sometimes they are used to stimulate exports and aim at switching foreigners' expenditure towards domestic output.

Both types of expenditure-switching policy may have direct impact-effects on residents' expenditure. Devaluation may result in increased expenditure from the initial income level, through the so-called 'terms-of-trade effect' of an adverse terms-of-trade movement in reducing real income and therefore the proportion of income saved. Trade controls will tend to have the same effect, *via* the reduction in real income resulting from constriction of freedom of choice.[13] In addition, trade controls must alter the real expenditure corresponding to the initial output level if they take the form of import duties or export subsidies uncompensated by other fiscal changes; this case should, however, be classed as a combined policy of expendi-

---

[13] These arguments conflict with the assumption, more frequently made in connection with trade controls than with devaluation, that the public will consume less because it cannot obtain the goods it prefers as readily as before. That assumption may well be valid in the case of a policy expected to be applied for a short period only, after which goods will become as available as before, or in the analysis of the short run during which the economy is adjusting to the change in policy; but it is invalid in the present context of flow disequilibrium, since it overlooks the effect of the policy change in reducing the future value of savings and hence the incentive to save. An example of this type of faulty reasoning is the assertion sometimes made that quantitative import restriction is particularly effective in under-developed countries because their economic structure allows little possibility of substitution for imported goods in either production or consumption.

One qualification to the argument of the text, which also applies to the final sentence of the paragraph, is that if the goods towards which domestic expenditure is switched are more heavily taxed than those from which expenditure is diverted (a type of complication which is ignored in the general argument of the text), real expenditure may fall rather than rise.

ture-change (unfavourable in the case of the export subsidy) and expenditure-switch.

Whether general or selective in nature, an expenditure-switching policy seeks to correct a deficit by switching demand away from foreign towards domestic goods; and it depends for success not only on switching demand in the right direction, but also on the capacity of the economy to make available the extra output required to satisfy the additional demand. Such policies therefore pose two problems for economic analysis: the conditions required for expenditure to be switched in the desired direction, and the source of the additional output required to meet the additional demand.

As to the first question, the possibilities of failure for both devaluation and controls have been investigated at length by international trade theorists, and require only summary treatment here.[14] Export promotion will divert foreign expenditure away from the country's output if the foreign demand is inelastic, while import restriction will divert domestic expenditure abroad if demand for imports is inelastic and the technique of restriction allows the foreigner the benefit of the increased value of imports to domestic consumers. Devaluation has the partial effect of diverting domestic expenditure abroad, *via* the increased cost of the initial volume of imports, and this adverse switch will not be offset by the favourable effect of substitution of domestic for foreign goods at home and abroad, if import demand elasticities average less than one half.

While the elasticity requirement for successful devaluation just cited is familiar, the approach developed in this paper throws additional light on what non-fulfilment of the requirement implies. From the equation $B = Y - E$, it is clear that, if direct effects on expenditure from the initial income level are neglected, devaluation can worsen the balance only if it reduces total world demand for the country's output. This implies that the country's output is in a sense a 'Giffen case' in world consumption; and that the market for at least one of the commodities it produces is in unstable equilibrium.[15] Neither of these ways of stating the conditions for exchange instability makes the possibility of instability as plausible *a priori* as their

[14] Impact effects on the level of expenditure from a given income level of the type discussed in the next-but-one paragraph preceding this one are ignored in this paragraph.

[15] *Cf.* E. V. Morgan, 'The Theory of Flexible Exchange Rates', *American Economic Review*, XLV, no. 3, June 1955, 279–95. Morgan's statement (285) that instability requires 'very strong and perverse income effects' is fallacious— all that is strictly necessary is a preference in each country for home-produced goods.

equivalent, reached through sectoral analysis, in terms of elasticities of import demand.

The second, and more interesting, analytical problem relates to the source of the additional domestic output required to satisfy the demand for it created by the expenditure-switching policy. Here it is necessary to distinguish two cases, that in which the economy is under-employed and that in which it is fully employed, for both the relevant technique of analysis and the factors on which the outcome of the policy depend differ between the two.

If the economy has unemployed resources available, the additional output required to meet the additional demand can be provided by the re-absorption of these resources into employment: in this case the switch policy has the additional attraction of increasing employment and income. The increase in domestic output may tend to raise the domestic price level, through the operation of increasing marginal real costs of production, and conversely the foreign price level may tend to fall, thus partially counteracting the initial effects of the switch policy; but such repercussions can legitimately be analysed in terms of elasticity concepts, since under-employment implies that additional factors are available at the ruling price.

If the economy is already fully employed, however, the additional output required cannot be provided by increasing production; it can only be provided through a reduction in the previous level of real expenditure.[16] This reduction may be brought about either by a deliberate expenditure-reducing policy introduced along with the switch policy, or by the inflationary consequences of the switch policy itself in the assumed full-employment conditions.[17]

If the increased output is provided by a deliberate expenditure-reducing policy, the nature of this policy will obviously influence the effects of the expenditure-switching policy, since the composition of the output it releases may be more or less substitutable for foreign output in world demand. Thus, for example, an expenditure-reducing policy which reduces domestic demand for imports and

---

[16] Recognition of this point may be regarded as the fundamental contribution of the absorption approach, though none of the authors cited seems to have appreciated all its implications: Meade, for example, analyses the case on the assumption that an appropriate expenditure-reducing policy is in effect, without examining the interdependence between the two policies or the alternative of inflation, while Alexander does not recognize that the effects of inflation on absorption could be achieved by policy.

[17] For analytical simplicity, both the possibility of increased production through 'over-full employment' and of direct expenditure-reducing effects of a switch policy (discussed earlier in this chapter) are ignored here.

exportable goods will be more favourable to expenditure-switching than one which reduces domestic demand for non-traded goods. The analysis of the effects of an expenditure-switching policy supported by an expenditure-reducing policy must therefore comprise the effects of the latter in determining the composition of the productive capacity available to meet the increased demand created by the former, as well as the elasticity relations which govern the effects of the interaction of increased demand with increased production capacity on the prices and volumes of goods traded.

If the expenditure-switching policy is not accompanied by an expenditure-reducing policy, its effect will be to create an inflationary excess of aggregate demand over supply, leading to price increases tending to counteract the policy's expenditure-switching effects. Inflation, however, may work towards curing the deficit, through various effects tending to reduce the level of real expenditure from the full employment level of output. These effects, which are familiar and have been analysed in detail by Alexander, include the effect of high marginal tax rates in increasing the proportion of real income absorbed by taxation as wages and prices rise, the possibility of a swing to profits increasing the proportion of income saved, and the effect of rising prices in reducing the real purchasing power of cash and government bonds held by the public, so reducing their wealth and propensity to consume. All of these effects, it may be noted, depend on particular asymmetries in the reactions of the sectors affected to the redistributive effects of inflation on real income or wealth, which may not in fact be present. The important point, however, is that these factors, on which the success of an expenditure-switching policy depends in this case, are monetary factors, and that the analysis required employs monetary concepts rather than elasticity concepts. As in the previous case, the elasticity factors are subordinate to the factors governing the reduction in aggregate real expenditure, in determining the consequences of the expenditure-switching policy for the balance of payments.

The argument of the previous paragraph—that in full employment conditions the success of expenditure-switching policies depends mainly on the effectiveness of the consequent inflation in reducing real expenditure—helps to explain both the prevalence of scepticism about, and hostility towards, exchange rate adjustment as a means of curing balance-of-payments disequilibria, and the fact that historical experience can be adduced in support of the proposition that devaluation is a doubtful remedy. The argument does not, however, support the conclusion frequently drawn from the analysis of devaluation in these circumstances, that import restrictions are to be preferred; this is a *non sequitur*, since import restrictions are equally an expenditure-switching policy. Rather, the proper conclusion is that expenditure-switching policies are inappropriate to full employment conditions, except when used in conjunction with an expenditure-reducing policy as a means of correcting the employment-reducing effects of the latter.

But what of the choice between devaluation and selective trade controls, to which reference has just been made? So far, it has not been necessary to distinguish between them, since from the point of view of the balance of payments both can be treated as expenditure-switching policies. It is from the point of view of economic welfare that they differ; and the arguments on their relative merits have nothing to do with the state of the balance of payments, except that if controls are preferable a deficit may offer an opportunity for introducing them with less risk of foreign retaliation than if trade were balanced.

The welfare arguments for controls on a country's international trade may be divided into two groups, those centring on controls as a means of influencing the internal distribution of real income, by discouraging imports consumed by the rich and encouraging those consumed by the poor, and those centring on controls as a means of increasing the country's gains from trade through exploiting its monopoly/monopsony power in foreign markets. The former are of doubtful validity, both because the ethics of disguising a real income policy as a trade policy are suspect, and because both the efficiency and the effectiveness of trade controls as instruments for governing real income distribution are dubious. The latter are valid, to the extent that the country has powers to exploit the foreigner and can use them without provoking sufficient retaliation to nullify the gains.

This is the familiar optimum tariff argument. Its application to balance-of-payments policy depends on the level of trade restrictions already in force, as compared with the optimum level of restrictions.[18] If an expenditure-switching policy is required to correct a deficit, and the level of trade restrictions is below the optimum, restriction[19]

[18] See S. Alexander, 'Devaluation versus Import Restriction as an Instrument for Improving Foreign Trade Balance', *International Monetary Fund Staff Papers*, I, no. 3, April 1951, 379–96, for a lucid and pioneering exposition of this principle.

[19] Generally, optimum trade restriction entails restriction of both imports and exports; but if the country's currency is over-valued it may imply subsidization of some or even all exports, and if the currency is under-valued it may imply subsidization of some or even all imports. (These conclusions follow from the fact that a devaluation is equivalent to an all-round export subsidy and import duty).

is preferable to devaluation until the optimum level is reached; in the opposite case, devaluation is preferable. But it is the relation of actual to optimum restrictions, and not the state of the trade balance, which determines whether restriction is desirable or not.

This concludes the analysis of alternative policies for correcting a 'flow' balance-of-payments deficit on current account. To complete the analysis of 'flow' disequilibria, it would be necessary to relax the assumption that international capital movements are confined to reserve movements between foreign exchange authorities, and to consider alternative policies for correcting a deficit on current and capital account combined. The central problem in this case is to determine the level of current account surplus or deficit, capital export or import, at which economic policy should aim. This raises two further problems too difficult to pursue here: the optimum rate of accumulation of capital for the community as a whole, and the degree to which it is desirable to discriminate in favour of investment at home and against investment abroad.

In conclusion, the argument of this chapter may be summarized as follows: formulation of the balance of payments as the difference between aggregate receipts and payments, rather than receipts and payments on international account only, has two major advantages. It brings out the essentially monetary nature of a deficit, which must be accompanied by dishoarding of domestic money or credit creation; and it relates the deficit to the operation of the economy as a whole. A deficit may reflect a 'stock' decision or a 'flow' decision by the community. The conditions which make a 'stock' deficit a policy problem indicate the use of direct control methods as against price system methods of correction. Policies for dealing with 'flow' deficits on current account may be divided into expenditure-reducing and expenditure-switching policies; in full employment conditions the latter must be supported by the former, or rely on inflation for their effect, which in either case cannot be analysed adequately in terms of elasticities. When capital account transactions are introduced into the analysis, the choice between policy alternatives requires reference to growth considerations not readily susceptible to economic analysis.

CHAPTER VII

The Transfer Problem and Exchange Stability[*][1]

THE transfer problem bulks large in the literature of international trade theory, both because international economic relations have abounded in transfer problems of various kinds and because the problem offers an attractive opportunity for the application of new theoretical techniques. My purpose here is not to survey the literature,[2] but to offer a straightforward and (it is hoped) simplified exposition of the theory of transfers in modern terms, based largely on recent literature but extending and unifying it in certain respects. In addition, it will be argued that transfer theory has a wider application than might appear at first sight and that, in particular, it can be applied directly to the problem of exchange stability.

In the context of modern international trade theory, the transfer problem can be posed in either of two ways—as a *real* problem or as a *monetary* problem. More precisely, it can be approached either on the classical assumption that the economic system works so as to maintain equality between income and expenditure at the level corresponding to full employment of resources in each country, or on the Keynesian assumption that the economy of each country is characterized by a perfectly elastic supply of labour and commodities at a fixed wage and price level,[3] so that output and income

---

[*] *The Journal of Political Economy*, LXIV, no. 3, June 1956, 212–25. The argument has been extended to include the application of transfer theory to trade intervention.

[1] This chapter was drafted during my tenure of a visiting professorship at Northwestern University; it has benefited greatly, though perhaps insufficiently, from criticisms of colleagues there and elsewhere in the United States and the United Kingdom.

[2] For such surveys see Jacob Viner, *Studies in the Theory of International Trade* (New York, 1937), chap. vi; Paul A. Samuelson, 'The Transfer Problem and Transport Costs', *Economic Journal*, LXII, no. 246, June 1952, 278–304, and LXIV, no. 254, June 1954, 264–89; and Gottfried Haberler, *A Survey of International Trade Theory* (Princeton, 1955).

[3] It is possible, but unnecessarily complicating, to assume a perfectly elastic supply of labour at a fixed money wage and an imperfectly elastic supply of output, as Keynes did in the *General Theory*. An analysis of this case may be

M

are determined by aggregate effective demand. In this paper the problem will be discussed from both approaches.

On either set of assumptions, classical or Keynesian, the transfer problem can be separated into two problems for analysis. The first is whether the process by which the transfer is financed in the transferor country and disposed of in the transferee will affect each country's demand for imports (at unchanged prices) sufficiently to create the trade surplus and deficit necessary to effect the transfer. The financing and disposal of the transfer will tend to reduce the transferor's demand for goods and increase the transferee's demand for goods; both effects will tend to improve the balance of trade of the transferor and worsen that of the transferee, and the changes may fall short of, or exceed, the amount of the transfer. Unless the changes in trade balances are exactly equal to the amount of the transfer, there will remain a balance-of-payments disequilibrium which must be corrected by some adjustment mechanism. In the classical model the adjustment mechanism is assumed to be a change in the terms of trade of the countries, brought about by price deflation and inflation;[4] in the Keynesian model the adjustment mechanism may be assumed to be either deflation and inflation of effective demand or a terms-of-trade change brought about by devaluation. In either model an alternative method of adjustment would be the tightening and relaxation of trade restrictions.

The second part of the transfer problem is whether the adjustment mechanism will be effective in restoring equilibrium. This problem really raises two subsidiary questions, one of direction and one of magnitude of influence. Taking the classical mechanism of a change in the terms of trade as an example, there is, first, the question whether a small deterioration in a country's terms of trade will tend to improve or to worsen its trade balance—the stability problem. Second, on the assumption that the balance would be improved by a small deterioration in the terms of trade, there is the question whether the trade balance can be improved sufficiently by this means to achieve a surplus of a given size. The same two questions arise with respect to the Keynesian mechanism of demand deflation and inflation, and also with respect to the use of trade controls of various kinds. It is obvious that the second question is an empirical one on

found in James E. Meade, *The Balance of Payments* (London, 1951), and its *Mathematical Supplement*.

[4] Strictly speaking, what must change is the double-factoral rather than the commodity terms of trade, since with non-traded goods the commodity terms of trade can change in either direction as the price level changes.

which theory can render little assistance, since it would always be possible to specify a surplus too large to be achieved by any method of adjustment. The question of direction of effect is, however, susceptible of theoretical analysis, and conditions for the mechanism to work in the right direction can be established.

To summarize, the transfer problem has two theoretical facets: whether the transfer will be undereffected or overeffected as a consequence of the process by which it is financed and disposed of (that is, the direction in which the adjustment mechanism will be required to operate) and whether the adjustment mechanism will operate in the direction of restoring equilibrium. This chapter is concerned mainly with the first of these problems, and the argument will assume that the adjustment mechanism will suffice. A large part of the answer to the second problem will, however, be provided by applying the results of the argument on the first problem to the general problem of exchange stability, and to the problem of the effect of various kinds of governmental intervention in trade on the trade balance.

The argument which follows makes the usual simplifying assumptions, namely, that the world consists of two countries, A and B, producing two commodities or commodity bundles, A-goods and B-goods, these being the commodities exported by A and B, respectively. It is assumed that A is the transferor and B the transferee.

I. THE CLASSICAL TRANSFER PROBLEM[5]

On classical assumptions, the question whether the transfer would be undereffected or overeffected at constant prices is extremely simple to deal with, since the assumption of automatic full employment implies that the transfer must be financed and disposed of in such a way as to reduce aggregate expenditure by the transferor and increase aggregate expenditure by the transferee by the amount of the transfer and thus rules out any multiplier effects. The transferor's balance of trade is improved both by the reduction in its expenditure on imports and by the increase in the transferee's demand for its exports. The total improvement, expressed as a proportion of the transfer, will be equal to the sum of the proportions

[5] This section reproduces, in a somewhat simpler form, the argument of my note, 'The Transfer Problem: A Note on Criteria for Changes in the Terms of Trade', *Economica*, N.S., XXII, no. 86, May 1955, 113–21. That note and some of the additional argument of the present section owe much to Samuelson's two masterly *Economic Journal* articles cited in n. 2.

of the expenditure changes in the two countries which fall on imports—more precisely, the sum of the proportions of the expenditure changes by which the receipts of the exporting country change. The transfer will be undereffected or overeffected, and the terms of trade will be required to change against, or in favour of, the transferor, according to whether the sum of these proportions is less or greater than unity. This general rule may be translated into several equivalent forms, by use of the fact that the proportion of the expenditure change which does not fall on imports must fall on exportable goods. The most convenient of these forms to work with is that the transfer will be undereffected or overeffected according to whether the sum of the proportions of expenditure change falling on the countries' export goods is greater or less than unity.

This rule, however, does not establish anything very interesting (beyond the demonstration that either result is possible), since nothing has been said about what determines the proportions of expenditure change. In general, these would depend on the nature of the transfer and the assumed conditions of international trade; as there is no reason for identifying the effects of the financing and disposal of a transfer with the effects of any other kind of economic change, nothing more can, in strictest generality, be said. Nevertheless, it is customary in the literature (and defensible in many cases) to identify the effects of the transfer on expenditure with those of an income tax and a subsidy. On this assumption the proportions of expenditure change can be related to the countries' marginal propensities to spend on exportables or importables, the precise relation depending on the assumed conditions of international trade. Three cases may be distinguished.

(a) Free Trade, No Transport Costs

In this case all expenditure on imports constitutes receipts for the exporting country, and the proportions of expenditure change are equal to the marginal propensities to spend. The transfer criterion is therefore whether the sum of the marginal propensities to spend on exportables is greater or less than unity.

(b) Tariffs, No Transport Costs

Tariffs introduce a difference between the price paid by residents of a country for imports and the receipts of the foreign exporters. In conformity with classical assumptions, the tariff proceeds cannot be allowed to disappear from circulation but must be assumed to be spent by someone. The simplest assumption is that they are re-distributed as an income subsidy and spent like any other increment of income, in which case part of the initial change in expenditure on imports associated with the transfer will wind up as a change in expenditure on exportables (out of redistributed tax proceeds). Consequently, the proportions of expenditure change falling on exportables will be larger than the marginal propensities to spend on exportables, and the transfer criterion is accordingly whether the sum of the marginal propensities to spend on exportables is greater or less than a critical value which will be less than unity.[6]

(c) Transport Costs, No Tariffs

In this case also there will be a difference between the price paid by residents for imports and the price received by the exporters, the difference representing the transport costs. To the extent that transport of exports utilizes the exported good, the transport costs will constitute receipts for the exporting country. In the extreme case where transport utilizes only the exported good, all expenditure on imports will be (direct, or indirect) receipts for the exporting country, the proportions of expenditure change will be equal to the marginal propensities to spend, and the transfer criterion will be the same as in the no-impediments case [(a) above]. But to the extent that transport utilizes the exportable good of the importing country,

[6] Let C and M be the marginal propensities to spend on exportables and imports and t be the proportion of the final price of imports taken in taxes. Then total expenditure at market prices will change by

$$1 + tM + (tM)^2 + \ldots = \frac{1}{1 - tM}$$

times the amount of the transfer, and the proportion of the transfer by which expenditure on exportables changes will be

$$\frac{C}{1 - tM} = \left(1 + \frac{tM}{1 - tM}\right)C.$$

Since the transfer will be undereffected or overeffected according to whether the sum of these proportions is greater or less than unity, i.e. according to whether

$$\left(1 + \frac{t_a M_a}{1 - t_a M_a}\right)C_a + \left(1 + \frac{t_b M_b}{1 - t_b M_b}\right)C_b \gtrless 1,$$

the critical value of the transfer criterion will be

$$C_a + C_b = 1 - \frac{t_a M_a C_a}{1 - t_a M_a} - \frac{t_b M_b C_b}{1 - t_b M_b}.$$

The right-hand side of this expression must be less than unity, since t, M, and C are all positive fractions.

transport costs constitute an indirect demand for that good; consequently, the proportions of expenditure change falling on exportables will be larger than the (direct) marginal propensities to spend on exportables, and the critical value for the transfer criterion will be something less than unity, as in the previous case.[7]

The transfer criteria derived in the three cases just examined suggest a reference to a question which has concerned many writers on the transfer problem, namely, whether, even though the classical proposition that the terms of trade *must* turn against the transferring country is erroneous, there nonetheless remains a presumption in favour of this conclusion. Fundamentally, this is a meaningless question, since only ignorance can come from ignorance and no satisfactory basis exists for assessing the likely magnitudes of the marginal propensities to spend which enter into the criteria, short of measuring them in particular cases, when no question of presumption would arise.[8] An argument from 'equal ignorance' might, however, be drawn on the following lines: given only that the sum of the marginal propensities to spend on imports and exportables is unity, equal ignorance would suggest no presumption that the average marginal propensity to spend on exportables is either greater or less than $\frac{1}{2}$. Thus in the no-impediments case there would be no presumption in favour of the classical conclusion; but there would be such a presumption in the cases of tariffs and of

---

[7] Let k be the proportion of the price of imports representing transport cost incurred in the importer's exportable commodity; then the proportion of the transfer by which expenditure on exportables changes is $C + kM$, and the critical value of the transfer criterion is

$$1 - k_a M_a - k_b M_b,$$

which is less than unity.

[8] Statistical estimates of marginal propensities to import in the interwar period (1924–38) have produced results for some countries well above the average of $\frac{1}{2}$ required by the criteria. For example, T. C. Chang (*Cyclical Movements in the Balance of Payments* [Cambridge, 1951], 37) found six agricultural countries with marginal propensities to import ranging from 0·52 to 0·73, though in all but one case (Denmark, 0·54) the estimates are based on relatively short series. More recently J. J. Polak (*An International Economic System* [London, 1954], 'Summary of Results', opposite 156) has obtained the following estimates: for the whole period, Denmark, 0·73; Norway, 0·67; for the 1920's Finland, 0·93; New Zealand, 0·65; Indonesia, 0·62; Union of South Africa, 0·57. While these estimates do not correspond very precisely with the theoretical concepts employed here (imports generally being valued c.i.f., which excludes tariffs but may include invisible receipts of the exporting country) and their application is complicated by the presence of many countries and many commodities, they are not inconsistent with the possibility that in some cases a transfer might be over-effected.

transport costs incurred in the exportable good of the importing country, since in these cases the transfer would be undereffected if the average marginal propensity to spend on exportables were exactly $\frac{1}{2}$. In the latter case the presumption would be reinforced by the fact that, if these transport costs absorbed half the delivered price of imports on the average, the transfer would necessarily be undereffected for any positive values of the marginal propensities to spend on exportables.[9]

A less controversial, more 'positive', approach to the classical presumption is to examine what it implies about the countries involved in the transfer. For this purpose it is convenient to use an alternative form of the transfer criterion, namely, that the transfer will be undereffected if the extra physical quantity of A-goods purchased (directly or indirectly) out of an increase in income in A is greater than it is in B;[10] that is, the transfer will be undereffected if the countries are biased (at the margin) toward the purchase of their exportables.

In the free-trade, no-transport-cost case the prices facing consumers are the same in both countries. Consequently, the classical presumption requires either that the countries differ in tastes and are biased toward consumption of their exportables or that, tastes being identical, the goods differ in degree of necessity and the country with the higher income per head produces the more 'luxurious' good for export. In the case of tariffs and of transport costs the relative prices facing consumers differ, each commodity being relatively cheaper in the exporting than in the importing country. Consequently, if the economies were on identical consumption indifference curves before the transfer, each would have the marginal bias *in direct consumption* toward the purchase of its exportable commodity required by the classical presumption. To put it another way, so far as *direct* consumption is concerned, tastes must be biased

[9] On the assumption that $k_a + k_b = 1$, the criterion of n. 7 becomes $k_a C_a + k_b C_b$, which is necessarily less than $C_a + C_b$.

[10] One formulation of the rule developed in the first paragraph of this section is that the transfer will be undereffected or overeffected according to whether the proportion of expenditure change in the transferor which falls on exportables is greater or less than the proportion of expenditure change in the transferee which falls on the transferor's exportables. Since the latter deducts tariffs and transport costs from the delivered price and adds back in transport cost incurred in the exported good, which amounts to measurement at factor cost in the transferor, deflation by factor cost gives the criterion stated in the text. Further, it follows that, since the sum of the proportions of expenditure change measured in this way must equal unity for each country, the condition respecting A-goods, as stated previously, implies the reverse for B-goods.

toward imported goods or the country with the higher income per head must produce the more necessary commodity if the classical presumption is to be invalid. But indirect consumption must also be considered. In the case of tariffs without transport costs, indirect consumption out of tariff proceeds is assumed to behave in the same way as direct consumption, leaving the foregoing argument unaffected. In the case of transport costs and free trade, the bias toward direct consumption of exportables induced by the difference in prices is reinforced if transport costs are incurred entirely in the exportable good of the importing country and mitigated—perhaps outweighed—if transport costs are incurred entirely in the imported good. The effects of transport costs incurred in both goods are too complex to be analysed here, though analogy with the tariff case indicates that, in the case of identical pretransfer indifference curves, a necessary condition for invalidation of the classical presumption is that transport is more 'import-intensive' than is marginal consumption expenditure in the importing country.

Before concluding this section, it is appropriate to consider briefly the effects of relaxing some of the simplifying assumptions. The possibility of varying home production of the imported good makes no difference, since this is conditional on the price ratio between the goods changing, which in turn depends on the criteria derived previously. The introduction of non-traded goods does alter the criteria, since changes in demand for such goods must be classed either as changes in (virtual) demand for exportables or as changes in (virtual) demand for imports, according to whether they are more substitutable in production and consumption for one or the other.[11] In both these cases, however, the direction of change of the commodity terms of trade is not uniquely determined by whether the transfer is undereffected or overeffected at constant prices. The introduction of more countries also alters the criterion, since the balances of payments of the two countries are no longer equal and opposite in sign. From the transferor's point of view, the transfer will be undereffected or overeffected (at pretransfer prices) according to whether the sum of the proportions of the transfer by which the transferor's expenditure on imports is reduced, and the transferee's expenditure *on the transferor's exports* (not on imports in general) is less or greater than unity. Again, the movement of the commodity

[11] If it can be assumed that non-traded goods are substitutes for exports, this strengthens the classical presumption that the terms of trade turn against the transferor; but contrary cases are conceivable (Samuelson, loc. cit., II, 288–9).

terms of trade is not decided by whether the transfer is undereffected or overeffected.

II. THE KEYNESIAN TRANSFER PROBLEM[12]

For the analysis of the transfer problem in Keynesian terms, it is assumed that output in each country is in perfectly elastic supply at a fixed domestic-currency price level, so that output, income, and employment are determined by the aggregate demand for output. It is also assumed that each country fixes its exchange rate and level of interest rates by appropriate monetary action, though its policy in this respect may change in the event of a continuing balance-of-payments disequilibrium, and fhat, apart from accommodating financial transactions between monetary authorities, international capital movements are independent of the levels of national incomes.

These assumptions permit the derivation of multiplier equations relating changes in the national incomes of the countries and in the balance of payments between them to the various autonomous changes in demands for goods and transfers which may occur. The equations may be written as follows:

$$\text{(1a)} \qquad Y_a = I_a + c_a Y_a + M_b + m_b Y_b,$$

$$\text{(1b)} \qquad Y_b = I_b + c_b Y_b + M_a + m_a Y_a,$$

$$\text{(1c)} \qquad B_a = M_b + m_b Y_b - M_a - m_a Y_a - T,$$

where Y_a, Y_b, and B_a are the total changes in the two countries' national incomes and in country A's balance of payments (all measured in international currency units); I_a and I_b are autonomous changes in the countries' demands for their own outputs; M_a and M_b are autonomous changes in their demands for each other's outputs; T is an autonomous change in capital movements from A to B; c_a and c_b are the marginal propensities to spend on the purchase of domestic output; and m_a and m_b are the marginal propensities to spend on imports. It is assumed in what follows that all marginal propensities, including the marginal propensities to save (represented below by s_a and s_b) are positive, an assumption which suffices to guarantee stability of the system. It should also be remarked that while the system is set up in the symbols of a simple Keynesian system (implying the absence of government, business, and transport

---

[12] This section enlarges on my note, 'The Reparations Problem: A Correction', *Economic Journal*, LXIII, no. 251, September 1953, 724–5.

sectors and the utilization of goods only for direct consumption), it can be extended simply by redefinition of symbols to represent aspects of more complicated economic systems, such as the presence of direct and indirect taxes (other than export duties, which would require modification of the balance-of-payments equation), the dependence of government and business expenditure on taxation and sales receipts, and the use of domestic and imported goods in the production process.[13]

The transfer problem in the Keynesian case differs from that in the classical (real) case in two respects. First, there is no reason to assume that the process of financing and disposal of the transfer leads to changes in aggregate expenditure in the two countries equal to the amount of the transfer—the funds may come out of dissaving or go into saving. Second, any changes in expenditure brought about by the financing and disposal of the transfer will have multiplier repercussions on the balance of trade between the countries. The problem in this case is therefore whether, when all multiplier effects have been taken into account, the changes in demands for goods which result from the financing and disposal of the transfer are less or more than sufficient to improve the transferor's balance of trade by the amount of the transfer—that is, whether the transferor's balance of payments worsens or improves as a consequence of the transfer.

To analyse this problem, it is necessary merely to substitute for the various autonomous changes in demands in the multiplier

[13] Let P represent the total change in sales proceeds at market prices, I and M autonomous changes in purchases of domestic and foreign output at these prices, h the proportion of a change in sales proceeds by which purchases of domestic output are further increased, and f the proportion by which purchases of foreign output are further increased. We may define h and f to include induced governmental expenditure from tax receipts, business expenditure from undistributed profits, and purchases of output for use in the production process, as well as final consumers' expenditure from disposable income. Then the multiplier equation for A, for example, may be written $P_a = I_a + h_a P_a + M_b + f_b P_b$. But since, for small changes, the change in national income at factor cost will be some given proportion of the change in sales proceeds, $Y = kP$, the multiplier equations based on sales proceeds may be rewritten in the standard form by defining

$$c = 1 - \frac{1-h}{k}, \qquad m = \frac{f}{k},$$

and

$$s = \frac{1-h-f}{k}.$$

Consequently, it is unnecessary to assume, as is generally done, that imports are used only in final consumption, to avoid input-output complications.

equations the proportions of the transfer by which the demands for domestic and foreign goods are reduced in the transferor and increased in the transferee. In doing so, however, it is most convenient to work with the changes in demand for imports and in saving associated with the transfer, using the property that the transfer must alter the demand for home goods, the demand for imports, or the accumulation of assets through saving. Representing the changes in demand for imports and in saving directly due to the financing or disposal of the transfer, expressed as proportions of the amount transferred, by m' and s', respectively, the multiplier equations yield the following solutions for the resulting changes in incomes and country A's balance of payments:

$$(2a) \qquad Y_a = \frac{1}{s_a}(B_a + s'_a T),$$

$$(2b) \qquad Y_b = -\frac{1}{s_b}(B_a + s'_b T),$$

$$(2c) \qquad B_a = \left(m'_a + m'_b - \frac{m_a}{s_a}s'_a - \frac{m_b}{s_b}s'_b - 1\right) \times \frac{s_a s_b}{\Delta}T,$$

where $\Delta = s_a s_b + s_a m_b + s_b m_a$. From this it follows that the transfer will be undereffected or overeffected according to whether $m'_a + m'_b$ (the sum of the proportions of the transfer by which expenditure on imports is altered by the financing and disposal of the transfer) is less or greater than

$$\frac{m_a}{s_a}s'_a + \frac{m_b}{s_b}s'_b + 1$$

(1 plus the sum of the proportions of the transfer by which saving is altered—expenditure *not* changed—by the financing and disposal of the transfer, each weighted by the ratio of the marginal propensity to import to the marginal propensity to save in the country concerned).

The criterion just established, like that established earlier for the classical model, permits the transfer to be either undereffected or overeffected, according to the magnitudes of various parameters. This result is contrary to the findings of Metzler and Machlup,[14] whose analyses led to the conclusion that the transfer would neces-

[14] Lloyd A. Metzler, 'The Transfer Problem Reconsidered', *Journal of Political Economy*, L, no. 3, June 1942, 397–414, reprinted in *Readings in the Theory of International Trade* (Philadelphia, 1949); and Fritz Machlup, *International Trade and the National Income Multiplier* (Philadelphia, 1943), chap. ix.

sarily be undereffected in the case under discussion (that is, on the assumption of positive marginal propensities to save in both countries).[15] This conclusion ran contrary to the findings of the classical analysis, a point of which Metzler, in particular, made much. However, the contradiction is attributable to the adoption of special assumptions, namely, that the financing and disposal of the transfer does not directly affect the demand for imports and that it changes the demand for domestic goods either by the amount of the transfer or not at all.[16] (In terms of the present system, the m'''s were assumed to be zero, and the s'''s to be either zero or unity,[17] which, with positive marginal propensities to save, insures that the transfer cannot be effected.) If, instead of these rather unrealistic assumptions, one version of the assumption of the classical analysis is chosen—that the transfer is accompanied by equal changes in expenditure in the two countries, divided in some way between domestic goods and imports—the criterion becomes the same as that for the classical case: the transfer will be undereffected or overeffected according to whether the sum of the proportions of the transfer by which import demands are changed is less or greater than unity. This is the assumption adopted by Meade.[18] One of its consequences is that the behaviour of incomes is determined by whether the transfer is undereffected or overeffected; it is obvious that this should be so, since the assumption reproduces the classical model, with the exception that switches of demand from one country's output to the other's influence outputs instead of prices.

The Meade-classical assumption, however, like the assumption of Machlup and Metzler, is only a special case. In general, there would

---

[15] Metzler (loc. cit., *passim*) showed that the transfer would be overeffected if one country had a negative marginal propensity to save (in his analysis, a marginal propensity to invest higher than the marginal propensity to save)—a possibility allowed by the stability conditions—and if in that country the financing of the transfer altered demand for home output to the same extent. Machlup (op. cit., 181) showed that the transfer would be exactly effected if the transferor had a zero marginal propensity to save.

[16] In the case of Metzler, this description refers to the mathematical analysis. Metzler's verbal argument identifies the effects of the transfer with those of other income changes—a case discussed in the next paragraph—rather than a change in demand for domestic output. As will be shown later, the two assumptions yield the same conclusions about the effects of the transfer on the balance of payments.

[17] Machlup (op. cit., 183) allows s' in the receiving country to be positive but less than unity; he also discusses the possibility of the transfer affecting the demand for imports directly, without realizing that this might permit the transfer to be effected by the income-effects alone.

[18] Op. cit., *passim*.

seem to be less reason in a Keynesian model than in the classical model for identifying the direct effects of the transfer on demand with those of any other economic change. But if the usual assumption of the classical analysis is chosen—that the transfer affects demands in the same way as any other change in income—with the difference that it also affects saving (that is, $m' = m$ and $s' = s$), the transfer cannot be effected if the marginal propensities to save are positive,[19] since the equation for the change in the transferor's balance of payments reduces to

$$(3) \qquad\qquad B_a = -\frac{s_a s_b}{\Delta} T.$$

For this particular case, it is obviously unnecessary to investigate the influence of tariffs and transport costs, since the effects of the transfer on the balance of payments are unambiguous, while the 'classical presumption' is a certainty. In the general case, analysis of these problems is possible, but too cumbersome to be worth pursuing here.

In concluding this section, it would be appropriate to comment on a paradox suggested to the writer by P. A. Samuelson, namely why, when the transfer is treated as an income change, the Keynesian analysis gives a definitely negative answer, whereas in the classical case the answer depends on the marginal propensities to buy foreign goods. To begin with, it may be pointed out that the transfer criterion for the Keynesian case can be made precisely the same as that for

[19] The results on this assumption are the same as on the Machlup-Metzler assumption, so far as the balance of payments is concerned, though the effects on income are different. This is not surprising, since the effects of the transfer in this case are the same as if the transfer financing led to an equal change in the demand for domestic output in each country, except that the first round of income change in each is wiped out. The conclusion that the transfer cannot be effected in this case can be generalized to any number of countries (see my article 'A Simplification of Multi-country Multiplier Theory', *Canadian Journal of Economics and Political Science*, XXII, no. 2, May 1956, 244–6, chap. VIII below).

The econometric model of the world economy constructed by H. Neisser and F. Modigliani (*National Incomes and International Trade* [Urbana, 1953]) can be applied to throw some statistical light on the extent to which the transfer might be undereffected in practical cases. Their Table 15 (93), which calculates the effects of income changes on trade balances in 1928, allowing for all repercussions on national incomes, implies that a transfer between England and Germany would improve one country's trade balance and worsen the other's by about 32 per cent of the amount transferred, while a transfer between the United Kingdom and the United States would alter the former's trade balance by about 30 per cent, and the latter's by only about $11\frac{1}{2}$ per cent, of the amount transferred.

the classical case, by re-defining the 'proportion of the transfer by which expenditure on imports changes' to allow for the indirect effect on import demand of the failure of the transfer to be fully reflected in a change in expenditure. This effect is represented in equation (2c) by the deduction from the direct effects of the transfer on import expenditure m' of the quantities $\dfrac{m}{s}s'$, which stand for the effects on import demand of the changes in income that would result from the missing changes in expenditure, if trade were kept balanced so that the closed-economy multipliers $\left(\dfrac{1}{s}\right)$ applied. If the terms $m' - \dfrac{m}{s}s'$ are taken as the proportions of the transfer by which expenditure on imports changes, then the Keynesian transfer criterion is the same as the classical, namely whether the sum of these proportions is greater or less than one. But where the transfer is treated as an income change, it so happens that the indirect effect exactly offsets the direct effect of the transfer on import demand, so that the total effect is zero.

There is in the Keynesian analysis, however, a more fruitful analogue to the 'sum of the proportions of expenditure changes falling on imports' criterion of classical analysis, which runs in terms of the proportions in which changes in saving are divided between holdings of domestic and of foreign assets; and the definiteness of the Keynesian answer turns out to be a consequence of the assumption stated at the beginning of this section, that international capital movements are independent of the levels of national incomes, which implies that all changes in saving consequent on the transfer go into or come out of domestic assets. If this assumption is relaxed to permit changes in saving to be divided between domestic and foreign assets, as they would be on the other assumptions of the model, the balance of payments multiplier equations presented above become:

$(1c)'\quad B_a = M_b + (m_b + k_b s_b)Y_b - M_a - (m_a + k_a s_a)Y_a$
$$+ (k_a' s_a' + k_b' s_b' - 1)T,$$

$(2c)'\quad B_a = (m_a' + m_b' - \dfrac{m_a}{s_a}s_a' - \dfrac{m_b}{s_b}s_b' - 1)(1 - k_a - k_b)$
$$\times \frac{s_a s_b}{\Delta}T + (k_a' - k_a)s_a' T + (k_b' - k_b)s_b' T,$$

$(3)'\quad B_a = (k_a + k_b - 1)\dfrac{s_a s_b}{\Delta}T,$

where k represents the proportion of a change in saving which is devoted to the purchase of foreign assets [and, in (3)$'$, $k = k'$]. It follows from (3)$'$ that, if the transfer is treated as an income change, it will be undereffected or overeffected according as the sum of what may be described as 'the marginal foreign investment ratios' is less or greater than unity; in other words, the transfer will be undereffected if there is a bias (at the margin) in each country towards investment in domestic assets—such as would result from additional ignorance and uncertainty about foreign conditions, or from exchange control, but not from difference in yields as such— and vice versa. In the more general case represented by (2c)$'$, if (as seems a reasonable simplification) the possibility of differences between the marginal foreign investment ratios applying to the initial and the induced effects of the transfer on savings is ignored, the transfer will be undereffected unless *either* the criterion discussed in earlier paragraphs is satisfied (for which a necessary but not sufficient condition is a marginal bias towards expenditure of transfer finance on foreign goods) *or* there is a marginal bias towards the purchase of foreign assets—but not if both occur together. More simply, unless there is some sort of marginal bias in the division of savings between domestic and foreign assets, no presumption is possible as to whether or not the transfer will be effected. Thus the division of savings between domestic and foreign assets plays a role in the Keynesian analysis analogous to that played by the division of expenditure between domestic and foreign goods in the classical analysis. This analogy will not, however, be pursued further here; nor will the remainder of the argument take account of the possibility that savings may be invested in foreign assets.

III. APPLICATIONS OF TRANSFER THEORY: THE EXCHANGE STABILITY PROBLEM

Transfer theory has generally been developed and applied in the analysis of such standard problems as reparations payments and international flows of long-term capital. It has, however, a far wider application in the field of balance-of-payments theory, since any actual balance-of-payments disequilibrium involves a transfer in some form from the surplus to the deficit country (or countries), and the problem of rectifying the disequilibrium can be framed as the problem of creating a transfer of equal amount in the opposite direction. Hence transfer theory can be applied to the analysis of methods for overcoming balance-of-payments disequilibria—whether automatic mechanisms of adjustment or planned governmental policies. For example, the analysis of the classical transfer problem shows that in a 'full-employment' world the deficit country does not necessarily have to turn its terms of trade against itself to correct the deficit and that the deterioration of the terms of trade will be less (or the improvement greater), the more the deflation of expenditure in the deficit country and the inflation of expenditure in the surplus country fall on imports rather than on exportable goods. The Keynesian transfer analysis shows that (with positive marginal propensities to save in both countries) changes in income taxation sufficient to yield changes in budget surpluses or deficits (at the initial income levels) equal to the initial balance-of-payments deficit will not suffice to remedy the disequilibrium, though changes in government expenditures of this amount may do so.[20]

The examples just cited involve adjustment mechanisms directed in the first instance at aggregate incomes and expenditures; a more interesting application is to the effects of changes in relative price levels on the balance of payments. Such changes in relative prices may be brought about either by deflation or inflation of domestic currency prices at a fixed exchange rate or by alterations in the exchange rate with domestic currency prices remaining unchanged. The latter case is the one more usually treated in contemporary theoretical analysis. The problem is formulated *either* in terms of the effects of devaluation on the trade balance *or* in terms of the stability of the foreign exchange market, the formulation depending on whether or not it is assumed that the monetary authorities intervene in the market to peg the rate of exchange.[21] In either case the central

[20] The Keynesian transfer analysis also shows that the gold-standard mechanism of adjustment (deflation and inflation of expenditure brought about by the effects of gold movements on interest rates) did not *necessarily* work by creating unemployment in the deficit country, as has often been alleged. This proposition requires a further assumption about the distribution of expenditure changes between importable and exportable goods.

[21] In the 'classical' case, analysis of devaluation must also assume some policy or process whereby the altered relations between national income and expenditure in the two countries inherent in a change in the trade balance are effected. This introduces an important complication, since the total effect of a devaluation will depend on the effect of the assumed policy or process on the trade balance as well as on the effect of the relative price change; and the effect of the supporting policy may be so strong as to reverse the effect devaluation by itself would tend to have on the trade balance. For example, if devaluation by A increased the demand for A's goods at the expense of B's, and the sum of the marginal propensities to spend on imports exceeded unity, restoration of equilibrium between aggregate demand and supply for each country's goods would require inflation of expenditure in A and deflation of expenditure in B, which

theoretical problem concerns the conditions under which a relative reduction in export prices would tend to improve a country's trade balance. This problem, which may be described generically as 'the exchange stability problem', also arises as a phase of the transfer problem, as the latter has been posed in the introduction to this chapter.

The exchange stability problem can readily be formulated in terms of transfer theory, and the criteria which determine whether the transfer will be undereffected or overeffected can be transformed into criteria for exchange stability. For simplicity of exposition, it will be assumed (in addition to the assumptions of the preceding sections) that trade is initially balanced and that there are no barriers to trade.

A reduction in the price of A-exportables relative to B-exportables carries with it a transfer from A to B equal in amount, so far as A is concerned, to the increase in the cost of A's initial volume of imports and, so far as B is concerned, to the reduction in the cost of B's initial volume of imports. With initially balanced trade and a small price change, these two measures of the transfer will be approximately equal. The transfer is 'financed' and 'disposed of' through the effects of the relative price change, which will have income and substitution effects on the demands of the countries for their own and each other's goods. Alternatively, the price change will affect the two countries' aggregate expenditures and expenditures on imports, these expenditures being evaluated at the pre-transfer prices because the effects of the price change on values are approximately subsumed in the transfer itself. For what follows, it is important to notice that if expenditure measured in exportables is constant in the face of an altered price of imports, expenditure measured at the initial price of imports alters by the amount of the change in the cost of imports, that is, by the amount of the transfer.[22]

would more than offset the effect of A's devaluation and leave A's trade balance worse than before. This complication is ignored in the following argument, which is concerned chiefly with exchange stability.

[22] Let $E = C + pM$ be aggregate expenditure, measured in exportables, where C and M are quantities of exportables and imports consumed, and p is the price of imports in terms of exports. Then the effect of a change in the price of imports (dp) is

$$dE = \frac{\delta C}{\delta p} dp + p \frac{\delta M}{\delta p} dp + M \, dp.$$

The first two terms on the right amount to the change in expenditure measured at the initial price of imports, the third is the change in the cost of the initial quantity of imports. These two changes will be equal in magnitude and opposite in sign if $dE = 0$.

N

The exchange stability problem is the problem whether the effects of the price change on expenditures will be sufficient to effect the transfer implicit in the price change itself. In the classical case the assumption that all income is spent insures that the transfer is accompanied by equal changes in the two countries' expenditures (valued at pretransfer prices). The transfer will be overeffected or undereffected and the exchange market stable or unstable[23] according to whether the sum of the proportions of the transfer by which the two countries' expenditures on imports change is greater or less than unity. These proportions are equal to the price elasticities of demand for imports of the countries,[24] so that the market is stable or not according to whether the sum of these elasticities is greater or less than unity.[25]

In the Keynesian case the transfer analogy leads to the conclusion that the exchange market will be stable or unstable according to whether the sum of the elasticities is greater or less than

$$1 + s_a' \frac{m_a}{s_a} + s_b' \frac{m_b}{s_b},$$

[23] In a real model, the exchange rate has no independent existence; what is really under discussion is the stability or instability of the underlying real equilibrium of international trade.

[24] The change in expenditure on imports, valued at the pretransfer price, is

$$p \cdot \frac{\delta M}{\delta p} \cdot dp = \eta_m \left(-pM \frac{dp}{p} \right),$$

where

$$\eta_m \left(= -\frac{p}{M} \frac{\delta M}{\delta p} \right)$$

is the elasticity of demand for imports. Since the implicit transfer is $-pM(dp/p)$, the change in expenditure on imports expressed as a proportion of the transfer is η_m.

[25] This is, of course, the familar Marshall-Lerner criterion. Since the elasticity of demand for importables consists of the sum of the marginal propensity to spend on importables and the 'compensated' or 'constant-utility' elasticity of demand, argument on the lines of the last part of the first section of this article shows that instability requires both a marginal bias toward the consumption of exportables and a low degree of substitutability between importable and exportable goods in consumption in the two countries. In the case in which both countries produce both goods, instability also requires a low degree of substitutability in production in the two countries.

It should be observed also that, though the argument of this section assumes the absence of trade impediments, the exchange stability criterion is unaltered by the introduction of tariffs or of transport costs incurred in the imported good, since the expenditure change in these cases depends only on the elasticity of final demand for imports.

where m and s, as before, represent the marginal propensities to save and to import of the subscript country; s_a' represents the proportion of the transfer by which saving from the pretransfer level of income is reduced (expenditure at pretransfer prices not reduced) in A by the increase in the price of A's imports; and s_b' represents the proportion of the transfer by which saving from the pretransfer level of income is increased (expenditure at pretransfer prices not increased) in B by the decrease in the price of B's imports. Alternatively, the s''s represent the effect of a decrease in the price of imports on saving or an increase in the price of imports on expenditure, from the initial income, divided by the initial value of imports.[26]

It was in the latter version that the exchange stability criterion for the Keynesian case was first published by Laursen and Metzler,[27] who saw correctly that any difference from the classical criterion hinged on the presence or absence of a terms-of-trade effect on aggregate expenditure and argued from the statistical evidence that (in the 'short run' of the cycle) a rising proportion of real income is saved to the conclusion that an increase in the price of imports would increase expenditure, thus making the critical sum of the elasticities of import demand greater than unity. Their conclusion has recently been disputed by White,[28] on the grounds that time lags make the long-run behaviour of the savings ratio relevant and that in the long run the ratio is constant.

Prior to the publication of Laursen and Metzler's work, Harberger published an analysis of the problem,[29] in which the apparatus of

[26] This follows from the fact that the constrasting signs of the savings changes, as defined, cancel the contrasting signs of the price changes and that the change in saving is equal and opposite to the change in expenditure.

[27] S. Laursen and L. A. Metzler, 'Flexible Exchange Rates and the Theory of Employment', *Review of Economics and Statistics*, XXXII, no. 4, November 1950, 281–99.

[28] W. H. White, 'The Employment-insulating Advantages of Flexible Exchanges: A Comment on Professors Laursen and Metzler', *Review of Economics and Statistics*, XXXVI, no. 2, May 1954, 225–8. I agree with the authors' 'Reply' in the same issue; but the evidence for, and theoretical explanations of, the constancy of the savings ratio in the long run are relevant to the present discussion of the exchange stability problem. In my review of Meade's *The Balance of Payments* ('The Taxonomic Approach to Economic Policy', *Economic Journal*, LXI, no. 244, December 1951, 812–32) I derived a stability criterion identical with that of Metzler and Laursen and adopted their conclusion about the direction of the terms-of-trade effect; the argument of that review is therefore open to the same sort of criticism that White expressed.

[29] A. C. Harberger, 'Currency Depreciation, Income, and the Balance of Trade', *Journal of Political Economy*, LVIII, no. 1, February 1950, 47–60. Harberger erroneously attributed the difference between his results and those of

formal value theory was employed to determine the effect of an increase in import prices on saving. Harberger assumed that saving, measured in exportable goods, is a function of real income only, changes in prices inducing no substitution between saving and consumption; that the marginal propensity to save for changes in real income due to changes in the terms of trade is the same as that for changes in output at constant prices; and that the effects of a change in the terms of trade on real income may be approximated by the change in the cost of the initial value of imports. On these assumptions each s' in the preceding formula becomes equal to the corresponding s, and the criterion of exchange stability becomes whether the sum of the elasticities of import demand is greater or less than 1 plus the sum of the marginal propensities to import.

All three of the assumptions by which Harberger derived this elegant result have recently been subjected to criticism. Day has argued that saving and imports may be substitutes, since imports may be consumers' durables yielding a flow of satisfaction comparable to the interest on saving.[30] Spraos has shown that, if this is so, the Harberger criterion overestimates the critical value of the elasticities, though he is sceptical of the importance of such substitution.[31] Pearce has shown that Day overlooks the effects of a change in the price of imports on the real value of interest and that, when this is recognized, no presumption as to the direction of substitution between imports and saving is possible.[32] Spraos has argued convincingly that the marginal propensity to save from a change in real income due to a change in import prices is likely to be substantially greater than the marginal propensity to save from a change in output at constant prices, thus making the Harberger criterion an underestimate. Both Spraos and Pearce have shown that Harberger's assumptions imply the presence of money illusion, since they ignore the effect of the increased price of imports in reducing the real value of saving.[33] Spraos attempted to correct for

earlier writers to the variability of production; in fact, this is merely a necessary condition, the fundamental explanation lying in the introduction of a non-zero effect of the terms of trade on saving.

[30] A. C. L. Day, 'Relative Prices, Expenditure, and the Trade Balance: A Note', *Economica*, N.S., XXI, no. 82, May 1954, 64–9.

[31] J. Spraos, 'Consumers' Behaviour and the Conditions for Exchange Stability', *Economica*, N.S., XXII, no. 86, May 1955, 137–47.

[32] I. F. Pearce, 'A Note on Mr. Spraos' Paper', *Economica*, N.S., XXII, no. 86, May 1955, 147–51.

[33] Harberger can be defended against this criticism by a careful reading of his argument. His 'saving' is described as 'hoarding' and is defined as the excess of income over expenditure; with initially balanced trade, current saving in this

this by raising the approximation of the real income loss to allow for an estimate of the loss of real value of saved (unspent) income, but, as Pearce shows, this preserves elements of money illusion in the savings function by leaving money rather than real savings a function of real income and by ignoring the effect of the price change on the real value of accumulated saving and consequently on the incentive to save.

If substitution effects between imports and saving and the 'Pigou effect' of import prices on saving are both ignored and if (following Spraos) it is assumed that saving is intended to be spent on imports and exportables in the same ratio as current consumption expenditure, the Harberger analysis can be reworked on the assumption that real, rather than money, saving is a function of real income, to yield this result:

$$(4) \qquad s' = \frac{\bar{s}}{1 - \bar{s}} (\epsilon_s - 1),$$

where $\bar{s}$ is the average propensity to save and ϵ_s is the income elasticity of demand for (real) saving.[34] This reworking reconciles the Harberger approach with that of Metzler and Laursen and confirms the latter in deducing the effect of devaluation on expenditure from the relation between the savings ratio and income. It assumes, however, that imports are demanded for consumption only. If some imports are required for investment and investment expenditure is fixed in real, rather than money, terms (an assumption supported by the assumption of fixed interest rates), a reduction in import prices affects money saving both by increasing consumers' real income and by reducing the cost of investment imports. The preceding result is then altered to

$$(5) \qquad s' = m_c \frac{\bar{s}}{1 - \bar{s}} (\epsilon_s - 1) + m_i,$$

sense and presumably accumulated saving also are zero. On this reading (which would make all expenditure consumer expenditure) a positive marginal propensity to save ('hoard'), whether in money or in real terms, is sufficient to make the critical value of the stability criterion greater than the classical unity.

[34] Let the initial volume of domestic output be Y and the initial quantities of domestic and foreign output consumed be C and M, respectively, these quantities being measured in units such that the initial domestic prices are unity. On the assumptions stated previously, real income, Y_r, may be measured by output deflated by a price index, so that

$$Y_r = Y \div \frac{C + pM}{C + M},$$

where p represents the (real) price of imports, initially unity; and real saving, where m_c and m_i are the proportions of the initial volume of imports devoted to consumption and investment, respectively. This last result suggests that, though the Harberger-Metzler and Laursen finding that the critical value of the sum of the elasticities of import demand is greater than unity implies a questionable assumption about the behaviour of the savings ratio, it can be supported by the introduction of investment imports.

IV. APPLICATIONS OF TRANSFER THEORY: TRADE INTERVENTION

Another problem to which transfer theory can be applied, and which may also itself be part of the transfer problem as the latter has been formulated in the introduction to this chapter, is the problem of the conditions under which various types of governmental intervention in international trade will tend to improve the trade balance. Like the problem of relative price level changes discussed in the previous section, this problem appears in two versions: if the authorities are assumed to peg the exchange rate, the problem is the effect of intervention on the balance of trade; if the exchange rate is free, the problem is the direction in which the rate must move to preserve

S_r, is a function of real income only and its money value (value in terms of domestic output) is

$$S = S_r \cdot \frac{C + pM}{C + M}.$$

Hence the change in money saving due to a reduction in the price of imports, expressed as a proportion of the initial value of imports, is

$$s' = -\frac{1}{M}\frac{\delta S}{\delta p} = \frac{1}{M}\left(\frac{YM}{C + M}\frac{\delta S_r}{\delta Y_r} - \frac{S_r M}{C + M}\right)$$

$$= \frac{S_r}{C + M}(\epsilon_s - 1)$$

$$= \frac{\bar{s}}{1 - \bar{s}}(\epsilon_s - 1)$$

where

$$\bar{s} = \frac{S}{Y} = \frac{Y - C - M}{Y},$$

and

$$\epsilon_s = \frac{Y_r}{S_r}\frac{\delta S_r}{\delta Y_r}.$$

equilibrium.[35] But the central theoretical problem is the same in both cases.

Governmental intervention in international trade may take a wide variety of forms, ranging from the 'classical' methods of import and export duties and export subsidies to more 'modern' methods of export and import licensing, 'directives', state trading, exchange control, and multiple exchange rates. For purposes of balance of payments theory, however, it is the objective rather than the form of intervention which matters;[36] and two types of intervention may be distinguished for analysis, according to whether intervention aims at improving the balance of payments by reducing expenditure on imports (through import-restriction) or by increasing export earnings. The latter comprises two sub-types, export-promotion to increase earnings by increasing the quantity of exports and export-restriction to increase earnings by increasing the unit value of exports; but since the conditions required for the one to succeed are clearly the conditions which will cause the other to fail, it is only necessary to consider one sub-type in detail. For contrast with the case of import-restriction, the case chosen for such analysis in this section is that of export-promotion.

Export promotion entails making the price of exportable goods to foreigners lower than their domestic value; the difference may be absorbed by the state (*via* an export subsidy, or a state trading or exchange authority loss) or it may be imposed on private citizens (*via* a lower profit margin on exports than on home market sales, or an excess of the price consumers would be willing to pay for the exportables they consume over the price charged to the home and foreign markets).[37] Similarly, import restriction entails making the domestic value of imports higher than the price paid to foreigners, the difference either being absorbed by the state (*via* an import duty, or a state trading or exchange authority profit) or accruing to

[35] The qualifications stated in Footnotes 21 and 23 above for the classical case, that rate-pegging must be supported by policies to effect the necessary alterations in the income-expenditure relations in the two countries, which policies complicate and may even reverse the results of other changes, and that the exchange rate has no independent existence, the analysis actually pertaining to the underlying real trade equilibrium, apply equally to the argument below.

[36] For an extensive and illuminating discussion of different forms of intervention and the economic problems of administration to which they give rise, see James E. Meade, op. cit., Part V, chaps. XX and XXI.

[37] The former assumes that exportables are 'directed' to the foreign market, the domestic price being allowed to ration out home market supplies; the latter assumes that the home market price is fixed at the same level as the export price, but domestic consumers are rationed in some more direct way.

private citizens (*via* abnormal profits to licensed importers, or an excess of the price consumers would be willing to pay over the price they actually pay for the imports they consume).[38] Where the difference between external price and internal value created by intervention is absorbed by the state, it will be assumed that the budgetary effect of intervention is offset by an opposite change in income taxation or government expenditure. In the classical case this assumption is necessary to preserve the equality of income and expenditure at the full employment level; in the Keynesian case, it is necessary to isolate the effect of intervention *per se* from the deflationary or inflationary effect of uncompensated increases in taxes or subsidies.

Though the effects of export promotion and import restriction on the balance of payments may each be formulated in terms of transfer theory, the formulation required is different in the two cases. It is therefore convenient to treat the two separately.

(a) Export Promotion

Export promotion by A entails a transfer from A to B equal to the associated reduction in the cost of B's initial imports from A (the value of A's initial exports to B). It is 'financed' by the reduction in private income or government expenditure in A required to absorb this cost reduction, and 'disposed of' through the income and substitution effects of the reduction in the price charged to B for its imports. The problem of whether export promotion will improve A's trade balance is therefore the same as whether the effects of the financing and disposal of the transfer on the two countries' aggregate expenditures and expenditures on imports (measured at pretransfer prices) will suffice to effect the transfer.

In the classical case, the transfer is accompanied by equal changes in expenditure (at pretransfer prices) in the two countries; and the transfer will be overeffected or undereffected according as the sum of the proportions of the transfer by which the two countries' expenditures on imports (at pretransfer prices) change is greater or less than unity. For A, where domestic prices are unchanged, this proportion is given by the proportion of the reduction in governmental expenditure which falls on imports, or by the marginal

[38] The former assumes rationing by price, the latter price control and some other form of rationing. A third possibility, that the difference accrues to the foreign exporters (which might happen, for example, if licences were granted to foreign exporters rather than to domestic importers) is ignored in the following argument.

propensity to spend on imports of the community, depending on how the transfer is financed; for B, the price of whose imports is reduced, the proportion is equal to the price elasticity of demand for imports (as in the case of exchange stability). Thus the transfer will be effected, and export promotion succeed in improving the trade balance, if the elasticity of B's demand for imports is greater than one minus A's (governmental or private) marginal propensity to import, or, what is the same thing, A's (governmental or private) marginal propensity to spend on exportables. Conversely, export promotion would fail (and export restriction succeed) in improving the trade balance, if the elasticity of B's demand for imports were less than A's (governmental or private) marginal propensity to spend on exportables.

In the Keynesian case the critical value for the sum of the proportions of the transfer by which import demands are affected is not unity but

$$1 + \frac{m_a}{s_a}s_a' + \frac{m_b}{s_b}s_b',$$

where the s''s represent, as before, the proportions by which the expenditure changes in the two countries fall short of the amount of the transfer. For B, where the transfer is received *via* a reduction in the price of imports, this proportion is determined by the reaction of savings to an improvement in the terms of trade, discussed in detail in the preceding section. For A, where relative prices are unchanged by export promotion, this proportion will be zero if the transfer is financed by a reduction in government expenditure, and equal to the marginal propensity to save if it is financed by increased income taxation—so that the term involving this proportion drops out in the former case, and reduces to the marginal propensity to import (which cancels out) in the latter case. In the former case, the transfer will be effected, and export-promotion successful, if the elasticity of B's demand for imports is greater than the proportion of the reduction of A's governmental expenditure falling on exportables, plus the product of the proportion of the transfer by which B's saving from the initial income level increases and the ratio of B's marginal propensity to import to its marginal propensity to save. In the latter case, the elasticity must exceed one plus the product of the ratios of saving change to transfer and marginal propensity to import to marginal propensity to save. It may be noted that if the defective Harberger approximation for the savings change ($s' = s$) is adopted, the criterion for the transfer to be effected becomes much simpler, since the term involving the change in B's saving reduces to B's marginal propensity to import, which can be cancelled against the income term in B's elasticity of import demand, making the requirement for success that B's 'compensated' or 'constant-utility' elasticity of demand for imports exceed the proportion of A's governmental expenditure reduction falling on exportables in the first case, and unity in the second case.[39]

(b) Import Restriction

Import restriction by A may be conceived of as comprising two changes, each entailing a transfer. The first is the equivalent of export restriction by B, entailing a transfer from A to B equal to the increase in value of A's initial quantity of imports due to restriction, financed and disposed of *via* the increased price of A's imports; the second is the transfer back to A of an equal amount, financed in the same way by B as the first transfer was disposed of, and disposed of by A in the same way as any other transfer. The difference between the two transfers lies entirely in the difference in their effects on A's demand for imports, the first involving an increase in the price of A's imports and the second involving no price change; and the net effect will be favourable or not, according as the effect of the first transfer in reducing A's demand for imports is greater or less than the effect of the second transfer in increasing it.

In the classical case, the first transfer reduces A's demand for imports by a proportion of the transfer equal to A's elasticity of demand for imports, while the second transfer increases A's demand for imports by a proportion of the transfer equal to A's marginal propensity to spend on imports, or to the proportion of the increase in governmental expenditure falling on imports, depending on how the transfer is disposed of. Since the elasticity of demand for imports exceeds the marginal propensity to spend on imports by the 'compensated' elasticity of demand, import restriction in this case must

---

[39] The analysis of the conditions required for export promotion to succeed also solves the problem, excluded in the previous footnote, of the requirements for import restriction to succeed when the difference between external price and internal value accrues to the foreigner, since that case amounts to export restriction by the foreigner and the conditions for success are the same as for export-promotion by the foreigner to succeed. Thus, in the classical case, A's balance of trade would be improved by such import-restriction if the sum of A's elasticity of demand for imports and B's marginal propensity to spend on imports from A exceeded unity, i.e. if A's elasticity of demand for imports exceeded B's marginal propensity to spend on exportables. An analogous condition holds in the Keynesian case.

improve the balance of payments if the transfer is disposed of *via* an increase in private income. Only if A's elasticity of demand for imports is less than unity, and the transfer is disposed of *via* an increase in government expenditure which falls more heavily on imports than would an increase in private expenditure, is it possible for import restriction to worsen A's balance of payments in this case.

In the Keynesian case, the reduction in A's demand for imports due to the first transfer is governed by the difference between A's elasticity of demand for imports and the product of the ratio of A's marginal propensity to import to its marginal propensity to save and the proportion of the transfer by which A's saving is reduced as a result of the adverse terms of trade change. Similarly, the increase in A's demand for imports due to the second transfer is governed by the difference between the marginal propensity to spend on imports or the proportion of increased government expenditure falling on imports, and the product of the ratio of A's marginal propensity to import to its marginal propensity to save and the proportion of the transfer by which A's saving is increased as a result of its receipt. Where the second transfer is matched by an increase in government expenditure, so that there is no change in A's saving, the condition for import restriction to improve A's balance of trade is that A's elasticity of demand for imports exceed the sum of the proportion of the increase in government expenditure devoted to imports, and the product of the terms-of-trade effect on its saving and the ratio of its marginal propensity to import to its marginal propensity to save. Where the second transfer accrues as private income, the proportion of the transfer by which A's saving increases is equal to A's marginal propensity to save, so that the term containing this effect becomes equal to the marginal propensity to import and so reduces the influence of the second transfer on A's demand for imports to zero; in this case, the condition for import restriction to improve A's balance of trade is that A's elasticity of demand for imports exceed the product of the terms-of-trade effect on its saving and the ratio of its marginal propensity to import to its marginal propensity to save. If the Harberger approximation were valid, this latter condition would always be fulfilled, since the criterion would reduce to the marginal propensity to import.

CHAPTER VIII

A Simplification of
Multi-Country Multiplier Theory[*][1]

IN recent years the theory of the foreign trade multiplier has been extended from the simple two-country case to the generalized n-country case, by the application of matrix algebra.[2] The following notes present an alternative and simpler proof of some of the more interesting conclusions which have been established by this technique.

I. NATIONAL INCOME MULTIPLIER THEORY

An autonomous change in demand for any country's output will have a multiplier effect on the outputs of all countries in the system. Let K_{ij} be the multiplier relating the total change in country i's output to an autonomous change in the demand for j's output, so that $Y_i = K_{ij}D_j$, where Y_i is the total change in country i's output and D_j is the autonomous change in demand for country j's output.

On the assumption that all marginal propensities to consume (home-produced or imported) goods are positive, the multipliers relating changes in national outputs to autonomous changes in demand will all be positive, that is, $K_{ij} > 0$ for all i, j.

On the assumption that each country's marginal propensity to

* *The Canadian Journal of Economics and Political Science*, XXII, no. 2, May 1956, 244–6.

[1] These notes were written during the author's tenure of a Visiting Professorship at Northwestern University. The author is grateful to his colleagues there for many helpful criticisms and suggestions.

[2] See L. A. Metzler, 'A Multiple Region Theory of Income and Trade', *Econometrica*, XVIII, no. 4, October 1950, 329–54; a special case was analysed earlier by F. Machlup, *International Trade and the National Income Multiplier* (Philadelphia, 1943), chap. VI and App. B. Essentially the same analysis applies to the theory of the multiplier in a multi-sectoral economy: see R. M. Goodwin, 'The Multiplier as Matrix', *Economic Journal*, LIX, no. 236, December 1949, 537–55; J. S. Chipman, 'The Multi-Sector Multiplier', *Econometrica*, XVIII, no. 4, October 1950, 355–74, and *The Theory of Inter-Sectoral Money Flows and Income Formation* (Baltimore, 1951). In the argument below, the word 'country' may be replaced by the word 'sector'.

save is positive, all multipliers will be finite ($K_{ij} < \infty$ for all i, j) and the multiplier relating the total change in a country's output to an autonomous change in the demand for its output will be:

(a) less than the reciprocal of the country's marginal propensity to save ('closed-economy' multiplier), that is, $K_{ii} < 1/s_i$ for all i. An autonomous change in demand must be offset by an induced change in saving, and since part of the change in saving will occur in other countries as their incomes change, the change in saving by country i will be less than the autonomous change in demand for country i's output; that is, $s_i Y_i < D_i$, and since $Y_i = K_{ii} D_i, K_{ii} < 1/s_i$.

(b) greater than the multiplier for an autonomous change in the demand for any other country's output, that is, $K_{ii} > K_{ij}$ for all $j \neq i$. An increase in demand for another country's output will induce both increased saving and increased consumption by that country; of the increased consumption, part will fall on this country's goods and part on the goods of other countries; the increase in income generated by the latter increase in output will also be partly saved and partly spent on consumption, and so on; so that the demand for i's goods will increase only by a fraction of the increase in demand for j's goods. Consequently, i's output will rise by less than it would if the demand for i's goods were increased by the same amount as the increase in demand for j's goods.

Property (b) means that an increase in the direct demand for a country's output would lead to a greater total increase in its output than would the same increase in the demand for any other country's goods, and vice versa. It also implies that a diversion of the demand of any country from the goods of country i to the goods of country j would reduce the output of country i and increase the output of country j.

II. BALANCE-OF-TRADE MULTIPLIER THEORY

A country's balance of trade is equal to the difference between its national income and aggregate domestic expenditure. The total change in its trade balance resulting from autonomous changes in demand will be equal to the difference between the total change in its income and the total change in its expenditure, or (cancelling out induced changes in expenditure) the difference between the total change in its saving and the autonomous change in its expenditure; that is, $B_i = s_i Y_i - E_i$, where B_i is the total change in country i's trade balance, and E_i is the autonomous change in expenditure by country i. Using national income multipliers,

$$(1) \qquad B_1 = \sum_j s_i K_{ij} D_j - E_i.$$

An increase in the demand of any country other than i for the output of any country in the system will turn country i's trade balance in its favour (since $E_i = 0$ by assumption); an increase in foreign demand for i's output will improve i's trade balance by more than the same increase in foreign demand for any foreign good (since $K_{ii} > K_{jj}$).

An increase in country i's demand for (expenditure on) any country's output will turn country i's trade balance adverse (since $s_i K_{ij} < 1$ and $D_j = E_i$); an increase in i's demand for its own output will turn its trade balance against it by less than would the same increase in i's demand for foreign products (since $K_{ii} > K_{ij}$).

A diversion of any country's demand from the products of other countries to the products of country i will improve country i's trade balance, and vice versa.

III. THE TRANSFER PROBLEM

Assume a transfer of amount T from country A to country B. The financing and disposal of the transfer will reduce A's demands for goods, and increase B's demands for goods, to an extent depending on the methods of financing and disposal employed. The effect of the transfer on A's trade balance will be given by the expression

$$(2) \qquad B_a = \sum_j s_a K_{aj}(m'_{jb} - m'_{ja}) T + (1 - s'_a)T$$

where m'_{jb} is the proportion of the transfer by which B's demand for j's goods is increased, m'_{ja} is the proportion of the transfer by which A's demand for j's goods is reduced, and s'_a is the proportion of the transfer by which A's total demand for goods is not reduced, as a result of the method of financing and disposing of the transfer. Country A's trade balance will improve by more or less than the amount of the transfer, and the transfer will be overeffected or undereffected, according to whether

$$(3) \qquad \sum s_a K_{aj}(m'_{jb} - m'_{ja})$$

is greater or less than s'_a.

This is the general case; the result indicates that the transfer may be either undereffected or overeffected. In the special case of a transfer the finance and disposal of which has the same effect on demand and saving as a reduction of income in A and increase in income in B, it can be shown that the transfer will be undereffected. The simplest way of establishing this result is to note that the changes in demands resulting from this method of financing and disposal will have the same effect on national outputs as a reduction in the demand for A's output and an increase in the demand for B's output equal to the amount of the transfer, except that the national incomes of A and B will not be decreased and increased by the amounts of the initial reduction and increase in demand for their products. In other words, the multiplier for the change in a country's income which would result from a reduction in its demands for goods and its saving in the same proportions as would be induced by a change in its income, will be one less than the multiplier for the change in its income that would result from a reduction in demand for its output. Consequently, the change in country A's income in this case will be $Y_a = K_{ab}T - (K_{aa}-1)T$. The change in country A's trade balance will be

$$(4) \quad B_a = s_a(K_{ab} - K_{aa} + 1)T + (1 - s_a)T = s_a(K_{ab} - K_{aa})T + T.$$

Since $K_{aa} > K_{ab}$, A's trade balance will improve by less than the amount transferred, and the transfer will be undereffected.

INDEX

o